D0754465

Self-Help Books

Self-Help Books

Why Americans Keep Reading Them

SANDRA K. DOLBY

University of Illinois Press

URBANA AND CHICAGO

Library of Congress Cataloging-in-Publication Data

Dolby, Sandra K., 1946–
Self-help books : why Americans keep reading them / Sandra K. Dolby.
p.   cm.
Includes bibliographical references and index.
ISBN 0-252-02974-7 (hardcover : alk. paper)
1. Self-help techniques—United States. 2. Psychological literature—
United States. I. Title.
BF632.D65   2005
646.7'00973—dc22   2005002017

Contents

Preface

In the pages that follow, I shall offer some conclusions that I have reached after surveying more than three hundred examples of popular nonfiction currently in print, all of which relate in some way to the American obsession with improving our practical and spiritual well-being. However, let me first say a little about why I have chosen to undertake this study. Recently my sister, Carol, was sorting through some of the accumulated stuff from one of the rooms of my parents' home when she found a box holding several years' worth of drawings, paper dolls, handmade books, and assorted glued things evidently contributed by my youngest brother and me when we were around six and nine years old. The cache contained an item that intrigued me beyond the expected nostalgia and reminiscence—a paper and pencil "newspaper" titled the *Sandra Dolby Press* (dated May 30, 1956) and bearing the headline "Mrs. Gertrude Dolby reads Bible through 5 and a half times." There followed front, side, and back view drawings of my grandmother (Mrs. Gertrude Dolby) and a short (very short) article announcing: "Every day Mrs. Dolby sits down and reads the Bible. She has never failed in reading it yet."

I've certainly seen far more impressive creations from nine-year-olds, but what intrigues me—beyond the perhaps interesting fact that indeed I did grow up to be something like a newspaper reporter—was the subject matter itself. I had forgotten how often I would go to my grandmother's house (she lived alone in the house next to ours) and find her reading the Bible. The reading was a kind of morning ritual, as was writing in her diary. Years later, and some time after my grandmother died, I asked my aunt Ann if I could have the many diaries my grandmother had written. I have them now—skeletal and suggestive reminders of those years when I was growing up, those years when I assumed that anyone who had the time must do that when they get older, must read and think and write.

Not all people do read and think and write, of course, and some who do are in fact young rather than old. Nevertheless, the idea that this trio of activities was somehow a good thing stayed with me. My sense of its "goodness" was fairly unsophisticated, tied as it was to my love and respect for my grandmother. Yet, increasingly, now as a scholar, a folklorist, with a wealth of tools and theories available to examine such things, I have continued to be intrigued by this process of self-education. This book is my indulgence of that abiding question: Why did my grandmother feel compelled to read and think and write about her own life? Why do humans find it necessary to educate themselves about life, about the spirit or soul, and then write about it? And what form has this urge taken now as one millennium has ended and another begun?

For my grandmother, all three activities seemed to be equally important and intertwined. It is too late now for me to ask whether it was important that the reading be from the Bible, though I know she often read poetry as well. It is too late to ask what form her thinking took, though I do know that until her very last years, she served as a teacher for the older adult Sunday school class at her church. Her thinking must have taken some form that could be adapted and discussed in a weekly class. And though I have her diaries, it is too late to ask how the events of her life and the lives of her friends and family affected her sense of how life is best lived.

But my grandmother was in many ways a part of the fin de siècle. She was born in 1879. Her cultural frame of reference included the introduction of the motorcar, World War I, the Jazz Age, Prohibition, the Great Depression, and finally World War II. The 1960s and everything since were not a part of her worldview, and this change-filled era of the 1960s has had a decided influence on the form and direction such introspective self-education has assumed among much of the American population during the last part of the twentieth century. It is my aim in this book to examine what I see as the late-twentieth- and early-twenty-first-century answer to this need for self-education: the popular nonfiction paperback, the self-help book. My argument is that, for many contemporary educated Americans, self-help books provide a welcome resource in the individual effort to grow in wisdom and lead a satisfying life. Furthermore, there are many writers of varying talent and insight willing to provide that accessible wisdom. Self-help books, whether we like it or not, are part of the continuing process of constructing and assessing an American worldview.

And I admit here at the beginning that my particular slant in the examination of this phenomenon—the rise of this body of popular nonfiction literature—is influenced by my own longtime interest in writers or story-tellers as "bearers of tradition," as we say in the discipline of folklore study. One effect of this slant, combined with my interest in written literature, is greater attention to the texts themselves and their writers rather than to the readers of such books. Thus I have not interviewed people who have read these books, as one would do in a typical ethnography, nor have I compiled statistics about the typical readers, as one might do in a sociological study. Instead, I have addressed a preliminary question, one that seeks to describe the content of these books, and I have aimed my discussion primarily at the general reader, anyone who might find the phenomenon of self-help books in America intriguing, either intellectually or personally.

As I have brought my thoughts on the subject to some sort of closure—at least enough to create a title and send off a manuscript—I have come back repeatedly to three books that have recently been published and now lie pro-vocatively on my table, tempting me toward three entirely different ways of treating the subject. One is fairly obvious—Tom Tiede's *Self-Help Nation*, published in 2001 with the telling subtitle *The Long Overdue, Entirely Justified, Delightfully Hostile Guide to the Snake-Oil Peddlers Who Are Sapping Our Nation's Soul*. Tiede's book, like Wendy Kaminer's *I'm Dysfunctional, You're Dysfunctional* published ten years earlier, heaps contempt upon the writers—and in fact the readers—of self-help books, gleefully airing all of the worst literary and conceptual sins of the writers and righteously outlining the char-acter weaknesses of the readers who would eagerly take in such rubbish. I will have more to say later about why it might seem tempting to simply pan the whole self-help movement as opportunistic on the part of writers and sheep-like and wimpish on the part of readers, but, in fact, the dismissive tone of Tiede's diatribe forcefully reminds me of what I, in contrast to Tiede, am about in writing this book. I am, above all, prepared to see the writers and the readers of self-help books as sincere and intelligent people who partici-pate in the formation and articulation of an American worldview. Writing and reading self-help books is part of that process, and the books at the cen-ter of that process need to be taken seriously rather than simply dismissed as modern-day "snake-oil" remedies. My aim is to examine those books care-fully and fairly, using the tools of folkloristics, my academic discipline.

I intend, then, not to write a popular critique such as Tiede's *Self-Help Nation*. A second book on my table is Douglas V. Porpora's *Landscapes of the Soul*, published in 2001. Unlike Tiede's book, Porpora's volume has two ap-pendices, copious endnotes, a large bibliography, and an index. This is clearly an academic work, and its subtitle, *The Loss of Moral Meaning in American*

Life, suggests that the author has undertaken his project with the utmost seriousness. Porpora's book is one easily listed as an important contribution to American studies. Its disciplinary ties are to the sociology of religion, along the lines of books by Robert Wuthnow or Robert Bellah. And like Wuthnow and Bellah, Porpora conducts both statistical surveys and individual interviews to gain information useful to his arguments on, in this case, why Americans have trouble articulating and acting with a sense of moral purpose. I like Porpora's book, but I am troubled by the way he elicits and uses the interview materials—a perennial problem in my own discipline, which routinely examines minutely the individual presentations of oral stories and other creative artifacts. As a folklorist, I expect much greater rigor in the process of eliciting and creating suitable "field texts," but I accept the obvious fact that Porpora's aims and methods are different from those a folklorist would use. On the more general question of what Porpora is about in writing his book, however, I would say we do share an important objective— the careful examination of the moral or spiritual dimension of an American worldview.

So I do intend to write something similar to Porpora's *Landscapes of the Soul,* an academic book suitable to a more popular audience simply because it addresses a concern that many Americans do see as important: their own personal sense (or lack) of purpose. This brings us to the third book on my table, André Comte-Sponville's *Short Treatise on the Great Virtues: The Uses of Philosophy in Everyday Life,* first published in France in 1996 but translated into English only in 2001. Like Porpora's book, *A Short Treatise* is a work intended for a well-educated readership, though it is clear that the author has tried to make his work accessible to the general reader rather than only to other scholars. What I especially like about Comte-Sponville's book is the intent indicated in his subtitle—the uses of philosophy in everyday life. Reading the book is a fairly demanding activity, even though the author hides many of his erudite expansions and much of his argumentation in the fifty pages of notes. But his intent is to demonstrate how eighteen ideas—named and discussed as "virtues" in this study—are used as part of the everyday personal philosophy of any ordinary individual. In other words, he provides a working list of the themes that are a part of most people's personal philosophies and gives us one template for the examination of a personal worldview.

Do I intend to write something like Comte-Sponville's *Short Treatise?* I wish I could, but no. However, I do see in his classification and examination of these common virtues a potential finding list useful for identifying essential components of varying worldviews. And, like Comte-Sponville, I am interested in how other writers have influenced the way people articulate their personal philosophies, their worldviews. It may seem a long stretch from Comte-Sponville's examination of the writings of noted philosophers to my examination of the writings of contemporary self-help authors—a long stretch from seeing ties to popular worldviews in the works of Plato and Aristotle, Kant and Spinoza, Sartre, or Henri Bergson to seeing such ties in the works of Wayne Dyer, Stephen Covey, Marsha Sinetar, or John Gray. But my argument is that there is a strong similarity. People use contemporary self-help books in their own learning projects, much as people have used classical philosophers and the Bible in the past. A first step in examining this process is an exploration of the books themselves.

One of the landmark books in this emerging tradition is Marilyn Ferguson's *Aquarian Conspiracy: Personal and Social Transformation in the 1980s* (1980). Ferguson wrote as a classifier and celebrant of what she saw as a new movement and gave a name to the shared vision behind this new quest:

> The paradigm of the Aquarian Conspiracy sees humankind embedded in nature. It promotes the autonomous individual in a decentralized society. It sees us as stewards of all our resources, inner and outer. It says that we are *not* victims, not pawns, not limited by conditions or conditioning. . . . The new perspective respects the ecology of everything: birth, death, learning, health, family, work, science, spirituality, the arts, the community, relationships, politics. (29)

This list of "everything" the new perspective respects is, in fact, a list of the topics addressed by the many authors writing books of popular nonfiction in the last four decades of the twentieth century and early years of the twenty-first.

In the process of speaking to these topics, the authors of popular self-help books, either knowingly or simply as human vehicles of the culture themselves, place before us many of the values typically identified as the basic stuff of a collective worldview—many of the "virtues" examined by Comte-Sponville, Porpora, Bellah, and others. Each self-help author offers his or her readers a focused meditation on how they might best act with prudence in their individual lives. Perhaps more crassly than do scholarly philosophers or theologians, each self-help author conspires to sell us wisdom—in most instances, wisdom we already own as part of our collective American heritage. I do not believe that readers are being led by the nose nor that their response to self-help literature is a kind of cultural determinism by which they acquiesce to a dominant ideology. Self-help books are a valuable cultural resource, and American readers have, through the marketplace, demanded that the resource be continually renewed and available. And self-help writers have willingly given us their wares, their interpretations of a tacit worldview in the form of guidebooks and philosophical reflection.

In the pages that follow, I shall examine how such writers draw upon the resources of American culture, consider them, and recast them into an emerging popular philosophy. I shall analyze the contents of these books that carry such appeal and inspiration for a popular American audience, an audience that, like my grandmother, feels a need to reflect upon life and become prudent, self-educated, self-reliant, perhaps even wise. Many of the themes Ferguson articulated in her 1980 publication will be sounded again and again. Many of the stories and sayings that are a part of American culture will be singled out as significant resources incorporated into these books of popular nonfiction. Ultimately, my own background as a folklorist will determine an emphasis on how narratives, sayings, and traditional values are used in conveying and articulating a common worldview. But the emergence of popular nonfiction is a phenomenon that invites the attention of all contemporary thinkers. I hope my folkloristic and descriptive look at the topic is a useful beginning.

Self-Help Books

Introduction: Self-Help Books and American Worldview

Do most Americans share a single, collective worldview? In other words, in the language of nineteenth-century ethnologists who gave us the word, are we Americans a "folk"? Most contemporary thinkers would argue that we cannot be viewed as a single entity—a folk. We are too diverse; we are the clearest example of multiculturalism in the world. And yet to outsiders, with every new Disneyworld or McDonald's that springs up on foreign soil, we export American values, American ideas—an American worldview. I suspect that both opinions are valid. Worldview is a slippery concept. I have chosen to use it here precisely because it is a slippery concept. It draws to it all the riffraff of ideas, behaviors, songs, tastes, maxims, stories, and rituals associated with a group of people.

Anthropologists have tried to make the study of worldview a more precise art. They have given us helpful units of comparison. But the study of worldview shared by a diverse and well-educated population is potentially much more complicated than would be the study of worldview shared by a homogeneous, traditional culture. And in either case it is not an easy task, as the "stuff" of worldview is embedded within the culture and is variously affected by the individual voices that are recognized as articulating it. Still, I think that some light might be shed on this complex issue of American worldview through an examination of the self-help books that are currently so popular. Ultimately, worldview is best studied through an ethnographic process—eliciting individual responses to a specific set of research questions. But a careful study of self-help books can be a first step in this process.

Because self-help books are so conspicuous in America, we can assume that, for many people, they figure into the mix of important influences in the

formation and articulation of personal philosophies—the building blocks of
a collective American worldview. Furthermore, I am prepared to argue that
the writers themselves are at every turn extracting elements of an existing
American worldview and incorporating them into their books. These writers are, in effect, giving back to their readers the worldview they and the readers already share. They are recycling an already well-established American
worldview.

Let us consider some of these books more directly. Everyone who visits a
bookstore has noticed them—the paperbacks offering advice and reflection
on topics as diverse as how to achieve psychological well-being, how to be
effective yet serene in the workplace, why the laws of physics are part of God's
plan, how to get along with your mate or with nasty bosses, how to reduce
stress and eat and exercise for optimal health, how to save the planet, why to
save the planet. Everyone has noticed them. My purpose here is to examine
them as a significant aspect of the contemporary American worldview, as a
reflection of some of our current concerns, hopes, and practices, and to offer some insights into the role such books play in popular self-education.

Many questions might be asked about these books, about their authors and
readers, but I am going to ask three basic questions: (1) Do these books represent a popular literary tradition, or is this a new phenomenon? (2) Can we
account for the success of these books? (3) What do these books tell us about
the popular wisdom of mainstream Americans? These three questions might
be seen as fundamental themes that wend their way through this entire study.
However, before I address them directly, I would like to briefly set the stage
for viewing books of popular nonfiction as cultural artifacts, as expressive
performances rather like the ballads, fairy tales, or legends that folklorists
usually study. I will not argue that they *are* examples of folklore but rather
that they can be seen as functioning as folklore and as having been created in
much the same way that folklore is created. Perhaps, like personal narratives—
stories people tell based on their own real experiences but incorporating the
frame of narrative borrowed from tradition—these popular self-help books
are neither fish nor fowl, neither entirely original nor entirely formulaic. But
they are surely popular expressive productions, and as such they both convey and incorporate elements of an American worldview.

The Appeal of a Proven Formula

As I was pondering why one encounters so many of these books of popular psychology, alternative medicine, inspiration and spirituality, business
advice, and even layman's science and theology as one browses the shelves

of various bookstore chains, I kept thinking of another popular American phenomenon—the urban legend. Urban legends are those realistic, disturbing stories that invariably happen to a friend of a friend and sometimes end up as the plots of movies. They are everywhere, and new ones arise daily. One of the latest has to do with the individual who wakes up in a bathtub of ice only to discover that one of his kidneys has been removed for sale in the illegal organ replacement market. Why would I be reminded of such stories when pondering the popularity of self-help books? It is not simply the stunning popularity of the two phenomena that is impressive. Rather, it is the fact that both phenomena can be analyzed and more clearly understood as examples of a folkloric process hard at work in American culture.

Before I develop this thesis, let me recount one of my favorite urban legends. Ideally, I would tell this in a much less formal setting—for example, sitting at a kitchen table, drinking coffee, and talking with my sister and her neighbor.

> Becky told me this about a friend of hers up in New Haven. This friend had gone to a party without her husband since he had the flu. The party was in Fort Wayne. She left the party to go home at about two in the morning. She gets into her car and notices that another car starts up right behind her. After a while it seems like this car is following her, so she starts speeding up to see if she can lose him. Pretty soon she starts running red lights and stop signs, but he just keeps right behind her. By now she's really scared. When she gets home, she pulls into the driveway and lays on the horn. Her husband comes out and says, "What the hell's going on here?" The woman gets out of the car and points at the car behind her. "This guy followed me all the way home." By now the guy in the car behind gets out, and the husband says, "What's the idea?" and sort of shoves his wife behind him. "Before you get mad," the other guy says, "let me say that I followed your wife because when I started my car up, I saw a man's head bop down in the back seat of her car. I wanted to make sure he didn't try to hurt her." The husband went over to his wife's car and opened the back door. There was a man with a knife in the backseat.

Granted, the outcomes of many such legends are much more dire—usually death or injury in some form. But the threat of death is here, and more important, we can see the structural pattern of the urban legend in this story as well as in any other. It is this pattern that leads us to suspect we have an urban legend even before other examples of "The Killer in the Backseat" have been collected. First, there is a risky situation (the woman out alone at two in the morning); then we are led to imagine a worst-case scenario (the woman is threatened with death or injury); and finally, there is an ironic twist at the end (the real threat was the killer in the backseat, not the man following her). The pattern itself has great appeal; it is what persuades us to call such stories a "genre" of folklore. And that pattern is what, to some extent, accounts for the popularity of these otherwise very unpleasant stories.

Can my discipline and I account for the popularity of not only urban legends (which are easily recognized as folklore) but also such books as M. Scott Peck's *Road Less Traveled* (1978), Stephen R. Covey's *Seven Habits of Highly Effective People* (1989), Susan Jeffers's *Feel the Fear and Do It Anyway* (1987), James Redfield's *Celestine Prophecy: An Adventure* (1993), Wayne W. Dyer's *Your Erroneous Zones* (1976), Marsha Sinetar's *Do What You Love, the Money Will Follow* (1987), Phillip McGraw's *Self Matters: Creating Your Life from the Inside Out* (2001), or Lynn Grabhorn's *Excuse Me, Your Life Is Waiting* (2000)? Evidently I think we can, or I wouldn't be writing this book. Part of this accounting is tied to the presence of a pattern, as with the urban legend. For people who tell and listen to urban legends, there is something in the artistic pattern of a risky situation, a worst-case scenario, and an ironic twist at the end that is effective aesthetically, even if the content is disturbing. And I would argue that there is a pattern characteristic of popular nonfiction that satisfies and draws readers to the genre and persuades writers to create new books with the assurance that they will please their audience.

One of the earliest studies to recognize the positive effect of a proven narrative formula was Vladimir Propp's *Morphology of the Folktale,* first published in Russia in 1930 but not translated into English until 1958. Propp demonstrated that European fairy tales all share a single structure. Later, in 1976, John G. Cawelti in his *Adventure, Mystery, and Romance: Formula Stories as Art and Popular Culture* brought the structural thesis to bear on these three genres of popular literature, and more recently Janice A. Radway (*Reading the Romance: Woman, Patriarchy, and Popular Literature* [1984]) has used the notion of formulaic writing to launch a fuller discussion of why readers (in this case, women) enjoy popular romances. It seems reasonable to me that there is a recognizable formula for writing an effective book of popular nonfiction as well.

What is this form or structure that characterizes books of popular nonfiction? Within each subgenre of popular nonfiction, there are traditional forms that can be identified—the pseudofable, the several steps program, the definition of parts. However, the basic structure of all varieties of self-help books in particular is much closer to the structure that Alan Dundes, in his study of North American Indian tales, identified as essential to all narrative: lack and lack liquidated (1965, 208). When applied to popular nonfiction, this basic structure becomes, first, a suggestion that something is wrong with us, with the culture that guides or programs us, or with our information about the world (lack); and second, a suggestion of what might be done to correct this problem (lack liquidated). As with our recognition of the basic structure of the urban legend, our recognition of this basic structure—a critique of the culture and a solution—allows us to compare the many books of popular nonfiction to each other in an increasingly meaningful way.

Whose Taste?

When Jan Harold Brunvand came out with the first of his many published collections of urban legends *(The Vanishing Hitchhiker)* in 1981, he said, "As tellers of American urban legends, whether adolescents or adults, *we* are a highly mobile and often fairly affluent folk" (19, my emphasis). Thus, he justified the frequency of "automobile legends" among the many legend types. But his statement also implies that he, an upper-middle-class, well-educated professor of English, could well be among those who tell and listen to such urban legends as "The Killer in the Backseat." Almost everyone can admit to being "taken in" by at least one urban legend. I remember believing that "The Hook" (in which an escaped sex maniac with a hook for one of his hands tries to attack a parked couple) was a true story and really did happen along Devil's Backbone, the local lovers' lane in the countryside just outside my hometown of Huntington, Indiana. Urban legends flourish among college students, office workers, assembly line workers, homemakers, teenagers who work at McDonald's, even college professors. However, because the genre and its formal "giveaway" features—especially the twist at the end—are becoming so well known, many people are less gullible than they used to be. Likely there is a trend among storytellers to claim a level of sophistication too high to actually believe such stories. There may come a time when only the most naive listeners will actually believe urban legends.

Still, there is no specific group that "owns" urban legends or even specific legends such as "The Killer in the Backseat." Folklorists often speak of an individual's participation in a "folk group"—for example, women as a folk group—even though any such group is an abstraction and rarely homogeneous in the way that the term "folk" might imply. Women might more likely tell "The Killer in the Backseat" since the cautionary lesson is directed at them. It could be argued that there is a "taste" that supports the telling of such legends among women. More often, however, the "conduits," as Linda Dégh calls them, responsible for the transmission of such stories are determined more by class and age than by any other factor.

If we look to the readership of popular nonfiction rather than to the participants in legend-telling, the importance of the question of taste is even more obvious. Herbert J. Gans, in his study *Popular Culture and High Culture: An Analysis and Evaluation of Taste* (1974), argues that

> the major source of differentiation between taste cultures and publics is socio-economic level or *class*. Among the three criteria that sociologists use most often to define and describe class position—income, occupation, and education—the most important factor is education (by which I mean, here and elsewhere, not only schooling but also what people learn from the mass media and other sources). (70)

If we substitute Gans's notion of a "taste culture" for the broader term "folk group" in folkloristics, we can see that there may be a group of people more inclined to read popular nonfiction than others and that the constituency of that group might depend upon, among other things, their level of education. It is a given that members of this group or "taste culture" must be literate and like to read (though, in fact, many of these books are available on audiotape or CD, often recorded by the authors themselves). It is telling, I think, that many of the writers of such books are themselves very well educated; many have advanced degrees and hold academic appointments. On the other hand, it is also interesting to notice that these books are considered "popular" rather than academic. Notes are few or absent; most lack a bibliography. One author, Deborah Tannen, on the flyleaf of her book *You Just Don't Understand: Women and Men in Conversation* (1990), separates one list of other popular books she has written from another list of "scholarly" or "edited" books that support her career as a professor.

One could easily suspect that some of these successful, highly credentialed authors might be feeling slightly ashamed of their popular writing. After all, it can be read and understood by people who are middlebrow, people who have not been trained to be quite so discriminating in their reading, people who do not demand much of their cognitive skills. Donald Lazere in his article on literacy and mass media reminds us that "most mass communication aimed at adults, both in television, radio, records, or film, and in print, is at a literacy level not much higher than that of children's programming. . . . Commercial media must appeal to the largest possible market, thus to the lowest common denominator of cognitive development" (1986, 289). Some writers whose writing styles are clearly suitable only for scholarly writing team up with popularizing editor-writers in an effort to meet the differing demands of this popular audience. From one perspective, this is an admission that scholarly writing is elitist, purposefully convoluted and obscure, and often not a joy to read. As David Damrosch says of the writing expectations placed upon graduate students (future scholars, learning to write in an academic style), they "must become less emotive, more analytic, and their work must move beyond a personal reaction to a text or an issue and situate itself explicitly within the scholarly debate" (1995, 149). But Lazere suggests that the difference is more than one of style. Damrosch's graduate students are learning to write for an audience that demands scholarly sophistication, and this includes a taste for analysis as a cognitive skill.

It was once assumed that anyone graduating from a liberal arts college would have developed a taste for analysis. Certainly "critical thinking" is still an aim of the curriculum at most undergraduate institutions. Damrosch seems skeptical. Are writers of popular nonfiction assuming the same taste for analysis that higher education cultivates? Or are they purposefully "dumbing down" their writing for the sake of that wider audience Lazere characterized as having the lowest common denominator of cognitive development? Does this mean that in self-help books, analytical argument is absent and anecdotal evidence and reliance upon a shared conservative "mythology" make up the rhetoric of choice? I'll have more to say in response to this question in chapter 2, where the primary features of the genres of popular nonfiction are outlined, and in chapter 3, where critiques of the genre are given greater attention. For now, I would ask that we remember that a preference for analysis is, in fact, a preference—a matter of taste. Many examples of popular nonfiction do exhibit analytical argument and certainly a process of cultural critique. But along with this, it may well be that the readers of popular nonfiction are pleased to find books that emphasize other ways of learning and teaching in addition to conspicuous analysis and critique.

By Whose Authority?

When a person tells an urban legend, usually someone else is credited as an earlier teller—the "friend of a friend" pattern. This pattern is now so widely recognized by folklorists that it has inspired its own acronym, FOAF. In my version of "The Killer in the Backseat" above, I mentioned (without further explanation) that "Becky told me this about a friend of hers up in New Haven." This motif of authentication is essential to the style of the legend. It adds significantly to the story's credibility. On the other hand, a listener is not usually expected to pursue the chain of transmission (as would a nosy folklorist); the detail is included purely for the sake of lending authority to the telling. The "authority" of this other teller is not a credentialed kind of authority; rather, the other teller is cited as someone who has passed along a truth, an ordinary person who does not make up stories but instead simply relates the latest news.

The system of authentication employed by those writing popular nonfiction is perhaps more complicated than this system of FOAF, but to some extent it amounts to the same thing. On the book jackets, for example, other writers of popular nonfiction are routinely quoted as recommenders of the jacketed work. And throughout many books, previous works by various authors of the genre are cited and used as sources in building an argument, much as in scholarly writing. Such "metacommentary" about the tradition itself within any given book is an important part of the process of promoting the tradition, as we shall see in chapter 2. A slightly different kind of authority acknowledgment is often featured on the covers of self-help books, however, than would typically be seen on academic books. It can be seen in the degree abbreviation—Ph.D. or M.D.—that often follows the principal author's name; the ghostwriter/second author is usually a published writer but not a credentialed authority. Scholarly books rarely announce the author's degree on the front cover since it is assumed that the author has an advanced degree.

It is this need to identify the authors of such books as "authorities" that so disturbs Wendy Kaminer in her 1992 critique of the genre, *I'm Dysfunctional, You're Dysfunctional.* I shall address Kaminer's critique more directly in later chapters, but for now we can acknowledge her complaint that the authors or publishers of popular nonfiction seem convinced that their readers are looking for people who can speak with authority, people who have better answers than they could come up with on their own. The easiest way to assure readers that an author is such an authority is to cite credentials (degrees) or include résumé-like details of past responsibilities in a brief biography. These, along with the book jacket recommendations, are convincing proof for the book buyer that the writer will have something worthwhile to say.

There is a temptation to view the entire enterprise of producing popular nonfiction as simply another profit-motivated business, like television or movie-making. The proof of the writers' "authority" is included to entice readers to buy the product, playing, as Kaminer suggests, on the readers' desire that someone else with authority tell them what to do. My own answer to this complaint is to view the buying of such books less as just another consumer activity and more as an exercise in self-education. There is a long tradition of self-education in America, and Joseph F. Kett, in his exhaustive 1994 historical study of the subject, *The Pursuit of Knowledge under Difficulties: From Self-Improvement to Adult Education in America, 1750–1990,* points to advantages individuals seeking to thus improve themselves have in tapping a known commodity—an expert—as a guide in their pursuit. There is an element of consumerism, but, as with instruction or advice offered in a regular classroom, it is up to the consumers (students) to decide whether what they are learning is worthwhile, no matter what kind of tributes were paid to the teacher or writer before the class began or the book was bought.

What Oft Was Thought

The familiar is not only comfortable but also necessary for things to be understood. Consider my version of "The Killer in the Backseat." There are many elements of the cultural frame of reference that allow the story to "work" as a narrative. Some parts of the cultural frame of reference are simply words or concepts that are shared as part of our "cultural literacy," as E. D. Hirsch (1987) would say—things such as our understanding of time and when people are normally home, what an automobile horn is and when one would use it, what it means to run a red light, and so on. Other elements of the cultural frame of reference that I have found particularly significant in oral narrative performances (see my *Literary Folkloristics and the Personal Narrative*) include more abstract features such as stereotypes, prejudices, customs, or beliefs.

In the case of "The Killer in the Backseat," it is necessary that listeners, like the story's "victim," assume that the person following the victim in the second car is male and that he intends the victim harm. As far as I know, the story has never been told with a man as the "victim" in the first car. Notions about gendered behavior and gender stereotypes are essential to the story. It is required that the listener share the teller's assumption that the male following the woman in the second car is a predator and that the husband would try to protect her from him if possible. Furthermore, for the story to be effective, both my listeners and I must share such ideas as "One way to escape from someone following you in a car is to run red lights, even though that is illegal" or "Two o'clock in the morning is not a good time to be out at night, especially if you are female" or "A man will come out of his house to see what's going on if he hears a horn blowing."

Similarly, in books of popular nonfiction, there will be many allusions to the cultural frame of reference. In effect, deciphering these allusions is my first task as a folklorist, since almost all of these elements of the cultural frame could be considered folklore. In chapters 5, 6, and 7, I look at some of the prominent kinds of folklore used in books of popular nonfiction—proverbs and sayings, personal and traditional narratives, traditional ideas and parts of a common worldview, and some of the motifs characteristic of popular nonfiction itself. I am convinced that the wealth of traditional materials—the comfortable frame of reference tied to an already familiar American culture—is significant in explaining why these books are so popular. People like to hear "what oft was thought" and to be drawn into a discussion along familiar lines before being introduced to anything new. Successful writers of popular nonfiction do this very effectively by highlighting elements of our shared cultural frame of reference.

Maintaining the Stability of Culture

In 1954, Berkeley anthropologist William Bascom wrote for the *Journal of American Folklore* his now classic article, "Four Functions of Folklore." He suggested that four general functions folklore serves are amusement or escape, validating culture, education, and maintaining conformity. He went on to say that the one overarching function of all folklore is to maintain the stability of culture. If we look at an example of folklore, such as "The Killer in the Backseat," we can see all four of the functions Bascom lists as possible interpretations of what is going on when the legend is passed along in a specific context, such as the one I described earlier. We can also see why Bascom would argue that the legend serves the overarching function of "maintaining the stability of culture." Stability is achieved in part by keeping what is already in place and working well, in place and working well. In other words, often folklore is a conservative force; it is there to ensure that what is a part of the culture stays a part of the culture.

In this light, "The Killer in the Backseat" stays a part of the culture precisely because it keeps certain beliefs, customs, attitudes, and stereotypes alive. Even though it varies from one telling to another, it is stable enough in content to serve as a vehicle for maintaining the stability of culture. People who pass along the legend are not consciously maintaining the stability of culture, but Bascom would argue that this is the legend's function nonetheless. For example, one traditional assumption maintained by the story is that women should not be out alone at night. Why? The legend also implies that our culture is a violent one, that many men are predators, that women need protection. The legend also preserves the more positive belief that a good man will assume the risk of protecting a woman he doesn't even know. And the rescuer was at some risk. He may have been wrong. He may have been perceived as simply harassing the woman himself, especially if the man in the backseat was there with the woman's permission—perhaps an inebriated friend she was giving a ride home. But the legend serves to maintain society's belief that there should be some men noble enough to take on that risk and protect those who need their protection.

The legend doesn't solve the problem of violence in American culture; in fact, it serves to maintain the assumption that violence is inevitable. And while the hero-rescuer motif is preserved as well, the worrisome effect of gender stereotypes is maintained with a vengeance. Folklore, in this instance, is a conservative force. But what of popular nonfiction literature? Is it, too, simply a conservative force, one that maintains the stability of the culture we already have? My answer to that is one that moves us to a consideration of the genre itself—the self-help book as a historical phenomenon emerging out of the 1960s and early 1970s and continuing in full force into the new millennium.

Collectively, books of popular nonfiction do, I think, maintain the stability of culture; they do ensure that some elements of past and current culture will be preserved into the next century, the next generation. But, to return to the self-help book's structural formula mentioned earlier, the problem or "lack" to which each self-help book is offered as a solution is formulated as a critique of the existing culture. As in any critique, the authors of self-help books select those elements of the culture that they believe need to be changed, and at the same time they highlight and reinforce those elements that serve in a positive way their own suggested solution. Popular nonfiction, then, does selectively maintain what is necessary and deemed "good" from the prevailing worldview. But self-help books are not simply straightforward expressions of worldview; they are works of analysis and interpretation and offer a cultural critique.

And in this cultural critique lies a clue to the popularity of these books of self-enlightenment. In the 1920s and 1930s, the fields of anthropology and folklore were immersed in the theories and practice of ethnography—collecting data and observing behavior in the field. By the 1960s, the subtext of a critique of Western culture so apparent in these ethnographies was emerging in popular writings as well—in books of popular nonfiction that carried on an examination of contemporary American worldview through a less rigorous yet telling comparison between modern Americans and earlier or less "sophisticated" peoples. George E. Marcus and Michael J. Fischer, in *Anthropology as Cultural Critique,* write, "They—primitive man—have retained a respect for nature, and we have lost it (the ecological Eden); they have sustained close, intimate, satisfying communal lives, and we have lost this way of life (the experience of community); and they have retained a sense of the sacred in everyday life, and we have lost this (spiritual vision)" (1986, 129). Much of the lament in self-help books is, as in this academic study, a lament for what has been lost, and there

is a call to reinstate certain traditions and beliefs that have been unwisely abandoned or neglected.

Writing as Performance in Context

I prefaced my recounting of "The Killer in the Backseat" with a brief description of a possible context—sitting at the kitchen table at my sister's house,
along with my sister and her neighbor. The unelaborated references to Becky
(my sister-in-law), New Haven, and Fort Wayne all presume upon knowledge
shared by the individuals in that particular context. But the role of context
in performance is more extensive than such simple allusions to shared knowledge would suggest. As a storyteller, I can assume that my listeners are not
simply using our shared frame of reference to understand what is happening in the story; I can assume that they are learning something new as an
interpretation emerges in that specific context.

And I can, if I stop to analyze the telling, realize that I am allowing a performance to emerge in that particular context that is uniquely suited to that
context and my personal performance goals. For example, in the story I include the unobtrusive detail that the woman's husband doesn't go to the party
with her because he has the flu. My inclusion of this detail represents to some
extent my understanding of the world (most men would not send their wives
off to a party alone unless something such as an illness interfered), and it also
represents my "reading" of my audience (my listeners would find the idea
of a woman going off to a party late at night without her husband a little
unrealistic; it would take away from the credibility of the story).

Listeners hearing my telling of "The Killer in the Backseat" will understand the story in a way that depends much upon what they, their culture,
and the immediate situation bring along to that brief storytelling session.
I can assume that my listeners will "hear" the stereotypes we share; I can
assume that they will know after I reveal that there was a man hidden in
the backseat that the story is over; I can assume that they will think twice
about leaving their cars unlocked the next time they go anywhere. These
and many other revelations emerge as the story is told. Usually we pay little attention to them; they simply add up to our vague sense of the "meaning" we think we are conveying as storytellers or believe we are hearing as
listeners. In general, we are so unconsciously immersed in our culture, in
our personal situation, even in the specific context of the telling, that we
are unaware of the effect that context has on our understanding of the story
we tell or the story we hear.

The writers and readers of popular nonfiction are immersed as well in a context, and that context has its effects. In this case, the actual response of the reader may be delayed, but the intimate connection between the content of the book and the context surrounding its writing and reading is still obvious. If a culturally charged word such as "God" or "spirit" is used in a book, the cultural frame of reference shared by the writer and reader comes into play, but so does the personal understanding of the reader. The reader's cultural and personal backgrounds are significant elements of the context in which the book is read. In an oral context, the storyteller can manipulate a number of performance characteristics such as timing, setting, visual cues, and gestures (see Bauman, 1992). But when a writer offers a book to a reader, any management of the content by the author or publisher must be accomplished through the words of the text itself. As they are writing, the authors have their only opportunity to really use the context they share with their readers. After that, the rest is up to the readers.

What this means for the popular nonfiction enterprise is that the context for the reception of popular nonfiction books is ultimately a phenomenon and influence shared by the author and the reader, even though the marketing division of the publisher may make great efforts to influence that context as well. It is the reader who decides to buy and read a given book, and it is the reader who does or does not incorporate the "content" of the book into his or her own body of knowledge. If we view the reading of a popular nonfiction book as the reception of a performance in context, we must regard the context as one over which the reader has had some element of choice. The decision to read the book and the reader's response to it are both aspects of what Allen Tough and a number of other researchers would call "self-directed education." Much of how the writer's "performance" is accepted and understood depends upon the reader's values that guided in the selection of the book and its reading. Reader-response theory (see Tompkins, 1980) in literary studies and performance theory in folklore simply reinforce the assertion that the meaning of a text is never solely in the hands of the writer.

One consequence of this is that readers create a mental list of books and writers they particularly enjoy. They read certain books over and over again, and they eagerly await new books by their favorite authors. In effect, they create for themselves what educators would call a "learning project" or personalized system of educational planning, a "self-directed" course of study that emerges from the specific context created by the reader's past and current situation. It is this self-educational context tied to the individual reader that is the new element in this emerging popular culture performance. I shall examine the relationship between self-education and popular nonfiction more closely in chapter 1.

Innovation, Transformation, Enlightenment

Popular nonfiction offers a critique of culture, a challenge to some of its traditional beliefs, and it offers a process of transformation or innovation as well. Twenty years ago, as the discipline of folklore was reexamining some of its primary assumptions, Barre Toelken posed what he called the "twin laws" of folklore process (1996, 39). According to this law, the presentation of folklore will routinely involve both the conservation of tradition and the innovation of new material or practice. Sometimes the person presenting the item of folklore will try to conserve tradition as faithfully as possible; sometimes the new presentation will seem far removed from its "original." Someone retelling "The Killer in the Backseat" will typically try to be true to the source. And yet, as Richard Bauman says of oral performance generally, the impact of the individual performer in a given context must always be taken into account. Otherwise, Bauman argues, "when one views the item of folklore as the collective product and possession of society at large, the performer is reduced to the role of passive and anonymous mouthpiece or conduit for the collective tradition" (1986, 8). Each telling, even of a traditional story such as "The Killer in the Backseat," incorporates the teller's personal response to what he or she perceives to be the full and significant context, and each performance is unique.

The authors of self-help books are eager to preserve and use whatever is useful from the past, but the programs or strategies they offer in their books are touted as "new." In the publishing world, if it is not new, it is plagiarism. It is incumbent on each author to present not necessarily a new theme but a new scheme. In fact, as we shall see, there is a fairly standard set of themes shared by the writers. Nevertheless, as with the authors of novels who dip into the storehouse of universal themes, these authors must create original and effective vehicles for presenting those themes. It is at this level that the books of popular nonfiction are most clearly seen as literary performances. Individual authors are entering an expressive arena as surely as they are entering a marketplace for didactic advice-giving. In chapter 2, I shall address some of the ways in which the writers of self-help books perform as authors intent upon expressing their own creativity as well as serving as teachers for their readers, and in chapters 5 and 8, I shall take up again the issue of what

I am calling here "creative cultural plagiarism," the often unacknowledged presentation of traditional material in newly authored texts.

Discovering Shared Assumptions

Taken collectively, the many urban legends that circulate in American culture (and throughout the world) contribute to a shared worldview; they serve to maintain the stability of culture. Every time I repeat a legend such as "The Killer in the Backseat"—no matter that I am doing so in a context of academic illustration—I add another chink to the wall of accepted violence, tolerated gender stereotypes, and unexamined mistrust already so much a part of the American worldview, what Linda Dégh, in her recent study of the legend, calls "the culture of fear." Still, as an educator, I have the opportunity to invite, even require, examination of those shared stereotypes and assumptions that comprise an American worldview. Together my students and I can hold the legend up to the light of reason and, more important, place it into the flask of compassion and see if it can be transformed into something of didactic value—an educational alchemy. "The Killer in the Backseat" can teach us something about ourselves and perhaps through its mixture of realism and fantasy inspire us to change the very "realities" we have accepted as part of our belief system.

This is precisely what the writers of popular nonfiction are trying to do; this is why I regard them as educators rather than merely opportunists jumping on the bandwagon of a profitable publishing enterprise. And, while I wouldn't go so far as to say along with Marilyn Ferguson that there is a "conspiracy" to support human social and spiritual evolution, I would argue that there is emerging from this boom in self-help literature a sense of community and a passionate drive toward enlightenment. Awareness of ideas, motifs, and beliefs already shared is a central part of this enlightenment. In chapters 5 through 8, I shall survey some of these traditional elements and examine how individuals creatively adapt them as they build their personal philosophies.

Experiential Reading: The Book as Text

Many years ago, folklorist Alan Dundes suggested that folklorists should always try to discover what people listening to an example of folklore thought the item meant. He called the methodological concept "oral literary criticism" (1966). It would be helpful indeed if we had a record of what people who hear

"The Killer in the Backseat" think the story says about American culture, about human nature, about gender differences. It would also be helpful if we had some sense of whether the teller is aware of the folkloristic nature of the story—if, for example, the teller commented in some way on the form of legends, saying something like, "You know, there's always a weird twist at the end," or, "You know, there's always a friend of a friend." Dundes called this second concept "metafolklore," and he thought that both concepts together spoke to the neglected reflexive nature of much folklore.

Similarly, the writers and readers of popular nonfiction are aware of the tradition in which they are participating by virtue of writing or reading self-help books. In effect, the writers and readers have already done, in a natural context, what other researchers and I are doing through more formal means. Books such as Gary Greenberg's *Self on the Shelf: Recovery Books and the Good Life* (1994) or the Garland annotated bibliography on *American Popular Psychology: An Interdisciplinary Research Guide* by Stephen B. Fried (1994) or *The Authoritative Guide to Self-Help Books* by John W. Santrock, Ann M. Minnett, and Barbara D. Campbell (1994) bring recognition to the ideational and literary pattern represented by the abundance of self-help books in our culture. Writers are aware of other writers, and readers are aware of the variety of books and authors available to them. The genre is an "emic" one; it is a genre named and recognized by the readers and writers themselves.

The genre is recognized, and yet the writers, readers, bibliographers, and researchers all appreciate as well the fact that each book is a separate and unique text, one that reflects the individual skills of the writer and represents a particular expression, a distinctive work. The experience of reading a well-developed book of popular nonfiction can be like the experience of reading a poem. I have not taken the time (and it would take much time and effort) to collect readers' responses to individual texts. What I will offer in this study is some discussion of the process of reception as well as my own literary critical response to some of the many works I have read for this project. I believe that in many instances, the quality of writing exhibited by these texts warrants both practical and literary attention. And I think that the readers, the people who buy these books and keep them in print, are themselves thus bringing a previously unrecognized discernment to their reading and voicing their own approval of the talents and efforts the writers bring to this enterprise.

Seeking Wisdom

Bascom argued that education was one of the four general functions of folklore. Those listening to a person telling a version of "The Killer in the Backseat" can be educated in an obvious way: they can learn to always check their backseats; they can remember the story as an important cautionary tale. Beyond this, however, listeners can also ponder the story, perhaps challenging in their own thinking some of the traditional ideas woven into the story and coming away instead with a new sense of how the world might work if we only tried to be more aware of our actions and beliefs.

The readers of self-help literature will have a similar opportunity to incorporate some new insights into their understanding of the world with each book they read. The writers, in their own way, will have that opportunity as well, for they are educating themselves even as they spell out their thoughts for their readers. The process of self-education is parallel in many ways to the age-old process of folklore transmission, folklore performance. The individual is both a part of a community and a solitary learner. Both aspects of the process are necessary—the communal and traditional, the unique and individual, the conservative and the innovative, the popular and the personal.

In the chapters that follow, I shall address some of these issues in more detail, bringing into the discussion examples from the many texts I have read for this study. My own readers will likely have other examples from texts I have not included or have failed to notice. This, of course, is precisely the beauty of such self-directed learning. My hope is that I have provided a framework of analysis that shines a light on the heart of this process—the creative use of cultural resources toward a goal of self-education.

1. American Popular Self-Education

My model for disciplined self-reflection—my grandmother, writing her daily entries in her diary—did not consider herself part of a literary tradition. She thought and wrote for her own sake with no intention that anyone else would read her thoughts. The writers of popular nonfiction are by definition intentional "authors" with every desire that their works be widely read and widely sold, even become best-sellers. This tradition of the popular nonfiction paperback has not always been a part of the American publishing scene. Just as German literary historian Rolf Engelsing argued in *Der Burger als Leser* that in Europe, the nature of reading as an activity was itself transformed by the greater availability of books in the nineteenth century (see Davidson, 1989, 15), we could argue here that the growth of the paperback book industry in the 1960s changed the nature of book buying and consumption in America. The low price and easy availability of paperback books in the past four decades means that readers can now easily buy books that, with little regard for cost, they may or may not read, may never finish, may sell to a used-bookseller or recycle at a garage sale, or may keep and treasure while buying a second or third copy to give to friends. The convenient technology and booming marketplace have supported the growth of popular literature, both fiction and nonfiction. It will be interesting to see how the Internet and desktop publishing will affect our literary behavior over the next few decades. The last half of the twentieth century may well represent a unique period in publishing history, one that fostered this boom in nonfiction paperbacks. But there are other catalysts that have in particular spurred the development of a popular nonfiction tradition in America, especially nonfiction usually designated (often on the back cover) as "self-help" or spiritual enrichment. Four elements are significant as we try to account for the burgeoning of this tradition in the latter half of the twentieth century: (1) individuality and the concept of self in community as part of the American worldview; (2) the tradition of adult self-education in America; (3) the literary tradition of the didactic essay; and (4) the new paradigm of social activism. These influences have steered the development of this popular literary tradition, and our fuller understanding of each can help us explain, in part, America's infatuation with the self-help book.

The Self and Community in American Society and History

A striking characteristic of nearly all of the works of popular nonfiction on bookstore shelves today is the focus on the individual, either directly as in self-help books or indirectly as in books of popular science or spirituality in which the enlightenment of the individual (in contrast to expansion of a discipline) is the objective. This attention to the self is significant; it is the selling factor behind this flourishing industry. And yet the notion of self invoked by these writers is not uniform. Represented in these books are at least four concepts of self that differ from one another in significant ways and determine to some extent the direction of argument presented by the authors. I shall call these four concepts the obligated self, the social self, the wounded self, and the detached self.

One of the earliest works to articulate the now-famous notion of "rugged individualism" as the predominant American character trait was the treatise *Democracy in America* by French philosopher Alexis de Tocqueville, published in 1835. In fact, though the concept of individualism had been around since the seventeenth century, it was not until Tocqueville undertook his study of American culture that a term seemed to be needed to describe this seemingly ubiquitous personality trait shared by all Americans (see Stewart and Bennett, 1991, 133–36). Much has been made of Tocqueville's concern with the dominance of individualism over community, especially in the popular 1985 study by Robert N. Bellah, Richard Madsen, William M. Sullivan, Ann Swidler, and Steven M. Tipton titled *Habits of the Heart,* a phrase they borrowed from Tocqueville. As can be guessed from the subtitle—*Individualism and Commitment in American Life*—Bellah and his colleagues view the historical strength of individualism in America as a worrisome challenge to the more traditional sense of commitment to community and to the general good of "others" in the nation.

Their concern echoes the dichotomy and worry of another nineteenth-century thinker, German sociologist Ferdinand Tönnies, whose classic work

Gemeinschaft und Gesellschaft (1887) posits the collective and cooperative notion of community *(Gemeinschaft)* against the individualistic notion of society, the isolation and self-centeredness of the single individual in the competitive marketplace (see Lasch, 1991, 139–43). And Bellah and his associates are not wrong—Americans do find it hard to abandon their individualism in favor of community. This is no more clearly apparent than in a contrast with the Amish, a religious group within the United States that explicitly maintains its opposition to the "doctrine" of individualism and insists, instead, that members suppress signs of individualism or "at least find fulfillment through collective objectives rather than personal ones," as Donald B. Kraybill argues (1989, 18). Except for such purposefully deviant groups as the Amish, Americans seem indeed to have embraced the notion of individualism and its veneration of the self since the earliest days of the Republic.

What this has meant for our study of popular nonfiction—of self-help books—is that an underlying assumption of all such books is the prominence of the self. Historically, Americans are attuned to the solo voice rather than the chorus; they expect writers to address the needs of the individual first and the community second. It is not that they—writers or readers—have no concern with community; instead, it is simply a matter of viewing the individual, the self, as the first order of business. Individuals must have their own house in order before they can sally forth to serve the community.

According to Sacvan Bercovitch, the Puritans were bound together by a "concept of representative selfhood."[1] Little wonder, then, that from the earliest days, Americans have felt a need to scrutinize the self and worry over the actions of the individual as they do or do not further the individual's progress along the path toward personal salvation. This attachment to the self shows up most clearly in a sense of obligation to improve the self. For example, in a well-known parable in the New Testament (Matthew 25), Jesus tells of the "wicked and slothful servant" who failed to invest the one talent that had been left to him and instead hid it in the ground. This story is often interpreted as a judgment against those who do not work to improve upon what they have been given; in other words, the individual has an obligation toward self-improvement. God expects us to seek to better ourselves, or so the roots of Puritanism would have us believe.

Among the current writers of popular nonfiction, it is in fact often the self-proclaimed Christian writers, such as Stephen Covey or Scott Peck, who assume from the very beginning that the need or obligation for self-improvement is a given. Their concept of self is not so much that of a sin-ridden soul in the hands of an angry God (the Puritan image made famous by Jonathan Edwards) but rather that of a favored and blessed servant who does as God expects, investing himself or herself in the worthy actions of progress and self-improvement. This first concept of self casts individualism as a primary and necessary focus, a personal responsibility, a means by which individuals meets their obligations to improve upon the raw materials God has given. This notion of the "obligated self" encourages a kind of introspection and programmatic effort reminiscent of traditional Christian regimens, Protestant or Catholic (as well as those central to other religious traditions). The focus is on the behavior and spiritual growth of the individual alone, especially as he or she is tested by the demands of the world.

A second concept of self recognizes the individual as accountable to society and therefore requires a balance between "rugged individualism" and community. Writers who adopt this concept offer suggestions for achieving self-fulfillment within the context of the larger community. This is the ideal of the balanced private/public self that many of the interviewees in the book by Bellah and his colleagues seek for themselves. There is still the same sense of obligation to invest the self or the soul as in the first concept, but now there is in addition a social obligation. As Anthony de Mello says, good works, charity, and service to the community are undertaken from the perspective of "enlightened self-interest" (1990, 20). Individuals will feel more content with their stewardship of the self if life includes some clear response to the needs of society.

This sense of social obligation is not so much a moral stance as a wise investment strategy, to return to the parable from the Book of Matthew. Writers of contemporary nonfiction who invoke this concept of the self see co-operation with society as a sound practice policy, a recognition of nature as it really is. They perceive that society is a hierarchy and that the wise person is the one who can balance self-interest and cooperation with the systems he or she encounters. Many of the writers who address their books to the corporate world are particularly aware of this social aspect of the self. Peter M. Senge in his widely read *Fifth Discipline: The Art and Practice of the Learning Organization* (1990) articulates a vision of "the learning organization" as part of a "profound evolution in the nature of work as a social institution," and within that vision the individual is charged with the responsibility to learn the systems that will lead to self- and corporate improvement.[2]

Others writers have adopted this view of the self, including Spencer Johnson and Kenneth Blanchard, whose *One Minute Manager* (1981) has sparked a series of books that instruct the individual in ways to balance personal and community needs. Almost always, achieving this balance involves learning and accepting one's place within a system that includes others. Mihaly Csikszentmihalyi writes, "A person who wants to make a creative contribution not only must work within a creative system but must also reproduce that system within his or her mind. In other words, the person must learn the rules and the content of the domain, as well as the criteria of selection, the preferences of the field" (1995, 47). And by "the field" he means very specifically the people who maintain the system within which the creative individual works.

The selves in this case are obligated to use talents they have been given, and through their own attachments and systems of response, they are tied to a community that offers a context for their efforts. This concept of self is clearly situated within a social world. The "social self" is instructed to be aware of community as a system to which a clear strategy of response can be and must be devised. It is a self that strives for commitment to and balance among, as Susan Jeffers says, the many and varied components of life, not simply personal growth (1987, chap. 8). At the level of academic philosophy, this concept of self is the one that serves the investigation of identity and morality and much of the language of contemporary discourse.[3]

The third concept of self is the one most commonly adopted by the authors of "popular psychology" books, by writers trained in the field of psychology. One might think of this concept of self as the "psychological self," but in fact almost always the concept involved sees the self as "wounded" or at least severely misled by the dysfunctional culture that feeds it. It is this concept of the self that so offends Wendy Kaminer—a view of self as victim, the wounded inner child, the "survivor," the codependent, the needy addict. Gary Greenberg in his study *The Self on the Shelf* argues that this often-invoked concept of the self represents a denial of the importance of "the Other," clearly at the base of modern philosophical discourse—the social self mentioned above.

The "wounded self" is immersed in culture but unable to relate to others in a healthy way. It is not surprising that many psychologists writing books of popular nonfiction view the self as wounded and in need of repair. The medical model of their discipline would seem to require such a notion. A cure comes in treating the wounded self, in analyzing the determining effects of culture, psyche, and personal history on the psychological state of the individual, not in addressing the connections between the individual and his or her community. James Redfield's popular *Celestine Prophecy* builds upon an understanding of the self as controlled by the circumstances of family "dramas," at least until enlightenment comes in the form of psychological education.

A fourth concept of the self is closely related to the third but casts a more optimistic portrait of the health or strength of the soul or spirit at the core of the self. This fourth view of the self is influenced by Eastern thinking. It combines a sense of detachment with an understanding of "the god with-in," or the notion that the self is indomitable and should act that way. I call this the "detached self." Some writers, such as Wayne Dyer or Ivan Hoffman, posit this observing or detached self as the ideal into which we can grow or perhaps to which we can return. This concept of self is closer to the notion of "soul" or "spirit"—the pure manifestation of the divine within every in-dividual, reminiscent of Wordsworth's "child" in "Intimations of Immortal-ity" or of Emerson's "oversoul."

A recent expansion of this concept is in the supposedly "channeled" book *Conversations with God: An Uncommon Dialogue* by Neale Donald Walsch. Like Jane Roberts some years earlier, Walsch claims to be simply taking dic-tation from a conversation with God (with Jane Roberts, it was a spirit named Seth). In Walsch's first book (there are several in the series), God tells him, "Upon entering the physical universe, you *relinquished your remembrance of yourself. . . .* You are, have always been, and will always be, a *divine part* of the *divine whole,* a *member of the body.* That is why the act of rejoining the whole, of returning to God, is called *remembrance*" (1995, 28, emphasis in original). In Walsch's book, God is the detached self, the observing spirit who knows all of life and of whom we are all a part, though we have forgotten. Though other writers may not take the notion quite so far as Walsch, those who adopt the concept of a detached self do share his understanding of the self as a di-vine soul capable of stepping aside from those attachments to the world that make us seem less divine than we are. Such writers hope to guide readers toward that lost but always-possible state of detachment. The detached self is one of potentiality.

The reliance upon these four concepts of self in the growing body of pop-ular nonfiction underscores the personal aspect of the subject matter. Wheth-er feeling obligated, social, wounded, or detached, the selves that read these books are presumed to be taking up these readings because the authors speak to their personal worries or needs and to their desire for a clearer sense of who they are, the nature of their world, and what they are doing here. In other words, the readers of popular nonfiction see their reading as part of a pro-cess of self-education through which they will learn more about the "selves" these writers have offered to help define, enlighten, and perhaps transform.

The Tradition of Adult Self-Education

Many of the products associated with American popular culture are intend-ed to entertain—movies, music CDs, television shows, comic books, paper-back novels. But the books we are considering here—books of popular nonfiction—are intended to educate the reader. Readers buy them not for their entertainment value but rather for their utility in various self-initiated programs of self-education. The tradition of self-education has been a part of American culture from the very beginning. Joseph Kett, in his study *The Pursuit of Knowledge under Difficulties,* traces the emergence of the more inclusive tradition of adult education out of the various societies for self-improvement that were a part of American culture from colonial days, phenomena like the well-known Chautauqua movement. The nonfiction paperbacks that have become so popular in the last four decades are a part of this tradition as well but a part that has usually been overlooked in research on adult education.

In *Adults as Learners: Increasing Participation and Facilitating Learning* (1981), K. Patricia Cross reviews the work of researchers such as Allen Tough and Malcolm S. Knowles who have focused on the phenomenon of "self-directed learning."[4] One of the striking features of adult education generally but self-directed learning in particular is that it is problem-oriented. As Knowles explains, the adult "comes into an educational activity largely because he is experiencing some inadequacy in coping with current life problems. He wants to apply tomorrow what he learns today, so his time perspective is one of immediacy of application. Therefore, he enters into education with a problem-centered orientation to learning" (1978, 58). The book of popular nonfiction, with its typical problem/solution structure, is a likely candidate for such self-directed learning. In fact, it would seem that such books become necessary as adult learners recognize their inadequacy in addressing *on their own* the kinds of problems featured in self-help books. Though Wendy Kaminer found this very reliance upon experts a shameful selling out of the much-vaunted American individualism, it seems an honest and utilitarian response to the nature of adult learning. Cross tells us that "self-directed learning is likely to be inefficient if the learner cannot define what he wants to know or needs help in locating the relevant resources. In such instances, the learner will be dependent on outside help" (1981, 194). These are precisely the two things that the author of a nonfiction book can do for readers—clarify the problem and offer an interpretative integration of sources as part of the solution.

The writer helps readers in this way but does not, on the other hand, take away the readers' initiative as "planners" of their own "learning projects." These terms—planner and learning project—are borrowed from Allen Tough's research on self-directed study among adults. In effect, by adopting these terms, we redefine the process of selecting and reading books of popular nonfiction as a freely chosen and deliberate educational endeavor planned by the reader, not simply a consumer response to effective marketing. Readers include the books they read as part of a planned reading program—a learning project—that they themselves design. Granted, they likely will not write out a syllabus, nor even keep a written bibliography, but for their own purposes they will have constructed "learning projects" that are accomplished as the various books they choose are purchased, borrowed, read, or rejected.

We might say that readers of popular nonfiction create their own curricula and course designs and independently integrate the various readings into cumulative "projects" that address the problems that motivated their reading in the first place. What they come to "know," then, is what they themselves accept as true from what they have read. They construct their own learning—at least on the subject of their project—through the process of self-directed reading.[5] Readers of self-help books are *active* learners; though they are not responding in a seminar nor experientially observing in the field, they are nonetheless the ones who choose the readings and move through their self-directed programs at the pace they set.

And the books they choose can be powerful components of the self-education program these readers adopt. Joseph Kett reports a belief, strongly adhered to by those who pursued self-education a century ago, that "books would transform individuals, almost like a conversion experience" (1994, 160). Certainly it is the aim of many writers that their readers, upon reading their books, be transformed and converted from their old unenlightened selves into new "improved" and educated individuals.[6] For most modern writers, there is a recognition that their readers are seeking wisdom through their process of reading. Their readers are not hoping to learn an academic discipline or body of information; instead, they are hoping to solve a perceived problem. The literary tradition that lends itself to that process is an old one.

The Literary Tradition of the Didactic Essay

The popular nonfiction tradition is a part of the literary tradition, not a branch of research or scholarship, though many of these popular paperbacks make use of scholarly sources and sophisticated research techniques and many of the authors wear the hat of a scholar in other contexts. This distinction between scholarship and the kind of writing we are examining here is a blurry one. Perhaps it would help if we specify the most significant differences between the two kinds of writing. Jacques Barzun and Henry F. Graff, authors of *The Modern Researcher,* describe conventional scholarship as follows: "Accumulation and verification must take precedence over literary skill, and encyclopedic thoroughness must become a commandment. To be scientific, a monograph must tell all about a single small subject, and what the work contains must aim at being definitive" (1985, 55). Not all scholarship meets this rigid outline, but the overview does suggest ways in which popular nonfiction writing differs from scholarly writing.

Building upon the description of scholarship offered by Barzun and Graff, I would suggest three important ways in which works of popular nonfiction differ from scholarship. First, authors of popular nonfiction write with the aim of articulating a problem of some personal significance to the reader and of offering a solution, of providing helpful guidance. In contrast, scholars hope to advance their disciplines or add to the cumulative understanding of a specific topic. Second, popular nonfiction, like all literature, hopes to be aesthetically appealing and to satisfy the reader's expectations for a competent, even artistic, literary performance. Scholarship is expected to be exhaustive and accurate, even to the point of tediousness if necessary. And third, writers of popular nonfiction use illustrations that effectively convey their ideas even at the expense of thoroughness of example (potentially invoking the reductive fallacy), while scholars are cautious about making generalizations and hesitate to let any one instance carry too much weight, even if the illustration is rhetorically persuasive.

This distinction between popular nonfiction and scholarship is an important one to establish before we consider the effect the tradition of didactic literature has had in the emergence of contemporary nonfiction. In viewing popular nonfiction as a continuation of a literary tradition, we ascribe to the writers the motives that inspire literature—a desire to express an idea or feeling, to persuade or move an audience, even to delight—rather than the more austere and formal motives of scholarship. Writers in the didactic tradition do have some more practical goals than those associated with, say, fiction writers or poets, but they do have every reason, nevertheless, to regard their written products primarily as pieces of expressive and rhetorical writing rather than scholarship.

Let us look at this didactic tradition. It is an ancient and respected one, starting, we must assume, well before the advent of writing. Long before the first Aesopic fables were written down, tales were told and proverbs were prescribed by community elders, parents, and others who had reason to instruct or advise. One of the age-old functions of all folklore is education, and performers who would amuse us are just as often eager to teach us as well. On the other hand, there are those who would argue that "literature"—true art—is never utilitarian, never purposeful, that writing intended to advise or persuade is communication or rhetoric but not literature.

Still, the line is a fine one, and the distinction is a matter of convention. Ancient myths, such as the story of Oedipus or the story of Noah and the ark or the many Native American stories of Coyote and the establishment of human practices—no less than Martin Luther King Jr.'s "I Have a Dream" speech or Henry David Thoreau's "Civil Disobedience"—involve an obvious aesthetic dimension; they are moving or entertaining as well as instructive. The didactic tradition has had to present itself in a palatable form and remain consistently appealing to its audience; otherwise, the didactic tendency would have died out long ago.

Not surprisingly, then, this didactic tendency is alive and well in contemporary America—in sermons, in public television broadcasts, in the public lecture hall, and particularly in the form of popular nonfiction paperbacks we are examining here. The tradition can be traced back through literature to Plato, and its most famous proponent in our more recent literary tradition is the British poet Alexander Pope, whose 1734 "Essay on Man" influenced many early American writers. The practice of didactic writing represents the continuation of a tradition explored and expanded by such notable American authors as Cotton Mather, Benjamin Franklin, Ralph Waldo Emerson, and Henry David Thoreau.

But what of these many didactic writers today? Are they, in the opinion of most people, writing literature? Certainly they are not writing didactic poetry as did Pope. In general, nonfiction, especially didactic nonfiction, has a hard time finding acceptance in the canon of respected literature. One wonders whether Emerson's "Self-Reliance" would be so easily accepted as an example of literary writing now, a century and a half later. The question is really whether the genre itself is viewed with prejudice. The authors of these current nonfiction paperbacks vary in their skills as writers, and any would, in my opinion, be hard-pressed to produce something as impressive as most of Emerson's work. Nevertheless, it is worthwhile to consider what it is they are about, to grant them the courtesy of a serious critique within the literary tradition they represent.

William Flint Thrall, Addison Hibbard, and C. Hugh Holman offer the following commentary on the nature of "didacticism" in *A Handbook to Literature:*

> Instructiveness in a literary work one of the purposes of which appears to be to give guidance, particularly in moral, ethical or religious matters. Since all literary art exists in order to communicate something—an idea, a teaching, a precept, an emotion, an attitude, a fact, an autobiographical incident, a sensation— the ultimate question of didacticism in a literary work appears to be one of the intent of the author or of his ostensible purpose. (1960, 144–45)

There is little doubt that contemporary self-help or enrichment authors intend their works to be instructive. What may be debatable is whether their works represent "literature" or whether, instead, they should be considered merely examples of "popular culture" along with the mysteries, romances, and westerns that John Cawelti groups together. In the next chapter, we shall address in greater depth this question of the artistry apparent in the genres of popular nonfiction.

Whether the authors intend their works to be seen as literature or not, they do intend them to speak to the concerns of what has come to be called "New Age" readers. This same concern was apparent as well in an earlier "new age" in America—Emerson's period of transcendentalism and what Lewis Perry calls "polite culture" that arose in the decades after the 1820s (1984, 207–59). During that earlier time, middle-class Americans clamored to learn how to be a more moral and enlightened people. Much of the "newness" of the period was to be found in its promotion of the individual and "feelings," two phenomena celebrated variously in such works as Emerson's essay "Self-Reliance" and Edwards A. Park's *Theology of the Intellect and the Theology of the Feelings,* published toward the end of the period in 1850. More recently, scholars have reassessed the effects of that period in America's intellectual history, especially as it has left its mark on the contemporary period. Francis L. K. Hsu, in *Rugged Individualism Reconsidered,* argues that "all of our major internal problems . . . are traceable, directly or indirectly, to that much extolled virtue of our Founding Fathers, rugged individualism" (1983, 4). On the other hand, as mentioned earlier, Robert Bellah and his colleagues contend that contemporary American values combine individualism and commitment in such a way as to continue the search for an individualized, morally and spiritually sound life so central to that earlier "new age" of Emerson and Thoreau.

What this means in the context of these many self-help and self-enlightenment books is that the authors of these works are able to draw upon a well-established tradition within the popular worldview. Americans are used to sharing a collective appreciation for "rugged individualism," whether it is necessarily good for us or not, and we continue to share a concern for our moral and spiritual behavior. By virtue of this literary and cultural tradition, we share the assumption that the maintenance of these values is each individual American's personal responsibility, that we, taking our cue from Emerson, must strive to be self-reliant and independent and to attend—each of us—to our moral and spiritual growth.

It is perhaps not at all surprising that one book among the many I have reviewed for this project is a reconsideration of Emerson's didactic essays in light of today's needs, Marianne Parady's *Seven Secrets for Successful Living: Tapping the Wisdom of Ralph Waldo Emerson to Achieve Love, Happiness, and Self-Reliance* (1995). While such modern didactic pieces are full-length books rather than essays, they continue a tradition of didactic literature that has always been a part of American culture. The relationship to the didactic essay tradition is perhaps clearest in those books that are collections of "meditations," such as Anthony de Mello's *Awareness* (1990) or Jon Kabat-Zinn's *Wherever You Go, There You Are* (1994). But all of them pick up the informal tone of the personal essay and insert that tone into a book-length piece that serves a didactic purpose.[7] The result is a new kind of book, one that adopts the tone and style of the informal essay, the problem/solution structure of the self-directed learning project, and the function of didactic literature.

The New Paradigm of Social Activism

Embedded in the function of didactic literature is the message that we should be about doing something—usually what traditional religious figures have called "good works." In her classic call to a "New Age," Marilyn Ferguson reviews some of the rich discussion of self-psychology in the work of Abraham Maslow and pays particular heed to his warning that "a fear of knowing is very deeply a fear of doing, because of the responsibility inherent in new knowledge" (1980, 146). Maslow and Ferguson seem to be in agreement that with new knowledge comes a responsibility to do something with that knowledge. Writers of popular nonfiction are, in effect, striving to erase the fear people would have of "doing" what needs to be done, of "knowing" that they are responsible. Inescapably, as Maslow argues, when a person knows the truth, he or she will feel compelled to act to bring about the changes that are needed. This is why various kinds of activism are a natural outgrowth of the self-improvement crusade.

For readers of books of popular nonfiction, the first order of business may well be changes in their own lives, often changes within the context of family and other immediate social relationships. However, for many readers there will be a pull toward some larger social commitment, as Bellah and his associates found, or toward some venue for service and contribution. Giving back to the social and physical environment is seen as essential. This is one of the instructions often offered by the authors of self-help books. Even the most crassly self-centered books advocate doing something for others, of engaging in social, community, and environmental service. Robert J. Ringer, in *Looking Out for #1,* says, "What is involved, at its highest level, is rational selfishness—acting on the belief that the good you hope to receive in return will be worth the time, effort and/or money you expend in doing something for the other person" (1977, 50). Spencer Johnson says much the same thing in *One Minute for Myself* (1985, 106). And these are just two of the books that claim to be completely self-serving rather than altruistic.

The consensus is that people gain something personally from service to others and to the earth, an idea clearly at the base of much of the community involvement sought by people interviewed by Robert Bellah and his associates. Wayne Dyer, in his 1997 book, *Manifest Your Destiny,* suggests that there are four stages in the growth of the enlightened individual: the athlete, the warrior, the statesperson, and the spirit. The third level—the statesperson, or the individual who seeks to serve or make a contribution—is the one to which most people aspire, he argues. And many writers would claim that youth is no barrier to being a "statesperson," that this "level" is instead a new paradigm that may be grasped by individuals at any time. It is the stage at which Marilyn Ferguson would describe members of the New Age "Aquarian Conspiracy." To repeat her definition: "The paradigm of the Aquarian Conspiracy sees humankind embedded in nature. . . . It sees us as stewards of all our resources, inner and outer. . . . The new perspective respects the ecology of everything: birth, death, learning, health, family, work, science, spirituality, the arts, the community, relationships, politics" (1980, 29). In effect, the new paradigm behind much of the popular nonfiction written today calls for some direct involvement in the process of social change.

Though this call for engagement is a tacit assumption behind much of the writing we are examining here, we can see some significant variation just in how the paradigm of social activism is invoked by various authors. One way alluded to above is what Ringer called "rational selfishness." I prefer a term that Ram Dass borrows from the Dalai Lama—"selfish altruism." In the preface to their book *Compassion in Action,* Ram Dass and Mirabai Bush offer the following:

> We are searching for a way of acting for social change in the world that is compatible with, in fact contributes to, psychological, intellectual, and spiritual growth, and acknowledges that, as Gandhi said, our life is our message. We are exploring what the Dalai Lama calls "selfish altruism": compassionate action is not done *for* others—it is done *with* others, *for* ourselves, because we can no longer avoid it. It helps fulfill our lives. (1992, xii)

This "selfish altruism" is motivated by a desire to feel good about ourselves. Anthony de Mello says, "Charity is really self-interest masquerading under the form of altruism," and he goes on to identify this altruism as a "more refined kind of selfishness" through which "I give myself the pleasure of pleasing others" (1990, 19). He and a number of other writers are very clear about the role social activism can play in fulfilling our own need for feeling useful. As Scott Peck says, "Virtually anyone who joins an organization . . . does so with two needs: to give something and to get something" (1993b, 33). Giving is as satisfying as getting.

A second embodiment of the paradigm is through the search for community, for the sense of *Gemeinschaft* articulated by Ferdinand Tönnies in the last century. Joseph Kett recognizes the call for "community education" in the early part of this century as a response to the need for loyalties and attachments formed within small face-to-face groups (1994, 314–15). Granted, those offering the "education" or, in modern instances, the social service are not really part of the group they serve. Nevertheless, they enjoy the experience of interacting within a community and of receiving the affectionate regard of those with whom they work. Robert Coles, in *The Call of Service,* writes at some length about the complexity of the relationship between volunteers and the people they serve (1993, 245–53). Most striking is his observation that, when interviewed, what people "being served" noticed most was the enthusiasm of the volunteers who served them; their "enthusiasm was one of the qualities they most admired and for which they expressed gratitude." Quite apart from the help that is given, volunteers are appreciated for their human interaction. And not surprisingly, this engagement in a community, this meaningful social interaction, is a large part of what the volunteers themselves find gratifying as well.

A third illustration of the paradigm of social activism is in what innovative educators in the 1960s called "experiential learning." Wilbert J. McKeachie, in the tenth edition of his classic manual for college teachers, *Teaching Tips,* includes a chapter on "Experiential Learning" and describes the practice as entailing "a broad spectrum of educational experiences, such as community service, fieldwork, sensitivity training groups, internships, [and] cooperative education involving work in business or industry" (1999, 154). And more directly, David H. Lempert has written a book (*Escape from the Ivory Tower: Student Adventures in Democratic Experiential Education* [1996]) entirely devoted to the development of experiential education opportunities for college students. Many of the courses he suggests are designed to take students into the local or global community to work with people outside the "ivory tower" and to participate in collaborative solutions to real social and economic problems.

Many organizations founded to serve various social and environmental needs attract adults who adopt this same service-oriented and experiential learning perspective—what Sam Rushforth, a conservation biologist at Brigham Young University, calls "activist pedagogy" (see Dolby, 1998). Some of the formal organizations that incorporate this view are Educators for Social Responsibility (Cambridge, Massachusetts), Learning Alliance (New York City), Earthwatch, and Habitat for Humanity. All such organizations regard participation as a learning experience and service as a cooperative venture through which the people served are simply aided in their own efforts. One objective—the one that ties such groups to much of the popular nonfiction we are examining here—is to experience effectiveness as a participant, to learn how collaborative work, often tedious and clumsy, is actually done in an effort to bring about needed change. A number of environmental, wildlife, and world hunger groups are attractive to people who seek to learn through first-hand experience the kinds of activities that promote positive change.

A fourth avenue by which social activism has emerged in the context of works of self-improvement and popular learning is in what has been called "liberation theology." Phillip Berryman has written the classic work on this movement, and he describes liberation theology "in terms of three closely related tasks: to reinterpret Christian faith in terms of the bleak lot of the poor; to criticize society and its ideologies through theology; and to observe and comment on the practices of the church itself, and of Christians" (1987, 87). One interpretation of this threefold charge is that offered by Paulo Freire, who set about the task of teaching adult peasants not only to read and write but also to address issues of vital importance to their lives, such as conflicts of power and land ownership.[8] The critique of society is a common theme of many works of popular nonfiction, of course. The new element here is in tying theology—usually specifically Christian theology—to an activist condemnation of poverty.

A similar notion urging activism in the cause of justice and the eradication of poverty is behind what religious adult educator Linda Vogel identifies as the "new earth" metaphor. She writes: "Participating in creating a new earth (the reign and realm or kingdom of God) requires a renewed faith and engagement in reconstructing society. People of faith are called to join together to . . . find a new freedom to live (and if necessary, die) as they invest themselves in working for justice" (1991, 88). The challenge to do "good works" has always been seen as a religious obligation, but this new application of liberation theology is taken on as an opportunity to serve by those who see injustice around them.

In many cases, one of these four kinds of social activism is apparent in the motivation for writing or reading a given book of popular nonfiction. Sometimes this motivation is clear in the title of the book, as in Karen Kissel Wegela's *How to Be a Help Instead of a Nuisance: Practical Approaches to Giving Support, Service, and Encouragement to Others* (1996). Through bits and pieces of biographical detail, we learn that many of the writers of books of popular nonfiction have participated in various social service or environmental activities. It is not surprising that they incorporate leanings toward such involvement into their books.

The popular nonfiction tradition that has expanded over the last four decades had its beginnings in the didacticism of ancient fables and proverbs. It has flourished for a number of reasons, but four ingredients that have been particularly influential are American individualism and the concept of the "self," the tradition of adult self-education, the literary tradition of the didactic essay, and the new paradigm of social activism. These factors, along with developments in book production and marketing, the proliferation of training and self-improvement workshops and classes, and a growing introspection among those responsible for American commercial and political activities, have encouraged the emergence of a popular nonfiction tradition. Especially since the terrorist attacks of September 11, 2001, people want to know how to solve our private and social problems.

2. The Books, the Writers, and Metacommentary

What is a "self-help" book? The term serves to identify (very loosely) a category of popular nonfiction. Upon checking Barnes and Noble's web site, I found more than 17,000 books among its holdings with "self-help" as the subject matter. In their *Authoritative Guide to Self-Help Books,* John W. Santrock, Ann M. Minnett, and Barbara D. Campbell surveyed 1,000 works they categorized as books on self-help topics. They include thirty-two subcategories within this larger category (ranging from abuse, addiction, and anger, through codependency, death, and dying, to intimacy, marriage, and sexuality), but they intentionally leave out books on such other topics as spirituality and medicine as well as popular books about the environment, science, creativity, and business.

The *Authoritative Guide* looks primarily at books of popular psychology, not other kinds of books that might be included in the general category of self-help, and the authors' objective is to offer lay people evaluations of those books informed by the elicited comments of mental health professionals. They do offer a definition: "Self-help books are books that are written for the lay public to help individuals cope with problems and live more effective lives" (1994, 4). This definition is in keeping with the problem/solution formula associated with the general category of self-help books, but in fact the kinds of problems addressed by the books Santrock, Minnett, and Campbell select are ones confined to what bibliographer Stephen B. Fried more precisely identifies as concerns of "psychological self-help."

It is good to be aware of the reason scholars in the field of psychology have concerned themselves with this boom in self-help books. As is clear in the definition offered above by the authors of the *Authoritative Guide,* psychological self-help books are intended to "help individuals cope" with problems, psychological problems. In fact, this objective is parallel to that of therapy and psychological treatment, of the clinical practice upon which many of the authors of self-help books draw for their rhetorically effective case studies. At issue for many scholars in the field of psychology is the growing use of self-help books *as a part of therapy*, as part of the "prescription" offered by practicing therapists.

Quite reasonably, I think, such scholars are worried that patients who are assigned or even simply encouraged to read self-help books will misdiagnose their own problems and misuse the suggestions made in the books. Many of the scholarly articles included in Fried's section on "Self-Help Books" in his annotated bibliography of *American Popular Psychology* address the problem of "bibliotherapy," the use of self-help books in therapy. With caution, however, some scholars, such as Steven Starker in his *Oracle at the Supermarket: The American Preoccupation with Self-Help Books* (1989), conclude that self-help books are already a part of the current cultural scene and that psychologists themselves need to be more aware of the values and applications conveyed through such books.

There is an important respect in which the larger category of "self-help books" takes some of the pressure away from this narrow concern over the use or misuse of such books in therapy. If we include in the category such other kinds of books as popular offerings on alternative medicine or business and management or books on spirituality, popular science, or creativity, then we can see that the intentions of the author and the actual use to which the book is put by the reader may be slightly or even very different. In other words, self-help books—specifically psychological self-help books—may function in ways that have little to do with their actual efficacy as tools of therapy.

What do we mean, then, by "self-help" book? In the fields of folklore and anthropology, scholars often differentiate between "etic" and "emic" genres. Etic genres are those categories of folklore that are identified and named by the scholar (or the scholar's discipline); they are used for cross-cultural comparative study, and usually their identifying characteristics are carefully outlined in a textbook definition of the genre. Thus, for example, the "legend" is an etic category identifying a particular kind of realistic traditional story, and scholars name such stories "legends" whenever, based on their understanding of the discipline's definition of the genre, they encounter "legends" in the field. Emic genres, on the other hand, are those categories of folklore identified and (usually) named by the people who create or use the folklore;

they are culture-specific and may or may not lend themselves easily to cross-cultural comparison.[1]

In the case of self-help books, there are a number of groups vying for the right to establish an agreed-upon understanding—an etic category—for self-help books. Publishers have a stake in influencing the market through the naming of their products; bookstores need to organize and promote their wares in an effective and appealing way; psychologists feel the need to distinguish between scholarly research in their field and books sometimes used in do-it-yourself therapy; and some individuals associate with a distinct activist "self-help movement" that works with nonprofit self-help groups (this last mentioned interest has very little to do with the books typically called "self-help" books; see Riessman and Carroll, 1995). Who gets to say what "self-help" really means? I have chosen to use the term because it seems closest to the earlier, perhaps more accurate term "self-improvement" used to describe the active intention of the reader as he or she engages in selecting and reading the book. For most Americans, "self-improvement" sounds a little stuffy; "self-help" is more direct, more honest. It describes what the reader is seeking and what the reader thinks the author and publisher are selling. Popular usage, then, allows self-help books to emerge as an emic genre, but as with most such categories, it remains only vaguely defined. I propose to borrow the emic term and make it a more precisely defined etic category, a popular literary genre, the self-help book.

The Books

The word "genre," borrowed from the French and meaning "type" or "kind," is often used in literary studies or art history or even the performance arts to classify styles or forms of expressive artifacts or performance. In folklore studies, both form and style are used in distinguishing genres but always with attention to content and function as well. Part of what separates self-help books from other genres of popular literature is the distinctiveness of these last two aspects—content and function. Or, more precisely, it is the unique combination of (1) self-improvement content; (2) an informal, rhetorical style; (3) the general problem/solution structure within some fairly predictable literary forms; and (4) an educational function that sets this category apart as a genre of popular literature and a distinct and identifiable element of American culture.

Before we look more closely at each of these features of the genre, let me propose a definition of self-help books modified from the one offered by

Santrock, Minnett, and Campbell in their *Authoritative Guide to Self-Help Books:* Self-help books are books of popular nonfiction written with the aim of enlightening readers about some of the negative effects of our culture and worldview and suggesting new attitudes and practices that might lead them to more satisfying and more effective lives. The desire for "more effective lives" seems essential to either definition. But the definition I propose here adds a purely educational dimension (enlightenment) to the process and admits that the reader's aim may be to lead a more satisfying as well as a more effective life. In effect, this expanded definition recognizes the self-help book's function as an educational and perhaps inspirational resource rather than as simply a remedy, even when the author may have intended the book to serve as a cure.

This quandary about the function and content of self-help books sometimes shows up symbolically on the back or front cover of a work where the publisher has tried to indicate the category to which the book belongs. For example, Stephen Covey's best-seller *The Seven Habits of Highly Effective People* bears the following identifiers at the top of the back cover: Self-Help/ Psychology/Inspirational. His more recent *Principle-Centered Leadership* (1990) is identified as Business/Self-Help/Inspiration. Stephen and Ondrea Levine's book *Embracing the Beloved: Relationship as a Path to Awakening* (1995) is classified as Spirituality/Self-Help, while Paula Payne Hardin's *What Are You Doing with the Rest of Your Life? Choices in Midlife* (1992) is marked with the label Personal Growth/Self-Help. Both Marsha Sinetar's *Developing a 21st-Century Mind* (1991) and Neil Fiore's *Now Habit* (1989) are classified as both Self-Help and Business books, but in Sinetar's case the business designation comes first while in Fiore's case "Self-Help" is listed first. Mark Goulston and Philip Goldberg's *Get Out of Your Own Way* (1995) is marked as both Self-Help and Psychology. Louis Janda's *Psychologist's Book of Self-Tests* (1996) is identified simply as Self-Help.

At play here is a certain uneasiness with acknowledging not amateurish but rather popular and applied research in some of the standard academic disciplines: business, psychology, religion, philosophy, education, medicine, sociology and anthropology, even physics, biology, and environmental studies. It is one thing to write informatively about one's discipline for a lay audience and yet another thing to write with the clear intention of offering guidance to each individual reader—to suggest ways that one's discipline or research might directly affect a reader's personal philosophy and day-to-day behavior in the world. The sermons of preachers and the lectures of teachers are probably the closest analogy to this kind of writing in contemporary American culture—perhaps the homilies of priests, rabbis, and preachers more clearly than the lessons of teachers. Their intention is to enlighten and persuade, and their content is, at least to some extent, the theology and discipline of their training.

We may expect preachers to offer homilies, but we typically expect scholars in a given discipline to write books that further that discipline, maybe even making that discipline more accessible to lay readers, but not to write books that guide readers toward more effective and satisfying lives—not to write self-help books. Authors who choose to write self-help books address not simply a different audience but also a different task than those associated with scholarly writing. Even a book like Paul Davies's *God and the New Physics* is written in response to the author's observation that "ordinary people" are "searching for a deeper meaning behind their lives" (1983, vii). The content of self-help books is both varied and consistent. It draws upon a variety of disciplines, yet it consistently emerges in the writing as the stuff of self-improvement—new insights, reconsidered conventions and ideas, more meaningful answers to questions about the world and the cosmos, suggestions on ways to change an attitude or behavior that may bring greater satisfaction to the reader's life. The basic content of self-help books is practical knowledge and insights that can be used for self-improvement.

The style of self-help books is decidedly informal in comparison to the formal, academic style of scholarly writing. Typically there are few if any footnotes or endnotes and often no bibliography. The style is also rhetorical rather than artistic, although some books may use language in ways that are appealing as well as persuasive. Authors often use second person in addressing their readers, and nearly all use a plural "we" to make themselves more an approachable part of the reader's circle of acquaintances. Self-help books frequently make use of trendy or colloquial language, sometimes even purposefully using popular or truly vulgar (in both senses) terms. For example, in *Breaking Free: A Prescription for Personal and Organizational Change,* David M. Noer uses the term "BSer" to identify people who respond to organizational situations with aggressive but shallow solutions. He says of his choice of usage: "We fervently sought a more scientific (if not more politically correct) term for this type but—based on input from colleagues, clients, and personal experience—could not discover a more descriptive label. We mean BSer in its common colloquial and fetid sense" (1997, 67).

Closely related to the style of self-help books is the form, or rather the variety of forms, of self-help books. At a deep level, all self-help books take the form (or more accurately, the structure) of the problem/solution puzzle: some troublesome or faulty belief or practice is a part of culture, and the author exposes this error in some effective way; the author then presents a solution to the problem and tries to persuade readers to accept it, or better yet to try using the proposed solution in their lives. Beyond this basic structure, however, there are a number of specific subgenres or forms that authors have chosen to use in taking on their literary task.

Out of the more than three hundred self-helps books I have read and the countless more I have browsed at bookstores, I have identified three general literary forms that are typically used by contemporary authors: the parable, the essay, and the manual or how-to book. We might expect to see most self-help books falling into the last category, but in fact relatively few do. Those that do tend to be in the field of business or time management, for example, Alan Lakein's *How to Get Control of Your Time and Your Life* (1973) or, more recently, Perry M. Smith's *Rules and Tools for Leaders* (1998). Actually, Smith's book, which is quite good, takes the form of the manual only in the substantial appendix A, which comprises a "Checklist and Guidelines for the Busy Leader." The main part of the book takes the essay form with divisions in the discussion falling into parts dictated by each of the "rules" included in the checklist. In a similar vein, Arthur L. Williams Jr.'s *All You Can Do Is All You Can Do but All You Can Do Is Enough!* (1988) offers a number of specific rules and formulas, as does Walter Anderson's *Confidence Course: Seven Steps to Self-Fulfillment* (1997), but in both books, each section or rule is bolstered by a short essay explaining why that rule makes sense.

Other books that take the how-to form are typically in the field of medicine or diet (Joan Borysenko's *Minding the Body, Mending the Mind* [1987]; Andrew Weil's *Spontaneous Healing* [1995]), child rearing (Benjamin Spock's *Baby and Child Care* [1946], since reprinted and revised many times), personal relationships (David J. Lieberman's *Never Be Lied to Again* [1998]), the more general "personal growth" (Ken Keyes Jr.'s *Handbook to Higher Consciousness* [1975] and *How to Enjoy Your Life in Spite of It All* [1980]), or, as we might expect, sexuality (Lonnie Barbach's *For Each Other: Sharing Sexual Intimacy* [1983]). Some books of popular psychology adopt the how-to form but expand each "step" in the how-to process into a fuller essay that serves to persuade rather than simply to instruct. For example, Sidney B. Simon's *Getting Unstuck* (1988) offers a number of specific strategies for overcoming eight "roadblocks" he outlines in the book. Simon, as one of the authors of the influential educational handbook on *Values Clarification* (1972), is quick to offer in *Getting Unstuck* exercises that he hopes will "teach" his readers the strategies he is presenting. This modified how-to book is actually more like a workbook, and there are a number of self-help books that borrow this classroom tool as part of their form and argument.

Like teachers who more often use the workbook form, self-help authors who incorporate exercises or workbook pages into their books are assuming a high level of instructive control even while they allow significant freedom in how the reader completes the exercises. The objective of such authors (for example, Julia Cameron in *The Artist's Way: A Spiritual Path to Higher Creativity* [1992] or Sam Keen and Anne Valley-Fox in *Your Mythic Journey* [1989]) is to guide readers through a set of learning strategies that can be applied in a variety of contexts. The reality of what exactly must be learned is quite different in such workbook-based books than it is in a typical how-to book. In fact, self-help books that use exercise and workbook pages are closer in many ways to the first category mentioned above—the parable. The notable difference is that the author of a parable presents a story without commentary (beyond that internal in the instructive story itself), while the author of a workbook-based book offers commentary on sample illustrations but leaves the choice of illustrations the reader creates up to the reader.

A popular example of the parable form of self-help book is James Redfield's *Celestine Prophecy*, as well as his sequels, *The Tenth Insight: Holding the Vision* (1996) and *The Secret of Shambhala: In Search of the Eleventh Insight* (1999). The unnamed narrator in *The Celestine Prophecy* tells of his adventures in Peru where he goes to discover more about an ancient manuscript. Nine important insights translated from that manuscript emerge as he moves about the country; all the while, he is pursued by the military and aided by various sympathizers who know about the manuscript. Redfield's book speaks to both spiritual and psychological concerns, but his mode of presentation is fictional. The form is similar to the novel, with a variety of characters introduced and at least minimally developed. However, within the narrative a clear catalog of lessons to be learned is apparent; in fact, the nine "insights" are the steps in the how-to formula that Redfield hopes to teach. Besides the two sequels, which are also parables, Redfield offers (with coauthor Carol Adrienne) a companion piece, *The Celestine Prophecy: An Experiential Guide* (1995). The *Experiential Guide* is a workbook intended for study groups or individual use. In effect, Redfield initially simply allowed the parable itself to influence readers as all literature does—through the appreciation and application the readers themselves were able to envision after reading the book. However, in the *Experiential Guide,* he makes those connections more explicit; he invites the readers to bring their own experiences and thoughts into play as each insight is discussed. Redfield has adopted a pedagogical perspective that assumes personal applications of a lesson are better than abstract ones, even better than concrete but fictional ones.

Redfield's use of a fictional narrative as the primary form for his self-help book is unusual but not unique. Other writers who have chosen the parable form include Wayne Dyer (*Gifts from Eykis* [1983]) and Dan Millman (*Way of the Peaceful Warrior* [2000]; *The Laws of the Spirit* [1995]), who presents sound bites of advice or "laws" through framing encounters with an old, eccentric gas-station attendant or a "mountain sage." Psychologist Carl Rogers calls Spencer Johnson's *One Minute for Myself* a "modern fable." Its characters—an unnamed businessman, Uncle, and Auntie—present the self-help content through their dialogue and embedded stories. Similarly, Richard C. Whiteley gives his recent book *The Corporate Shaman* the subtitle *A Business Fable for the Modern Age* (2002). I have chosen to use the term "parable" for these instructive narratives because parables are most often presented without further explanation; the teller allows the listener's own perceptiveness to determine how effective the parable is.

The most famous raconteur of parables is, of course, Jesus, who adopted the traditional use of such stories from his own Jewish background. Jesus tells his disciples why he chooses to speak in parables: "This is why I speak to them in parables, because seeing they do not see, and hearing they do not hear, nor do they understand" (Matthew 13:13 RSV). And later he says to his disciples, "But blessed are your eyes, for they see, and your ears, for they hear." It is almost as though Jesus was aware that, for people not already tuned into his message, his stories needed the informed explication that would occupy preachers for the next two thousand years and more. Some texts are meant to be like poetry—rich with a myriad of possible meanings. Parables are constrained somewhat because they are intended to be instructive rather than simply expressive, but they do through their narrative form allow for more than one interpretation.

A more common form for the self-help book than either the parable or the how-to book is the less blatantly instructive essay form. Traditionally, an essay is a short piece written on a single topic but offered with no presumption of thoroughness or scientific rigor. An essay is not a treatise or dissertation; it is not a monograph or even a "study." All of these alternative terms are used in discussing works that are intended to treat a subject in an exhaustive manner. An essay can be quite serious, but it need not presume to present the reader with anything like a complete report on the topic, not even a complete report on the author's own thinking on the subject. This is why self-help book authors can easily write three or four bestsellers on much the same topic; the form is open-ended and friendly to the practice of recirculation, expansion, revision, or even simply restating in a new way. Each book is its own performance without being the definitive statement from the author.

Julia Cameron's *Artist's Way* is an example of a self-help book that uses the essay form in a *workbook subtype*. Here, exercises, fill-in charts, journal assignments, and check-in quizzes are inserted in the ongoing series of essays on such topics as the sense of integrity, the sense of abundance, or the sense of identity. The author does offer her own commentary on the topics selected, but she requires the reader to create and provide the "texts" that illustrate the points she makes. A closely related subtype is the *story collection subtype*. Here, the self-help book offers a number of short narratives from various sources and follows each with some commentary that collectively supports the book's educational objective. Jack Canfield and Mark Victor Hansen's immensely popular *Chicken Soup for the Soul* is this kind of book, as are their many other *Chicken Soup* books.

The *textual interpretation subtype* is a third variation of the essay form. Here, the author selects one text to serve as a basis for discussion throughout the entire book. One example that I, as a folklorist, found particularly interesting is Marsha Sinetar's *Living Happily Ever After: Creating Trust, Luck, and Joy* (1990). In this book, the author uses the Brothers Grimm version of the fairy tale "Hansel and Gretel" as the textual basis for her discussion of the themes of trust, luck, and joy. At the beginning of each chapter, she relates another part of the story and then proceeds to show how the strategies adopted by Hansel and Gretel can be useful to readers in their own daily lives. Other examples of the textual interpretation form include Robert Bly's *Iron John* (1990) or Benjamin Hoff's *Tao of Pooh* (1983) as well as Marianne Parady's interpretation of the works of Ralph Waldo Emerson (*Seven Secrets for Successful Living*). Perhaps even Wess Roberts and Bill Ross's *Make It So: Leadership Lessons from Star Trek, The Next Generation* (1995) could be included here, along with the many more group-specific interpretations and applications of religious texts.

A special category recently adopted with vigor and offering in some ways a peculiar spin on the interpretation of a religious text is a fourth category I will call the *dialogue subtype*. The startlingly successful example of this form is the *Conversations with God* series of books (1995, 1998a, 1998b) by Neale Donald Walsch, as well as two additional "conversations" called *Friendship with God* (1999) and *Communion with God* (2000). He subtitles each of these books *An Uncommon Dialogue*, and he presents each book in the form of a conversation between two individuals (one of whom is God, the other the author). Each speaker has his own font; it is quite clear who is speaking when. Walsch claims that he is writing God's part of the conversation through the process of dictation, a claim very similar to one made some years ago by Jane Roberts when she dictated the Seth books. A less belief-challenging example of the dialogue form is a book by Matthew Fox and Rupert Sheldrake called *Natural Grace* (1996). Here again, each "speaker" has his own font. The form itself is clearly in the tradition of the famous dialogues offered by Plato as a means of presenting the philosophy of his teacher Socrates, as well as his own.

Perhaps the form best-suited to the aims of the self-help book tradition is the *meditation subtype*. Here, the author brings together a series of his or her own short essays loosely grouped by subject matter and presents them as a sequence of personal reflections. The hope, of course, is that the reader will find some or all of the meditations helpful and enlightening. As a rule of thumb, I would suggest that whenever the book includes more than a dozen chapters, it very likely falls into the category of the meditation subtype.

One enormously successful book of this subtype is Richard Carlson's *Don't Sweat the Small Stuff . . . and It's All Small Stuff* (1997). Carlson's book has one hundred short chapters (usually only two or three pages long). In fact, he stays with that formula of one hundred chapters in his many other *Don't Sweat* books. Others authors who use this form include Jon Kabat-Zinn *(Wherever You Go, There You Are)*, Buddhist monk Jack Kornfield (*A Path with Heart: A Guide through the Perils and Promises of Spiritual Life* [1993]), and Catholic priest Anthony de Mello (*Awareness; The Way to Love* [1991]). Occasionally, even some scientists or physicians present their ideas in this meditation format; for example, science writer Richard Morris calls one of his books *Cosmic Questions: Galactic Halos, Cold Dark Matter, and the End of Time* (1993) and groups together a number of short essays, each of which speaks to some aspect of several large issues, such as "Why do we exist?" or "Knowing the mind of God." Similarly, Herbert Benson offers in his book *Timeless Healing: The Power and Biology of Belief* (with Marg Stark, 1996) a number of short essays grouped by topic in which he reflects on issues related to mind/body matters now very much a part of contemporary medicine. The form is an ideal one for expressing thoughts in brief, memorable bites. The power of the book is in grouping them together in a way that again loosely directs the reader's attention toward an overall area of enlightenment or change in perspective and behavior.

The last two subtypes of the essay form are not always easily distinguished from one another. I call them the *expanded essay subtype* and the *academic study subtype*. Again, these are formal categories within the genre of the self-help book, and perhaps stylistic categories within the essay form itself. I will have to admit that any hope of keeping a consistency—even a foolish consistency—in the designation of these categories is futile. There is an inevitable messiness about them. As Martin Gardner says in his preface to *Great Essays in Science,* "As a literary form the essay has always had irresponsible boundaries" (1994, xiv). Still, I think there is a shared though loose understanding of what an essay is. John Gross, in the introduction to his anthology *The Oxford Book of Essays,* comments on the "central tradition of essay-writing" influenced so profoundly by the sixteenth-century French writer Michel de Montaigne: "No matter how large its subject, the distinguishing marks of an essay by Montaigne are intimacy and informality" (1991, ix). A larger work (book-length) that exhibits these hallmarks of intimacy and informality along with a focus on a single topic might well be seen as simply an expanded essay.

Most self-help books, I would argue, are of the expanded essay subtype. One of my favorites is the short (104 pages) book by Ivan Hoffman called *The Tao of Love* (1993). Actually, the last 20 pages of the book offer several how-to suggestions, so the main "essay" is actually about 75 pages long. What Hoffman does in this expanded essay is move in an intimate and informal way through the development of his thesis, offering illustrations from his own life and bringing in appropriate quotes and images from other authors in an effort to support the insights he articulates. His thesis is that we need to learn how to love and that learning to trust is the essential first step in learning to love. Though the discussion is very informal and even in such a short work never rushed, all is directed toward leading the reader (perhaps even seducing the reader) into an acceptance of this thesis.

Rhetoric is the winning card in a good essay. The essay form invites the writer to pull out all the stops; it is nonfiction's poetry, the writer's chance to use language and effective example to intrigue, stimulate, and ultimately persuade the reader. Little wonder, then, that many of the most successful self-help books adopting the expanded essay form are often metaphorical even in their titles: James A. Kitchens's *Talking to Ducks* (1994); Wayne Dyer's *Your Erroneous Zones* or *The Sky's the Limit* (1980) or *Real Magic* (1992); Sam Keen's *Fire in the Belly* (1991); Claudia Bepko and Jo-Ann Krestan's *Too Good for Her Own Good* (1990); Harriet Goldhor Lerner's *Dance of Anger* (1985) or *The Dance of Deception* (1993); Lillian B. Rubin's *Intimate Strangers* (1983); Gary Zukav's *Dancing Wu Li Masters* (1979) or *The Seat of the Soul* (1999); Robert H. Hopcke's *There Are No Accidents* (1997); Wayne Muller's *Legacy of the Heart* (1992); even Scott Peck's *Road Less Traveled* or John Gray's runaway bestseller *Men Are from Mars, Women Are from Venus* (1992). The objective in all such expanded essays is to sell the thesis, to persuade readers toward a new, enlightened perspective, and perhaps as well to convince them to try new behaviors that just might lead to a happier life.

But not all writers of self-help books are eager to take on the role of nonfiction's poets. Some prefer the more sober form of the academic study subtype, the form closest to the scholarly genres they may be used to. The style, content, and function of the academic study subtype, nevertheless, are different from those associated with model academic studies written by scholars with the aim of addressing some thorny and unresolved issue in their discipline. It is a fact, however, that the academic study subtype of the self-help book is usually written by a Ph.D. who has put on his or her popular writer hat or teamed up with a second writer or editor whose writing style is more suited to a lay audience. The distinctive feature of the academic study subtype is the book's emphasis on information over instruction. While it is clear that the author has presented the material in such a way that the reader will find it easy to "use" it—that is, the information is more accessible than would be a more scholarly presentation—still, the author has not assumed a more direct instructive role. The book is intended to enlighten, and the author seems motivated by a desire to help people improve their understanding of life or the cosmos, but it is left up to the reader to determine how that new enlightenment might be applied in daily life—the opposite extreme of the how-to book.

One author who uses the academic study subtype very effectively is Mihaly Csikszentmihalyi, a productive scholar with hundreds of publications in traditional academic journals and university presses. However, his first really popular publication with a trade book press (Harper and Row) was *Flow: The Psychology of Optimal Experience* (1990). In his preface to that book, he articulates a position that I believe is held either consciously or implicitly by most writers who use the academic study form:

> This book summarizes, for a general audience, decades of research on the positive aspects of human experience—joy, creativity, the process of total involvement with life I call *flow*. To take this step is somewhat dangerous, because as soon as one strays from the stylized constraints of academic prose, it is easy to become careless or overly enthusiastic about such a topic. What follows, however, is not a popular book that gives insider tips about how to be happy. . . . There is no promise of easy short-cuts in these pages. But for readers who care about such things, there should be enough information to make possible the transition from theory to practice. (xi)

Csikszentmihalyi goes on to explain that he has tried to make the book "user-friendly," having avoided "footnotes, references, and other tools scholars usually employ in their technical writing" but including easily accessible endnotes and a substantial bibliography. He examines the topic of his book through the process of summarizing past research and integrating its lessons into his own thesis. He is eager to bring enlightenment to his readers, but he leaves the "transition from theory to practice" up to them.

Other examples of the academic study subtype include such books as Gail Sheehy's bestselling *Passages: Predictable Crises of Adult Life* (1974), Ellen J. Langer's *Mindfulness* (1989), Robert L. Van de Castle's *Our Dreaming Mind* (1994), David Darling's *Soul Search: A Scientist Explores the Afterlife* (1995), and Paul Brockelman's *Cosmology and Creation: The Spiritual Significance of Contemporary Cosmology* (1999). Some authors, such as Peter Senge (*The Fifth Discipline*) and Daniel Goleman (*Emotional Intelligence* [1995]), follow their popular research-based books with a related workbook or guide that makes suggestions on how to apply the material presented in their earlier books (Peter Senge, Art Kleiner, Charlotte Roberts, Richard B. Ross, and Bryan J. Smith, *The Fifth Discipline Fieldbook* [1994], and Daniel Goleman, *Working with Emotional Intelligence* [1998]).

The academic study subtype of the self-help book is the one most obviously in the tradition of self-improvement established early on in American culture through the Chautauqua movement and other such forums for involved public intellectuals. Lectures in that context were expected to be informative, not necessarily instructive. Similarly, some self-help books are offered in something very much like that traditional academic study form. The author has confidence in the effectiveness of the academic study form and chooses to write in a form as close to it as possible. Yet in choosing to address a popular audience, the writer, in a way, sets aside for the moment full participation in the culture of his or her discipline and instead moves into another culture group—that of self-help book writers—and brings along a form that can serve there as well. Still, books in the self-help tradition are distinctive by more than form alone.[2]

Along with content, it is the function of self-help books that sets them apart. They are intended to be educational, and supposedly, when effective, they will not only enlighten the reader but also transform or convert the reader into a happier and more successful person. In terms of the actual consequences of reading self-help books, there is little research available to document how effective such books are, little proof that people do in fact change their behavior as a result of reading self-help books. On the other hand, there is abundant anecdotal evidence that people have become self-help "literate" by virtue of having read many such books. They know what is supposed to be good for them, and they have enhanced their knowledge and understanding of the cosmos, relationships, and good mental, emotional, and spiritual health. They have gained some level of enlightenment. Clearly self-help books are successful at educating readers. But what exactly have they learned? We shall return to this question of applied self-education briefly in chapters 4 and 8.

The Writers

One latent function of self-help books is that they provide their authors with an opportunity to bear witness to their own transformation or conversion. This may go far in explaining why the expanded essay form is so popular among self-help authors. The intimate, personal tone of the essay permits the unabashed enthusiasm and sense of epiphany the writer is often required to keep subdued in more scholarly writing. Often the sense of personal ardor, even proselytizing, is apparent throughout a given book—for example, in Anthony Robbins's *Awaken the Giant Within* (1991) or Marsha Sinetar's *Ordinary People as Monks and Mystics* (1986) or Margaret J. Wheatley's *Leadership and the New Science: Learning about Organization from an Orderly Universe* (1992). Such authors typically include in their books not only a "story" about a particular incident that, like James Joyce's epiphanies, captures the essence of their conversion to the idea presented in the book but also a recurring tone of earnestness and zeal that conveys the authenticity of their emotional involvement with the topic at hand.

I shall say more about authors' use of personal narratives in chapter 6, but I would like to cite one example here—Wayne Dyer's account of finding and visiting his father's grave. In his book *You'll See It When You Believe It* (1989), Dyer relates the story in great detail, though he refers to the incident again in later books. In telling his story, he also comments on how the incident fits into his own decision to write the kind of books he is now best known for. He begins the narrative after relating how he, his mother, and his two brothers had been abandoned years before by his father.

> In 1970 I received a call from a cousin I had never met, who had heard a rumor that my father had died in New Orleans. But I was in no position to investigate it. At the time I was completing my doctoral studies, moving to New York to become an associate professor at St. John's University, going through a painful divorce, and "stuck in place" when it came to my writing. In the next few years I co-authored several texts on counseling and psychotherapy. I knew that I did not want to continue writing for strictly professional audiences, and yet nothing else would come to me. I was stuck, personally (divorce), physically (overweight and out of shape), and spiritually (a pure pragmatist with no thoughts about metaphysics). (4)

Dyer goes on to tie the finding of his father's grave to his own eventual success as a writer of self help-books:

> In one pure honest moment I experienced feeling forgiveness for the man who was my father and for the child I had been who wanted to know and love him.

I felt a kind of peace and cleansing that was entirely new for me. Though I was unaware of it at the time, that simple act of forgiveness was the beginning of an entirely new level of experiencing life for me. I was on the threshold of a stage of my life that was to encompass worlds I could not even imagine in those days.

When I went back to New York, miracles began to appear everywhere. I wrote *Your Erroneous Zones* with ease. An agent arrived in my life through a series of "strange" circumstances at exactly the right moment. . . . In the years that followed, my writing seemed to be taking me in new directions. I went from writing about "How to" utilize specific strategies in self-understanding to "How to" become a more assertive human being. I went from telling people how to do something to writing about the importance of being at transcendent levels as a human being. (7–8)

Dyer's own "conversion" has clearly been significant in bringing him into the society—or as Marilyn Ferguson calls it, the "conspiracy"—of self-help book authors. Most of the successful writers in the genre are people like Wayne Dyer—professional or academic individuals who experience their own enlightenment as a motivation, a force compelling them to educate others about the good effects their new understanding can produce if given a chance. And they are keenly aware that writing in the stuffy, though rigorous and academically sound, style of the scientist is no way to bring new converts into the fold. They take on the mantle of the self-help writer with all the earnest goodwill of a newly enlightened prophet.

Who are these writers? Some have started to attain a kind of cultural currency similar to that awarded literary figures or public intellectuals in the last century. When a book has had a significant impact, the author's name is remembered the next time a reader visits the bookstore, and if a new book by that same author is on the shelf (or the Internet list), it too will go into the shopping cart. Many authors have several books in print. Others become household names with the publication of only one very influential book. Some of these most successful authors are Joan Borysenko, John Bradshaw, Nathaniel Branden, Joyce Brothers, David Burns, Leo Buscaglia, Jack Canfield, Rachel Carson, Deepak Chopra, Norman Cousins, Stephen Covey, Mihaly Csikszentmihalyi, Ram Dass, Barbara DeAngelis, Larry Dossey, Wayne Dyer, Robert Fulghum, Daniel Goleman, John Gray, Gerald G. Jampolsky, Susan Jeffers, Spencer Johnson, Jon Kabat-Zinn, Sam Keen, Ken Keyes Jr., Jack Kornfield, Peter Kramer, Harold Kushner, Alan Lakein, Harriet Goldhor Lerner, Phil McGraw, Thomas Moore, Scott Peck, Tom Peters, James Redfield, Anthony Robbins, Lillian Rubin, Theodore Rubin, Robert Schuller, Martin Seligman, Peter Senge, Gail Sheehy, Barbara Sher, Bernie Siegel, Marsha Sinetar, Deborah Tannen, Neale Donald Walsch, Marianne Williamson, and Gary Zukav.

Most of these are living authors; some are perhaps busy even now writing new books in the genre. And every month new writers offer their bid at selling wisdom to an eager public. I hesitate to suggest a profile for these writers. They are varied in background and personality, and yet there are some shared characteristics among them. They tend to be well educated. Though there are quite a few women among the authors of self-help books, there are more male than female authors. Most are white—not necessarily Anglo-Saxon, but white (though the number of African American writers is growing); most are heterosexual and married, though often it is clear that they are in a second or third marriage; and almost all of them have found ways to promote their ideas through other media, lecture tours, workshops, and often even entire institutions established to teach their insights. Many of them are quite wealthy as a result of their writing.

These writers often represent a kind of popularizer only grudgingly tolerated within their academic disciplines. Some, like Wayne Dyer, can claim the privilege of writing for a popular audience by virtue of having already paid their dues to their discipline. Some, like Deborah Tannen, continue to write both scholarly and popular works, satisfying both "communities" of which they are a part. But in every discipline there is at least one ancestor, one figure of some stature, who broke away from the confines of scholarly writing and presented the discipline in a way that was both interesting and useful to readers outside the field. Earliest in American tradition was probably Benjamin Franklin. His autobiography and many essays and aphorisms continue to influence thinking in the business community (see, for example, Peter Baida's *Poor Richard's Legacy: American Business Values from Benjamin Franklin to Michael Milken* [1990]). I have already mentioned the importance of early essayists such as Emerson and Thoreau, and certainly Sigmund Freud, Carl Jung, and William James must be counted among the ancestors. But writers from the earlier part of the twentieth century are the more likely candidates for the title of ancestor, or perhaps literary mentor, people such as Abraham Maslow in psychology, Bertrand Russell in philosophy, C. S. Lewis in religion, John Dewey in education, Ruth Benedict in anthropology, Douglas McGregor in business, or Thomas Merton on the ascetic life. The more general category of "personal growth" as a subject has its outstanding mentors as well: Dale Carnegie, Norman Vincent Peale, and Maxwell Maltz, author of one of the earliest popular pocket-size paperbacks, *Psycho-Cybernetics* (1960).

These writers—both those who wrote the classics in self-help literature and the writers living and writing today—drew upon a tradition of scholarship and popular literature and upon their own experience. Often it has been the experience of seeing the effects of their educational or therapeutic activities in the lives of real people that has compelled these authors to write their first self-help books. Susan Jeffers comments in a later book on why she wrote her first self-help book, *Feel the Fear and Do It Anyway.* She recounts a story of how she decided quite spontaneously to offer a course at the New School for Social Research:

> Teaching that course was a turning point in my life. My experience was so positive and felt so right that I decided to leave my job of ten years to become a teacher and a writer of self-help books. It is significant that the name of that first class I taught was Feel the Fear and Do It Anyway! I often wonder if I had *not* listened to my intuition that fateful day, if the book of the same name or any of my other books (including this one) would ever have been written! (1996, 84)

Clearly, for writers such as Susan Jeffers or Wayne Dyer, the decision to write a book that serves a different function, that takes them into a different community of writers, and that allows them to make what they see as a needed contribution is a decision made almost as a reluctant surprise, even to themselves. It is this quality that gives their decision the flavor of a conversion experience. And it is this experience of being converted or born into a new community of practitioners that comes through in the related practice of metacommentary both in the books themselves and more strikingly on the front and back covers of these popular paperbacks.

Metacommentary

In the middle of the twentieth century, there emerged in many disciplines an interest in the "meta-" dimension of subjects of research—metalanguage, metacommunications, metanarrative, metafiction, even metafolklore (see Dundes, 1966). "Metacommentary" would be commentary about commentary. In the case of self-help books, metacommentary has been an essential element in promoting, authenticating, and maintaining the practice of writing self-help literature. The most visible instance of metacommentary occurs on the front and back covers of self-help books, and often inside on the first few pages of front matter as well. Here we find quotes praising the current or past books of the jacketed book's author along with an identification of the author of each quote via the title of one or more of his or her own self-help books. It is assumed that the potential buyer of the book will recognize some or all of the names and books of writers offering brief commentary through these quotes. It is an important means of promoting the book as well as of authenticating the author as a writer known and appreciated by other successful self-help book authors.

I was cheered by one particularly apt example of metacommentary in the introduction to Richard Carlson's *Don't Sweat the Small Stuff . . . and It's All Small Stuff.* Carlson writes:

> I'd like to share a personal story that touched my heart and reinforced an important lesson—a story that demonstrates the essential message of this book. As you will see, the events of this story planted the seed for the title of the book you are about to read.
>
> About a year ago a foreign publisher contacted me and requested that I attempt to get an endorsement from best-selling author Dr. Wayne Dyer for a foreign edition of my book *You Can Feel Good Again.* I told them that while Dr. Dyer had given me an endorsement for an earlier book, I had no idea whether he would consider doing so again. I told them, however, that I would try.

Carlson then relates how he tried to reach author Wayne Dyer but failed to get an answer. He told the publisher to leave the endorsement off, but it was put on the cover anyway. Upset, he called his agent and had the books pulled. He continues:

> In the meantime I decided to write Dr. Dyer an apology, explaining the situation and all that was being done to rectify the problem. After a few weeks of wondering about what his response might be, I received a letter in the mail that said the following: "Richard. There are two rules for living in harmony. #1) Don't sweat the small stuff and #2) It's all small stuff. Let the quote stand. Love, Wayne."
>
> That was it! No lectures, no threats. No hard feelings and no confrontation. Despite the obvious unethical use of his very famous name, he responded with grace and humility. (1997, 2–4)

This is not to suggest that the writers of self-help books do not have egos. Still, the overwhelming message conveyed through most of the books is that writers in the field of personal growth and self-improvement constitute a supportive community, one that rejoices in each new addition to the collective insights that draw them together. Metacommentary in the books themselves often reinforces this message. For example, Susan Jeffers, in *End the Struggle and Dance with Life,* tells the following story:

> A while ago, I gave a talk at an all-day symposium. Three other speakers were on the schedule, all of whom were household names in the self-help field. As I was getting ready to walk on the stage to face three-thousand people sitting in the audience, my adrenaline was flowing big time! My husband, Mark, kissed me on the cheek and whispered in my ear, "You'll be the best."
>
> In the past I had loved hearing that, I *needed* to hear that! But this time, something didn't feel right about it. I suddenly became aware of the negative con-

sequences of trying to be "the best." It created tension; it created alienation from the other speakers; and it took me off my Higher-Self purpose, which was to help others. As this Aha! hit me, I whispered in Mark's ear, "Thanks for the loving support, but next time just say, 'You'll be good enough.'" And with that letting go of my need to be the best, I walked confidently onto the stage, knowing that my only purpose was to put love into this world, *not to compete with other people who are trying to put their love into the world as well.* (1996, 36–37)

Often authors refer to one another's work in their own books, or, more often, they offer the reader a quote from a given author without in fact identifying the source beyond simply listing the author's name. Another kind of metacommentary that highlights the sense of community among self-help book writers is the growing number of anthologies or edited interviews that bring together some of the better-known individuals in the field of personal growth and spirituality. *Handbook for the Soul,* edited by Richard Carlson and Benjamin Shield (1995), for example, includes short essays by Lynn Andrews, Angeles Arrien, Sydney Banks, Melody Beattie, Jean Shinoda Bolen, Joan Borysenko, Nathaniel Branden, Jack Canfield, Richard Carlson, Stephen Covey, Wayne Dyer, Betty Eadie, Matthew Fox, Robert Fulghum, John Gray, Gerald G. Jampolsky, Jon Kabat-Zinn, Elizabeth Kubler-Ross, Harold Kushner, Linda Leonard, Stephen Levine, Thomas Moore, Ram Dass, Anne Wilson Schaef, Benjamin Shield, Bernie Siegel, Brian Weiss, Marianne Williamson, and Marion Woodman. All are writers whose books (as well as lectures and workshops) have brought them a certain celebrity status and have given them a ticket of admission into the club of self-help writers.

A few journalists have taken on the task of interviewing and writing about some of these popular authors. William Elliott, in his book *Tying Rocks to Clouds: Meetings and Conversations with Wise and Spiritual People* (1995), interviewed many of the people Carlson and Shield included in their anthology (more than twenty in all). And Tony Schwartz, in *What Really Matters: Searching for Wisdom in America* (1995), interviewed and researched the work of many of the individuals well known as wisdom writers or wisdom seekers. Though journalistic in tone and purpose, both books point to an emerging intellectual history of this often maligned and trivialized domain of popular discourse. And such historiography is the first necessity for identifying a field of study as having come into its own. It is the quintessential metacommentary.

All is not as rosy as it may seem, however, as there has long been an abiding disparagement of self-help books, whether subtle or not so subtle, even by popular writers themselves. Often there seems to be an effort on the part of some writers to claim a more "scientific" or rigorous methodology than that other writers have used. Daniel Goleman, in the introduction to his immensely popular *Emotional Intelligence,* for example, says:

> I have had to wait until now [1995] before the scientific harvest was full enough to write this book. These insights are so late in coming largely because the place of feeling in mental life has been surprisingly slighted by research over the years, leaving the emotions a largely unexplored continent for scientific psychology. Into this void has rushed a welter of self-help books, well inten- tioned advice based at best on clinical opinion but lacking much, if any, scien- tific basis. Now science is finally able to speak with authority to these urgent and perplexing questions of the psyche at its most irrational, to map with some precision the human heart. (1995, xi)

Despite Thomas Kuhn having pretty much laid to rest back in 1962 the idea that even the hard sciences would ever be "finally able to speak with author- ity" on the various scientific enterprises, Goleman seems willing to adopt something akin to a "more scientific than thou" attitude with regard to oth- er writers in the popular arena.

Interestingly, to my mind, what is happening here is an inappropriate ex- tension of the perceived need for scientific rigor associated with disciplin- ary scholarship into an area of rhetorical performance that serves quite a different purpose and calls for quite a different set of "rules" for competen- cy in that performance. The "clinical opinion" and especially the case stud- ies used as illustration in typical self-help books are persuasive for many read- ers. However, like the authors of the *Authoritative Guide to Self-Help Books,* Goleman sees only the testable curative results of applied research as wor- thy of serious attention, even among a popular audience. His own academic colleagues may require such evidence, but his popular audience is more likely persuaded by the effectiveness of his choice of illustrations than by the quan- tifiable data that supports his own conclusions.

I'll mention one last kind of metacommentary that, I think, plays much more effectively upon the popular appreciation for self-help books than does Goleman's vaguely defensive comment. Peter D. Kramer became a house- hold name soon after the publication of his book *Listening to Prozac* (1993). On the opening page of a more recent book, Kramer makes the following comment:

> I ask Lou, whom I consider my mentor, should I or should I not write a book of advice? I have written a best-seller, and when a psychiatrist writes a best-seller, he is urged to write a book of advice. . . . I broach the idea in a cautious way, through raising technical concerns about books of advice. I am suspicious of

the form—the chain of illustrative vignettes, too convenient to be fact, too predictable to be decent fiction. I have trouble imagining writing in the second person, the way advice books are written: You have this problem, you have that. I have more trouble yet deciding what it is I might know. (1997, 15–16)

Kramer then proceeds to offer his reader a wonderfully creative book (I would classify it as a parable) in which his fictionalized mentor presents him with a kind of "dry run" on writing a self-help book, a book of advice. His mentor asks him to "advise" an acquaintance who seeks some help with answering the question "Should I leave?"—that is, should I end an intimate relationship? His mentor tells him that the person will come to see him in two hours. During that time, Kramer imagines who the acquaintance might be and writes out twenty different possible scenarios. The book is excellent, and it examines both the nature of advice itself (and by association the self-help book tradition) and the varying kinds of response to the question that make sense in light of each hypothetical situation and current psychological wisdom. Kramer's book playfully but effectively raises a serious question about whether academics—or anyone else—should take up this practice of writing self-help books.

In the next chapter, we shall look in earnest at some of the critiques that have been aimed, either directly or indirectly, at the self-help movement.

3. The Critics, the Simple Self, and America's Cultural Cringe

Many people seem to be annoyed and embarrassed by the fact that self-help books are so popular in America. And it is not that such books cannot be found elsewhere. I have spent time in Australia, England, and Norway, and many of the same books found on the shelves in America are found in these countries as well, along with local contributions to the growing international library of self-help literature. I even noticed that, in Norway, some popular titles such as John Gray's *Men Are from Mars, Women Are from Venus* and Neale Donald Walsch's *Conversations with God: Book 1,* have been translated into Norwegian, even though a high percentage of Norwegians read English. All the same, people do associate the genre with America. Most of the authors are American, and evidently so are most of the readers.

The Critics

One researcher who shares my respect for the self-help book is Tom Butler-Bowdon, a writer who has selected, summarized, and reviewed examples of what he calls "the literature of possibility." In his *50 Self-Help Classics: 50 Inspirational Books to Transform Your Life* (2003), he offers informative, Cliffs-Notes-style commentary on the books and brief biographies of the authors. The book functions as would any other self-help book; the primary difference is that the author bases each chapter of his own volume on the work of another author and builds his own insights from that base. In general, he champions the books he has selected, and he offers little negative criticism of any of the works or authors he reviews. Another supportive researcher who examines self-help literature seriously is Wendy Simonds, author of the 1992 study *Women and Self-Help Culture: Reading between the Lines.* As a sociologist, Simonds is interested in the role such books play in the lives of women who read them. She offers a good starting point for ethnographic work among readers.

Surprisingly, however, there have not been many genuine critiques of the self-help literature. It seems rather to be a matter of damning by neglect, or occasionally by parody and sarcasm, but rarely even by faint praise, at least among scholars—the people who usually review books of nonfiction. And yet, it is good to remember Steven Starker's comment in his review of the genre, *Oracle at the Supermarket:*

> It is too prevalent and powerful a phenomenon to overlook, despite belonging to "pop" culture. Inasmuch as self-help books are dispensing advice to millions on matters physical, psychological, and spiritual, they cannot responsibly be ignored by social scientists and health care practitioners. Questions regarding their relative merits and potential dangers deserve careful consideration. (1989, 10)

Wendy Kaminer was one of the first to take up Starker's challenge with the publication of her book *I'm Dysfunctional, You're Dysfunctional* in 1992. Tom Tiede's more recent *Self-Help Nation* and a few parodies, such as Herman Minor IV's *Seven Habits of Highly Ineffective People* (1994) or comedians Ben Stiller and Janeane Garofalo's *Feel This Book* (1999), suggest that the genre is hardly worth taking seriously. All seem to agree that the popularity of such books reflects poorly on the American people. Intellectuals in particular seem eager to distance themselves from any personal interest in self-help literature. As Kaminer was quick to point out: "I have read self-help books only as a critic" (1992, 1).

Why would educated Americans be embarrassed to admit they had read a self-help book? What is it about the genre that makes intellectuals want to affect a stance of disdainful superiority? Why are the few critics who have addressed the genre at all seriously so relentless in their negative evaluation and sarcasm? Are the books really that bad? I would like to consider some of the charges that are levied against self-help books, either directly or indirectly, by their critics.

The few critics who have addressed the genre at some length (for example, Kaminer, Tiede, Starker, Gary Greenberg) would barely make up a good-sized seminar on the topic. Understandably, then, the primary points of criticism themselves have not been outlined, so I will begin there. Wendy Kaminer comes closest to having voiced most of them, though her often disparaging tone casts a defensive pall over her critique and, I think, detracts from the effectiveness of her commentary. Nevertheless, she has put her finger on what I believe is the primary fear behind the scholarly disdain for the genre. She says, "An apolitical movement [the recovery or self-help movement] that helps shape the identities of a few million people will have political conse- quences, and the ideology of recovery makes me question what those conse- quences might be" (1992, 152). Like Tom Tiede, Kaminer is concerned that Americans seem to be losing their sense of direction, their democratic ideal of self-determination, their strength of character. In short, she is convinced that Americans are being led astray by the same "snake-oil peddlers who are sapping our nation's soul" that Tiede worries about.

Kaminer does not say what she thinks the consequences of so many Amer- icans being thus led astray might be, but she suggests that the consequences might be political. She fears, it seems, that even the fairly well-educated, read- ing American public will allow these self-help writers to lead them insidiously into—what? Populism? Communism? Andrew Jackson–style democracy? At best, she sees Americans as forfeiting their intelligence for gullibility. It ap- pears that she is allowing her own discomfort with democratic reality to in- fluence her thinking on the matter. American democracy has always had to contend with the freedom of its people to read what they like, learn what they like, and elect into office people who espouse the ideas they like. I do not share her fear of this process (though I often find it hard to live through), but I do recognize the need for a critique of the materials that are brought into or reinforce an American worldview through the avenue of self-help books. With that aim of offering a review of this important influence on and com- ponent of an American worldview, let us examine some of the characteris- tics of self-help literature that seem most troublesome to our hypothetical seminar of critics.

Five points of concern or potential areas of discussion addressing the body of self-help literature would be (1) the issue of authoritarianism versus self- reliance; (2) a perceived poor level of writing skills and level of analysis; (3) lack of originality; (4) the ready acceptance of a medical or "therapy" model; and (5) a primarily female rather than male readership. Such issues are ones that would be of interest to social and literary critics. They are not, on the other hand, concerns typically addressed by the "customers" who offer their reviews of specific books on-line through such media outlets as barnesandnoble.com or amazon.com.

One worry is that self-help books reflect a growing "tendency toward au- thoritarianism," as the promotional blurb on the back cover of Kaminer's book claims. The readers of such books are seeking out experts rather than relying on their own common sense, wisdom, and personal convictions. They are abandoning the self-reliance Americans are supposed to be known for and instead eagerly accepting the authority of their supposed betters. Coming to this issue from a different perspective, I see the reading of self-help books as part of a loose tradition of self-education, and the idea of education has always involved seeking out someone more expert than the student on a given subject. Even informally, people often go to others for advice, so I think the claim of authoritarianism is something of a red herring. It seems that the worry over authoritarianism has more to do with a questioning of the quality of "expertness" of the experts rather than a fear that people will suddenly start following in lockstep the dictates of self-help book writers. In other words, critics of the self-help movement worry that readers will accept as "experts" writers whom the critics regard not as "authorities" but rather as second-rate scholars or slack researchers.

In writing this book, I am, of course, casting myself as well in the role of critic or reviewer, and to some extent a kind of intellectual snobbishness is required or at least expected of someone taking that role. In the rather broad and stereotypical terms sociologist Herbert Gans uses to identify various classes of people in the United States, I am of the "educated class" and therefore a proponent of "high culture," and furthermore, I am presuming to speak as an informed critic—a scholar, a professional—about a certain group of objects in the culture. As Gans says, "Critics are sometimes more important than creators, because they determine whether a given cultural item deserves to be considered high culture" (1974, 78). I am aware of this role, and I am aware of my own "risk" in being perceived as a traitor to my class (my profession) by voicing sincere appreciation for self-help books as objects and by siding with the buyers of such books as creditable individuals who do in fact know what is good and useful and proper. Actually, I am not so much taking a risk as hoping to use my advantage as a credentialed critic to widen the circle of appreciation for this genre of popular nonfiction.

Gans goes on to shed some light on why the popularity of self-help books might seem to fly in the faces of contemporary intellectuals:

> High culture's prime allegiance is to its own creator-oriented public, but it also perceives itself as setting aesthetic standards and supplying the proper culture for the entire society. . . . This is not to say that high culture deals with all fundamental questions and that lower cultures ignore them. Moral issues are constantly treated in popular entertainment fare and philosophical issues come up as well, typically exemplified in concrete cases. Conversely, high culture does not often address itself to prosaic issues like making a living, because such issues are not problematic for its public. (1974, 78–79)

Though Gans emphasized in his book that he saw "high" and "low" as neutral terms, clearly there is a value judgment. High culture is better. In the hegemony of intellectual exchange, those who share the taste (and distaste) of the professional class are those whose opinions matter.

The threat inherent in popular nonfiction, then, is that this more refined "high culture" opinion will be ignored. Instead, consumerism will determine that self-help books are acceptable. As Steven Starker admitted, perhaps reluctantly, self-help books are "too pervasive and influential to be ignored." And as Gans reminded us, the public that has made self-help books so popular is indeed concerned with the "prosaic issues" of making a living, building satisfying personal relationships, avoiding fights, deciding how to spend their time and effort, even learning what they truly think about health and sickness, life and death. It is at that boundary where the prosaic slides into the profound and meaningful that intellectuals take umbrage at this intrusion into their territory. How can writers who ignore the requirements of academic rigor presume to contribute to our understanding of the human condition? Will they not simply mislead the masses who look so easily to authority rather than demand the proof of professional practice and academic accountability? This, to me, is the charge that Wendy Kaminer in particular makes against self-help writers.

And yet the greater concern seems to be that intellectuals themselves might be drawn in, might offer the stamp of approval to self-help writers and their unmonitored mentoring. As I have worked on this project, I have had a number of highly respected scholars admit to me in private that they have read various specific self-help books and found them helpful in their personal lives. Yet they often seem conflicted, as though they were admitting to trying a folk cure rather than visiting a medical professional. This, I think, is the source of much of the offense many intellectuals take when faced with the self-help book phenomenon. Like nineteenth-century intellectual Sir Burnett Edward Tylor, who studied folklore in order to stamp it out, contemporary critics of self-help books accept as their duty the eradication of rather than the support of "unscientific" theories and ideas. Nevertheless, they, like "the masses," may find themselves persuaded by some of the writing they feel compelled to condemn. My colleague Gregory Schrempp has examined this more general academic conflict in some detail and observes that "even in scientific societies a relatively small part of life is comported according to the formal scientific procedures" (1996, 192). In other words, when it comes to how they determine to live their own lives, even intellectuals may resort to the popular or "folk" procedures of self-help mentoring.

Authority, then, is at best a spurious issue, one that hides a worry over the way the writers of self-help books choose to persuade their readers. The cry of the 1960s was "Question authority," and it seems unlikely that the readers of self-help books—many of whom are from that generation—would abandon the habit of questioning authorities of whatever sort. Instead, what really seems to concern critics is that readers, despite their education and familiarity with proper research techniques, will nevertheless find persuasive the writings of those who do not use the prescribed avenues of scholarly writing (in which authority certainly counts for much). Critics are unhappy not with authoritarianism but rather with the choice of people who are honored as authorities and with those authorities' methods of persuasion. This brings us to the second issue that goads the critics of self-help literature—poor writing and lack of rigorous analysis.

Among self-help authors, there are individuals who give clear evidence of being very careful writers, and there are other individuals who are easily pegged "poor writers" by anyone used to evaluating writing. Most readers of popular nonfiction are not necessarily accustomed to evaluating writing, at least not consciously. As a university professor, I have the perhaps unfortunate predilection to always judge other people's writing as part of my stock-in-trade. Critics of the self-help phenomenon have this predilection as well, even if they claim only to be objecting to the kind or quality of ideas expressed through self-help books. For people like me (and I assume other critics of the genre) who value what we consider to be "good writing," it is a disheartening truth that even poor writers manage to be persuasive and to find publishers. This truth does not make me value good writing any less, but it does suggest to me that some readers of self-help books may have other priorities and a capacity to respond positively to other kinds of writing than the kind I prefer.

I say "some" readers because I do think that there are many readers of self-help books who are just as discriminating in their preferences as I am. And I would also argue that there are many self-help writers who are quite talented and have learned to persuade as well as to inform in ways much more appealing to a general reading audience than the typical style of most academics. On the other hand, I have often found myself wondering at the seeming success of certain authors, bewildered at how they could have satisfied any readers' needs or expectations. It is when I face this question that I go back to my earlier assertion that what self-help writers are about is providing the resources, curriculum, and methods for their readers' self-education. With that thought in mind, I would recast the issue of "poor writing and lack of analytical rigor" as an illustration of the variety of ways of learning that different people find effective.

In chapter 2, I discussed some aspects of style characteristic of the genre; here, I would like to single out three features shared by many examples of such writing that seem to "work" well for most readers, even if not for me. My claim is not that these are features of "good writing," at least as I understand it, but rather that they are features that some writers obviously consider effective teaching tools, persuasive rhetorical strategies. It should be instructive, I might add, that these stylistic features are the very ones that critics find most irritating about the genre: a tendency to assume a generalized reader (use of "you" and the inclusive royal "we"); a tendency to oversimplify, repeat, and "dumb down" the writing; and the use of anecdotes as though they were proofs. In other words, practices such as these, which many critics would call aspects of "poor writing," seem in fact to be quite effective as rhetorical devices in self-help books.

The first and third of these features are sins that show up regularly in the writing class I teach every summer. I know that students argue privately among themselves that I am simply asserting my own preferences on these matters as though they really were laws of acceptable writing. Self-help writers would probably agree with these disgruntled students, and for the world outside of academe, such complaints are probably justified. The second feature, however, represents my own pet peeve with the genre. As a teacher, I recognize the value of repetition, of simplifying ideas, especially of breaking complex ideas down into simpler ones that can be grasped more easily. However, I also know all too well that students will feel insulted if they are spoken down to, if the line between helpful repetition or simplification is crossed, if the teacher "dumbs down" the lesson.

Why are the readers of self-help books not insulted by the oversimplified writing so characteristic of much popular nonfiction? Actually, I suspect that often they are insulted, or at least irritated. But unlike my university students who often seem so ready to take personally the way I might treat them in class, readers of self-help books seem willing to forgive their authors or, perhaps more telling, to assume that someone else in the reading audience must need that kind of simplification. This came home to me most clearly when I bought and started reading Gerald G. Jampolsky's *Shortcuts to God: Finding Peace Quickly through Practical Spirituality* (2000). The title of this book alone was enough to challenge my willingness to stay immersed in this topic. And, not only did the title promise shortcuts to a complex and profound idea, if not a divine being (God), but the book included cartoonlike illustrations and lots of power-point boxes and highlighted text that severely tested my intention to keep my own reactions to the books for this project in the background. Like my students, I found it hard not to be personally insulted when someone seemed to be talking down to me.

Jampolsky, a psychiatrist, is one of those writers often cited by other self-help writers, especially for his first book, *Love Is Letting Go of Fear,* published in 1979. He has had a long career as a medical doctor, founder of a health center, worldwide lecturer, and writer. He works with both adults and children who are facing life-threatening illnesses. This last bit of information gave me pause as I pondered how he could possibly imagine himself an effective writer, how he could convince himself that a book such as *Shortcuts to God* could avoid the clear likelihood of insulting his readers. I can only assume that Jampolsky has seen this style of presentation achieve the goals he set for it. For some readers—perhaps for those who, like many of his patients, are facing death or debilitating disease—these rhetorical techniques are effective. And, just possibly even for some other readers who simply do not let themselves be insulted by a writer's choice of style and presentation, there are still worthwhile lessons to be learned through reading *Shortcuts to God.* Regarding this one, I will have to conclude that beauty (and effectiveness) is in the eye of the beholder.

Like many other critics of the genre, then, I find it a challenge personally to get around the poor writing I perceive in some of the self-help literature. I expect a book to exhibit features of good writing rather than to reflect the author's decision to publish a workshop presentation in a written format (which I suspect is often the case). Nevertheless, I come back to two reassuring points: some writers in fact are quite good as writers and have found a new way to use their talents in a popular medium, and even those authors I perceive as poor writers create texts that are evidently effective for some readers. But, what are we to make of the closely related question about the content of self-help books? What about the lack of originality in most of this body of literature? What about the charge that when self-help writers are being overly simplistic and repetitive, they are also being banal and unoriginal, merely offering their readers platitudes they already know?

As will be even more apparent in chapters 5, 6, and 7, I am convinced that the traditionality of much of the content of self-help books not only accounts for their success but also serves the process of creativity that does indeed lead to small innovations in personal thought and collective worldview. But before I argue this assertion, I will quote directly one critic, Wendy Kaminer, who sees the situation very differently:

> We should be troubled by the fact that the typical mass market self-help book, consumed by many college-educated readers, is accessible to anyone with a decent eighth-grade education. We should worry about the willingness of so many to believe that the answers to existential questions can be encapsulated

in the portentous pronouncements of bumper-sticker books. Only people who die very young learn all they really need to know in kindergarten. (1992, 7)

This last sentence is a witty reference to Robert Fulghum's *All I Really Need to Know I Learned in Kindergarten,* published in 1989. Fulghum is arguing that essential lessons for a good life are of course simple (a child can understand them) and traditional. He is arguing on behalf of the best parts of folk wisdom. Some critics of the self-help literature have no patience with this blatant recycling of old truths. Even more offensive to the critics, however, are the self-help writers who believe they are offering new insights to their readers when in fact they are not. In either case, critics would fault self-help writers for contributing nothing new to our popular philosophy—and yet, like most professional philosophers, self-help writers are simply offering old wine in new wineskins. Their contribution is in making the old truths appealing to a new generation.

If pressed, most critics of self-help books would back off from the worry over originality. A more telling concern is with the medical or therapy model at the base of much self-help writing. It is no surprise that many self-help authors are psychologists or physicians, and it should be no surprise that these writers are eager to offer cures or solutions to their readers' problems. Critics see the ready adoption of this therapy model as an unfortunate move away from the pervasive stoicism that characterized Americans of an earlier era. In *Self-Help Nation,* Tom Tiede says: "Great numbers of Americans before the 1960s were not fixated by what was wrong, but by what was right. They were individualists in a common struggle. They were taught self-responsibility rather than self-help" (2001, 10). Perhaps this is so, or perhaps it is only with the rise of this body of self-help literature since the 1960s that we have before us in print a vast archive of this aspect of the American worldview. Certainly, the suffering, depression, marital problems, and child abuse that are often cited in self-help books are not new phenomena; they have been with us from colonial days, whether acknowledged or not. But the assertion that one should stoically endure and say nothing has perhaps been abandoned and replaced with the self-help message that it is good to talk about problems and try to solve them.

Self-help books would seem to be anathema to those who celebrate the rugged individualism and manly stoicism of a John Wayne. Little wonder, then, that a final important issue for critics of self-help literature is what Kaminer identifies as "the feminization of popular culture" (1992, xvii). Critics envision the typical reader of self-help literature as female rather than male. Whether this is actually true or not, we do not know. I suspect that there are many more men than women who read self-help books concerning life in the corporate world, and probably more women than men who read books on personal relationships. Some books are written specifically for women— for example, *Secrets about Men Every Woman Should Know* by Barbara DeAngelis (1990) or *Living with the Passive-Aggressive Man* by Scott Wetzler (1992). And yet the self-help addict with whom Tom Tiede opens his book—the person who went into debt while spending some $12,000 on over six hundred self-help books—was male. "Feminization," however, is a charge levied at any behavior or expression that favors the soft over the hard, the emotional over the logical, the therapeutic and verbal over the stoic and reticent. Self-help books are perceived as feminine even when they are written by men (as many of them are). Self-help books are anything but manly, and they promote a worldview, a culture, that appeals to women rather than to men.

Is this perception accurate? Perhaps with additional research, we can say with some certainty whether more women than men read self-help books. However, the perception that it is a feminine genre is definitely out there, and not just among critics. In fact, I would guess that much of the disdain accorded the genre is a result of this assumption that self-help books, like romances, are women's literature—that is, literature that women would read and that men, therefore, would not. In my own earlier research of the personal narrative as a folklore genre, I have been puzzled by a similar unease with a kind of storytelling that is often perceived as characteristic of women rather than men. Despite clear evidence that there are many men who do tell personal narratives and many men who do read self-help books, the perception persists that to be interested in the "personal" or to seek solutions for personal problems is to be behaving as women behave, and men as well as many women active in the professional realm do not want to be seen as "acting like women." Granted, this opinion is simply an opinion. I have not researched this question (but see Stanley Brandes's discussion in *Metaphors of Masculinity* [1980]). Nevertheless, it seems to me that at least some of the critical distaste for the self-help book can be attributed to this lingering prejudice against things perceived as feminine rather than masculine. The critical reception of self-help books suffers from this stereotype still a part of our culture, even our "high" and academic culture.

The supposed female reading audience, along with charges of a therapy model and associated psychobabble, a lack of originality, often poor writing, and a flight from the virtues of stoicism and self-reliance, then, are some of the perceptions that cause critics to be wary of saying anything good about self-help books. Is there any clear contribution the genre makes that could be held up in contrast to these perceived weaknesses? Is there any saving grace to be found in the self-help book's obvious popularity, or is it, as some critics suggest, a national shame? As a folklorist, I am as content to study the self-help book as a part of America's expressive culture as I am to study legends or children's riddles, protest songs, or blond jokes. Self-help books draw upon and perpetuate an American worldview. But do they add anything new? And, if not, why are they so avidly read by so many people?

The Simple Self

The self-help book's popularity reflects a paradox at the heart of Americans' perception of themselves. Americans think they are simple selves—broad-shouldered, active, natural, and unreflective—but the popularity of the self-help book demonstrates that they are not. The paradox is not in this contradiction but rather in the very self-consciousness that arises with every agreement to look to and evaluate the "self"—in other words, with every self-help book that is written and read. I describe this process as a paradox because the ultimate message of all self-help books is that individuals must detach themselves from the conditioning imposed by the surrounding culture. To be happy, to be effective, to be truly a success, the individual must become a "simple self," a person free of attachments to the values of the outside culture and responsive only to his or her own basic and honest presence in the world. And yet, of course, with every self-help book such a person reads, the "self" becomes self-conscious and the "simple self," if it were ever a possibility, is lost. In fact, we could say that readers of self-help books become addicted to the very process of examining, pouring attention on, even chastising themselves—the internal, personal, subjective self.

The two important ingredients in this paradox are the "ultimate message" of all self-help books and the simple self. Earlier I discussed the basic structure of the self-help book, the problem/solution formula. But the "ultimate message" is something other than this structural requirement. There are a great many problems posed by the authors of self-help books, a great many topics or issues addressed through the basic problem/solution structure. These problems, though varied, do all arise through the process of enculturation—the education and socialization of individuals into their own culture, in this case, into American culture. The message that self-help authors collectively offer their readers in response to these many problems is that their readers must divest themselves of their need to be accepted, approved, applauded, or loved by the community that has given them their culture. They must detach themselves from their own informal education handed to them by their families and society and instead learn a new set of values freely chosen without the pressure of cultural sanction.

What exactly does this mean? How are Stephen Covey's *Seven Habits of Highly Effective People* or Wayne Dyer's *The Sky's the Limit* or Susan Jeffers's *Feel the Fear and Do It Anyway* examples of this message of detachment? Covey's seven habits are certainly not new. That was one of Wendy Kaminer's complaints about his book. But Covey's suggestions, the habits he would teach people to adopt, can only be approached by his readers after they have abandoned the "bad" habits they already have. In other words, as Gloria Steinem says, "Before we can learn, we must unlearn." The underlying message of all self-help books is that readers must no longer be attached to their former values, tastes, habits, or even loves if they are to learn new ones. No matter that the new ones are not really new. The principle remains that people must unlearn their culture before they can benefit from the teachings of their self-help mentors.

The irony is that this ultimate message is doomed to failure. People cannot really cast off the culture that has made them human. Self-help writers are fighting a losing battle, and some of them know it. Nevertheless, each book begins with the requisite effort to make the reader aware of the effects of cultural conditioning and ends with some hope-inspired effort to teach more "reasoned," more effective, ways to be and act in the world. But it is the awareness itself that is the ultimate message of each self-help book. And while it is true that some individuals will drop certain "old" habits or values and adopt new behaviors or attitudes upon reading a given book, the primary achievement of the self-help writer is in making the reader aware of how cultural conditioning works. And once readers are aware, they will never again be "innocently" a product of American culture. Instead, enlightened readers will now bear a responsibility for consciously changing the "self" in some way, or for continuing, with eyes wide open, to choose the culture that influences who they are and what they do.

A self-conscious "self" cannot be simple. In his study of the "great virtues," André Comte-Sponville writes, "Simplicity means forgetting oneself, forgetting one's pride and fear. . . . [The simple self] sees no point in self-examination. . . . He does not take himself seriously or give tragic dimensions to himself or to his life. . . . He has nothing to prove, since he does not seek to impress. . . . Simplicity is the virtue of wise men and the wisdom of saints" (1996, 156). A person who reads a self-help book is not an unselfconscious, simple self. And yet, to be a "simple self" free of the attachments learned through enculturation is the goal set for their readers by most self-help writers. Anthony de Mello, in *The Way to Love*, writes, "In order to be genuinely happy there is one and only one thing you need to do: get deprogrammed, get rid of those attachments" (1991, 23). This piece of advice is repeated in some guise in all self-help books, but the ideal to which it points is a person who would never read a self-help book. A simple self would not seek to change himself or herself or solve some problem in his or her life. As Comte-Sponville says, the simple self "is not interested enough in himself to judge himself" (156).

The paradox, then, is that self-help books perpetuate a complexity and self-consciousness of character that they advise against, and the writers of such books depend upon a culture that fosters self-absorption. This is why their efforts in bringing about change are, at least in general terms, doomed to failure, but it is likely also why self-help books are with us in such abundance. A simple self would have no use for self-help books, but the complex and self-conscious selves that most of us are would seem to require them like a daily bread. They nourish our hunger for self-examination and cultural critique.

America's Cultural Cringe

Here let me introduce the concept of "cultural cringe," for the concept will, I hope, be useful in outlining the analytical process at work in most successful self-help books. Several years ago I spent some time in Australia, studying some of the differences between Australians' perception and use of their "national character" and our own view of ourselves here in the United States. In that context I often heard the term "cultural cringe" used to express the feeling of inferiority or at least neglect attributed to the culture of Australia when compared to British or American culture. In other words, Australians often saw their own culture as coming up in second place when measured against the culture of "the mother country" or the upstart United States. And therefore, they perceived an expectation that they would or should "cringe" when their own culture was thus exposed as second-rate.

Obviously, the idea that a nation would act as an individual might act—either cringing in shame or putting a chip on its shoulder—is ludicrous, but I have always been struck by the image nonetheless. Australia has many wonderful traditions that are characteristic of and unique to that culture, and yet this sense of something faulty in its culture was common enough to have earned it a name—cultural cringe. Australians have clearly asserted a much more positive national self-image since then, but why would such a judgment of national character develop in the first place? Where does this deprecation of one's own culture come from?

To folklorists, it seems an obvious first step to look to the folklore of a nation to see how a sense of identity is expressed. From the earliest days of folk-lore and anthropological research, there has been an underlying belief that the "primitive" or "folk" traditions—the culture of the common people—was perhaps exotic or quaint but almost always inferior and flawed, backward, or even dangerous. Learned gentlemen studying the natives of Borneo or the peasants of Transylvania saw in the culture of "the other" countless examples of inferior and erroneous beliefs and practices. Ethnocentrism—the belief that one's own culture is superior—was a standard assumption on the part of Victorian scholars studying the culture of others, even the culture of their own "lower classes." Unlike the Australian cultural assessors mentioned above, educated Europeans of the later 1800s saw their own elite culture as safely ensconced at the height of civilization and progress. It was the "other" more lowly cultures that needed to be turned from their superstitious ways toward the light of educated, civilized behavior.

Some early folklore scholars, such as Sir Edward Burnett Tylor, set about collecting folk traditions—even the traditions of the uneducated people of their own countries—with the aim not of preserving those traditions but instead of eliminating them. In 1871, Tylor wrote that his purpose was "to expose the remains of crude old culture which have passed into harmful superstition, and to mark these out for destruction" ([1880] 1924, 16). With time, that same zeal for reforming folk cultures came to be applied to modern Western culture itself, due in part to the challenges of socialism, communism, and civil protest movements but also in response to a rise in existential philosophy and a growing acceptance of cultural relativism. No longer was it permissible to posit "our" culture as the only standard simply because it was ours. Other people have a right to see things differently from the way we do, and their customs and beliefs are not necessarily wrong or inferior, simply different. Thus argued the cultural relativists.[1] One effect of this relativist stance was a willingness to examine our own culture, not simply with an aim toward political or social change but rather with a growing recognition of how cultural conditioning influences our behavior. And often that behavior is not what we would like it to be. We have come to experience a kind of cultural cringe.

As noted earlier in considering the structure of self-help books, the authors and the readers of popular nonfiction depend upon a framework of problems in need of solution. That problem/solution framework is the formula for a self-help book. The specific problems, the illogical or unloving behaviors about which Americans are cringing, will need to be identified and perhaps accounted for before the writers can offer their suggestions of how to deal with those problems. In other words, it would seem that one significant way in which self-help book authors help their readers is in identifying the traditions or conventional ways of thinking that are already a part of the culture and that are contributing, through the process of cultural conditioning, to their problems. The problem is cultural conditioning, and the sources of that conditioning are the traditions that surround us from birth on.

Popular writer Scott Peck begins his book *A World Waiting to Be Born* with "There is an illness abroad in the land." Later, on that same page, he says again, "Something is seriously wrong" (1993b, 3). He is clearly prepared to tell us what the problem is, and, as do most self-help authors, he adopts what has come to be called the "medical model," an assumption that there is apparent in people's behavior a disease that needs to be treated. He proceeds to describe the disease, and he posits a kind of "psychospiritual" (his word) healing as a solution to this disease that has been introduced through the process of American enculturation. In adopting this metaphor, he is in good company. Most social scientists have used a disease model as well. Many writers in both popular and academic circles have agreed at least in spirit with Sir Edward Burnett Tylor—that the worldview maintained through American culture is the "problem" and that getting rid of the faulty folklore, innocent as it may seem, is the only solution.[2]

For early reformers like Tylor, it was relatively easy to identify the "units" of cultural behavior that were perceived as harmful; beliefs, practices, and behaviors in general that were different from those found among "civilized" peoples were the things that needed to be stamped out. Thus, many of the traditions typically called "folklore" were considered the units of transmission for harmful ideas and attitudes. And Tylor, like a modern self-help book author, was eager to undertake careful research; to identify the offensive superstitions, beliefs, and practices of the "peasants"; and to enlighten them with news of knowledge and innovations they would surely find preferable to their own benighted folkways.

Actually, Tylor was emphatically not writing for the often illiterate "folk" whose customs he studied. But contemporary self-help book writers *are* writing for the modern, urban, quite literate, and sophisticated "folks" whose behaviors, beliefs, and practices they are bringing under question. And for contemporary writers, the easy identification of folk traditions as the units through which these "erroneous" ideas are maintained is not so immediately apparent. Most writers—other than folklorists—do not usually think of contemporary, educated people as having folklore, beyond maybe a few harmless home remedies for hiccups and maybe some jokes and urban legends.

There are a few self-help book writers who do in fact perceive of the problematic patterns of thought they are addressing as folklore. Ken Keyes Jr., for example, claims that reading his book *How to Enjoy Your Life in Spite of It All* will "help in freeing you from buying into any folkways in our culture that increase your separateness, alienation, neurosis, sickness, and unhappiness" (1980, 119). That is a heavy load to lay upon the sweet songs, charming tales, and beautiful epics we usually think of as folklore. How could "Down in the Valley," "Br'er Rabbit and the Briar Patch," or the legend of Johnny Appleseed produce separateness, alienation, and neuroses? But of course Keyes is right; ideas grounded in the "stuff" of folklore are indeed responsible for many of the problematic aspects of American worldview. In fact, the ideas themselves are traditional, are folklore, but we often do not use the term "folklore" to identify abstract ideas that are embedded in the materials of song or story or the behavior of ordinary people.

It might be helpful to look briefly at how the concept of "tradition" arose in folklore study. Even the word "folklore" has not always been with us. It was coined in 1846 by William Thoms, an Englishman who wanted a less cumbersome term than "popular antiquities" to identify the materials he was studying. Even in that earlier term, an adjective—antiquated—was being transformed into a noun, or more precisely, the descriptive feature of oldness, of continuity over time, was set aside as a category of things—popular antiquities are "items" that can somehow be corroborated as having existed in the minds of people for generations. It is that process of corroboration, of demonstrating repetition, that is the primary contribution the field of folklore study has made to the larger intellectual enterprise. Folklorists have spent two hundred years trying to perfect a system for identifying tradition. It is not as easy as it may seem.

Earliest efforts simply involved locating analogues of sayings, beliefs, customs, rhymes, or rituals that could still be found among the peasants of Europe. But the process became much more complicated as scholars tried to find parallels of stories and songs in earlier written records or in the oral performances of contemporaneous cultures. Then the challenge became one of first identifying the unit of comparison: Do we compare only whole stories or songs with one another, or do we break the story down into smaller units, such as specific actions or characters, and compare those? How do we know when something is traditional, and how do we know how to describe or list the essence of a narrative idea as a "tradition"? Is something like "death from humiliation" (AT type 885A; see Aarne and Thompson, 1981, 302) a tradition? Is "compassionate youngest son" (motif L13; see Thompson, 1955) a tradition? How do we know when we have encountered in a story an example of the motif "death from humiliation" or "compassionate youngest son"? Such motifs are ideas, but it is usually some outside observer, a scholar, who decides that they are ideas that have been repeated, handed down from one generation to the next or passed along from one group of people to another.

Stith Thompson, in the 1930s, believed it important to create indexes that would help in the effort to identify whole narratives or parts of narratives as "traditional." His six-volume *Motif-Index of Folk Literature* (1955–58) is an impressive testimony to his conviction that scholars could identify a tradition when they saw one. But perhaps more important, the motif index suggests that thousands of ideas have been transmitted through the agency of the human mind, that people have grasped certain ideas, even psychologically significant ideas such as humiliation or compassion, and passed them on to other people as though they were tangible objects with an existence of their own. Or, to go back to Ken Keyes and his warning about the hazards of folklore, we can see in the motif index that there are countless "traditions" that have embedded in them significant, sometimes even dangerous, ideas that people are ready to accept and take into their lives simply because they are so seductively a part of their culture.

In the early 1970s, folklorist Alan Dundes suggested the term "folk idea" for more abstract yet traditional units of worldview, and more recently Hasan El-Shamy has expanded Thompson's concept of motif to include key principles from cognitive psychology as classificatory devices (1995, 1:xiii). In effect, El-Shamy has identified such psychological concerns as literally "dying from shame" as traditional narrative units; they have been found to be a part of, in this case, Arab culture. Clearly, folklorists have been struggling for a long time with the problem of identifying tradition, especially tradition that is abstract in content—an idea, an attitude, or a perspective on life. And it is precisely these units of ideology that show up in self-help books.

Much more recently, another term has been suggested for a concept closely aligned with "tradition." The term "meme" was suggested, almost offhandedly, by British biologist Richard Dawkins in the last chapter of his book *The Selfish Gene* (1976). Since Dawkins was writing about a biological process rather than a cultural process through most of his book, his coining of the term "meme" (from the Greek *mimeme*) to identify a unit of culture that is passed on by imitation remained largely undeveloped until the 1990s. Douglas Hofstadter, Daniel C. Dennett, Mihaly Csikszentmihalyi, Aaron Lynch, and Susan Blackmore have all written on the concept in the last decade. In Lynch's book, *Thought Contagion: How Belief Spreads through Society, the New Science of Memes* (1996), his discussion pointedly takes up the urban legend as an example of "thought contagion"—essentially the movement of abstract ideas through time and space. More telling than the urban legend, which has specific narrative content, is the great variety of "ideas" large and small that are considered examples of memes that, like legend types and fairy tale motifs, take on a life of their own—ideas that become identifiable and parasitic "traditions."

One of the earliest writers to take up Dawkins's notion of the "meme" was psychologist and self-help writer Mihaly Csikszentmihalyi. In his 1993 book *The Evolving Self: A Psychology for the Third Millennium,* Csikszentmihalyi writes, "Although we might initially adopt memes because they are useful, it is often the case that after a certain point they begin to affect our actions and thoughts in ways that are at best ambiguous and at worst definitely not in our interest. . . . Once a meme is well-established, it tends to generate inertia in the mind, and forces us to pursue its logical consequences to the bitter end" (123–24). The example Csikszentmihalyi offers to illustrate the point is the development of weaponry—the evolution of the idea that a projectile, such as a stone, can increase the destructive power of an individual. He then reviews the slow growth of the idea from arrows to cannonballs to bombs to incinerating laser rays. The frightening conclusion, then, is that it is the *meme* that lives and it is the people, whose minds help in the meme's survival, who are its servants.

This is the worrisome theme of a more recent book on the topic, Susan Blackmore's *Meme Machine* (1999). Blackmore, sounding very much like anthropologists of half a century ago, speaks of memes as "selfish" (from Dawkins), as "wanting" to be passed on to the next generation. She writes, "When you imitate someone else, something is passed on. This 'something' can then be passed on again and again, and so take on a life of its own. We might call this thing an idea, an instruction, a behaviour, a piece of information . . . but if we are going to study it we shall need to give it a name" (4). Not only had folklorists gone through this process of recognizing repeated patterns long before the word "meme" was coined, but William Bascom had articulated in 1954 the same concern with the seeming organic need of traditions to maintain themselves. Or, as Bascom said, the one overarching function of all folklore is to maintain the stability of culture (1965, 297). In this "organic" view, the urban legend of "The Killer in the Backseat" stays a part of the culture because the idea or expectation of violence against women is already a part of the culture, and the legend functions to keep it a part of the culture.

Much earlier in the study of folk traditions, particularly folk narratives, folklorists grappled with the notion of automigration, the rather mystical idea that stories moved through time and space more or less on their own. As folklore theorists considered the real process of transmission, they found this idea more and more absurd. In 1945, Swedish folklorist Carl Wilhelm von

Sydow published a paper in which he stated flatly that we must always take into account the individual who "passes along" an item of folklore—the active storyteller, the proverb teller, the pot maker. Granted, patterns can be recognized and indexes can be created to help us identify traditions *as traditional.* But it is an individual who at every turn is responsible for deciding that the tradition will be passed along and that it will be modified and presented in a certain way.

The upshot of this controversy is that, while we must recognize that memes or traditions or floating fairy-tale plots like "Cinderella" do exist, an individual is still needed to bring them to form, to performance. What this means for our study of the self-help book is that the process of cultural enlightenment can be tied to the individual. The author of a self-help book can, in effect, halt the "meme machine" or the forward march of tradition long enough for the individual to become aware of his or her own role in the process. The individual is not simply a cog in the wheel of traditional ideas rolling through a given culture. The individual self-help book reader, in particular, can be taught "metacognitive skills" that make the unofficial learning process more transparent.[3]

Though most self-help book writers are eager to offer solutions to the problems they identify and discuss, they are also in general quite aware of the process of learning that is at the heart of their readers' engagement with the book. They know that it is up to each reader to pull himself or herself away from the traditional thinking that is causing the problems that are the subject of the book. Anthony de Mello says, "All I can do for you is help you unlearn" (1990, 17). Unlearning the folklore, unlearning the worldview they have accepted so easily into their daily lives, is the task self-help book authors set for their readers. And the effective writer guides the reader through a necessary process of cultural enlightenment that breaks the chain of cultural determinism, at least for that individual—and perhaps, if for that individual, then for the human species. That is the hope of self-help book writers— that they will be able to convince their readers that changing the way they think, making them more aware of the relationship between belief and behavior, will change their lives for the better. That is their own quest and inspiration.

How do self-help book writers accomplish this task? Most use the precepts of cognitive psychology; that is, they introduce the reader to new ways of thinking and in the process challenge old, troublesome ideas, stories, or beliefs. In effect, they argue that despite the many cultural influences that are always in force in our daily lives, we can learn to recognize when we are letting "culture" determine our thinking and behavior and instead do what a culturally enlightened person would do.

Writers who do this most effectively usually follow a seven-step sequence: (1) They identify a given problem—for example, poor time management, failed intimacy in personal relationships, a tendency to overwork or underachieve, worry about death, general unhappiness. (2) They explain the problem's strength and endurance as a consequence of faulty thinking. (3) They account for both the presence and persistence of the faulty thinking itself by examining the traditional (or sometimes inherent or archetypal) sources that maintain that thinking in the culture. (4) If possible, they offer vehicles for alternative patterns of thinking—often stories, slogans, or sayings. (5) They interpret the information they have presented to the reader as supportive of the new, enlightened thinking they hope to promote. (6) Often, they then suggest changes in behavior and practice that will move the reader away from the old thinking and reinforce the new. (7) Finally, they include an epilogue or conclusion in which they remind the reader that the message of the book can only be realized in the reader's own application. This is the writer's last word—the rhetorical and inspirational send-off.

Crucial to the process is step 5—interpretation. This is what makes the self-help book didactic rather than solely informative or inspirational. The writer clearly intends to teach, to enlighten the reader. And, again, the aim is to teach for the sake of the reader's own personal learning and application, not for the sake of furthering the author's discipline or simply adding to our general body of knowledge (though it may do these as well). The stuff of tradition is examined with the hope that enlightenment may come to the reader. It is a teacher's goal more than a healer's; or, perhaps it is a recognition of the power of enlightenment to heal. America's cultural cringe is accepted, even exploited, as a part of the process of cultural enlightenment.

4. Giving Advice and Getting Wisdom

One of my favorites among the books I have read for this study is one I mentioned earlier, Peter Kramer's provocatively titled *Should You Leave? A Psychiatrist Explores Intimacy and Autonomy—and the Nature of Advice.* In the first chapter, he writes, referring to his popular 1993 volume *Listening to Prozac,* "I have written a best-seller, and when a psychiatrist writes a best-seller, he is next urged to write a book of advice" (1997, 15). Kramer addresses the significant difference between offering advice to a real "other" and simply writing in general terms as one would in a self-help book. In fact, he creates fictional "you"s in the remaining chapters of his book and addresses his advice to these hypothetical people, claiming, "One way or another, I must come to know you. Otherwise I will be limited to something that is not quite advice—perhaps the transmission of values; because what passes for advice outside the individual encounter is often just the transmission of values" (34). Nevertheless, because his advisees are fictional, Kramer is doing very self-consciously what fiction writers do perhaps more intrinsically as part of their craft—incorporating values and concerns of society and human nature into the lives and actions of their works' dramatis personae. And, he is as well characterizing for his readers some of the leading theories of his discipline and demonstrating their application to hypothetical cases. He is offering advice packed with a wealth of intended contextual richness.

And yet I would be surprised to hear that Kramer intended his book primarily for other psychiatrists who hoped to enter the general advice-giving game. This was not written as a how-to book for advice columnists or self-help book writers. A few other writers, such as Robert J. Wicks (*Sharing Wisdom: The Practical Art of Giving and Receiving Mentoring* [2000]) or perhaps

Marsha Sinetar (*The Mentor's Spirit: Life Lessons on Leadership and the Art of Encouragement* [1997]), do seem to be writing for others who hope to mentor and offer advice, but most self-help writers, including Kramer and other scholars conscious of their disciplines, are writing with the general middle-class American reading public in mind. They are writing a very successful kind of meta-nonfiction. Kramer is simply more up-front about the way he is using the tradition itself, more forthcoming in his simultaneous advice-giving and scrutiny of the practice of writing of self-help books as a means to guiding others.

In chapter 2, I mentioned the abundance of "metacommentary" throughout the many self-help books I have examined. Often, this metacommentary identifies the people who comprise the network of self-help writers. Other times, it simply states some observation about self-help books, noting their popularity, their typical subject matter, even their noted failings. Unlike footnoting in clearly academic writing, this system of referencing other writers and other self-help books serves to reinforce the tradition itself rather than to acknowledge previous research. Self-help writers are sometimes, as in the case of Peter Kramer, almost painfully aware of the tradition in which they are writing, and they comment on that tradition in terms that acknowledge its inadequacy to the task of advising unknown readers. And yet, they proceed with the task at hand; they write and publish self-help books. Why? Is it simply to make money? Is it to enhance the ego with a popular publication? Is the tradition itself a flawed form of pop culture peddled like snake-oil remedies to a gullible public, as Tom Tiede would have us believe?

Careful and dedicated writers such as Kramer or, say, Robert C. Solomon (*About Love* [2001]) are enough to convince me otherwise. I believe that they do see themselves as educators. The missing element in any self-help book is, as Kramer laments, the advisee's life story, the context or real-life situation of the reader. The writer must persuade his or her readers to bring their own lives and their own questions to their reading of self-help literature. It is the perennial dilemma of the teacher who lectures to a class of five hundred—how can an educator ensure that each student gets the most he or she can from the lecture?

The dean of faculties office at my university recently granted me a summer fellowship in support of my efforts to create a graduate course to be offered via the Internet. As I worked on the course design and lessons, I realized that I had never taught a course to students I would never see. When I stopped and thought about it, I found the notion strangely disconcerting. I enjoy teaching; I enjoy the interaction; I enjoy the feeling that I am contributing in some way to the lives of my students. In teaching an Internet course, would I still experience that sense of engagement, or—and this was my real worry—would I instead feel that I was simply putting some specialized knowledge out on the market, "selling wisdom" to people I would never meet face-to-face? I am more sanguine now about the issue, but initially I felt much as I suspect many of the writers of popular nonfiction feel—slightly awkward in my role as a "distance" educator.

Not all self-help book writers see themselves first and foremost as educators, and likely not all readers of self-help books approach their reading in the spirit of a student. Perhaps there are some who, like the desperate seekers Wendy Kaminer envisions, are simply looking for a stereotypical shaman, a *curandero,* a psychological folk healer who has the power to cure their ills, whatever they may be. But if that is indeed what they are seeking, they will find relatively few of the writers of self-help books who offer that brand of faith healing; most writers are eager to teach rather than to simply offer formulas. Most clearly see themselves as concerned—if distant—mentors, as teachers, or, if as healers, then as healers who educate rather than as conjurors who prescribe magic rituals and practices to obedient believers.

Many self-help book writers state directly that they perceive their role as that of educator. Longtime editor of *Parade* magazine Walter Anderson titled his book *The Confidence Course: Seven Steps to Self-Fulfillment,* and the book jacket calls the book "the most important class you never took in school." In her book *Feel the Fear and Do It Anyway,* Susan Jeffers says, "You may be surprised and encouraged to learn that while the inability to deal with fear may look and feel like a psychological problem, in most cases it isn't. I believe it is primarily an educational problem" (1987, 4). Marsha Sinetar explains that she writes self-help books as a consequence of her own early habit of seeking education and mentoring through impersonal sources, such as books:

> Not until 1993 did I scale back my corporate practice to accommodate a growing desire to write. In my youth, however, encouragements were rare and came primarily from the mentor's *spirit:* impersonal love. I mean by "impersonal" those positive forces all around us, even from dispassionate or inanimate sources like the people we don't know—poets and actors—or books and cultural icons. Through high school and college I was prematurely self-supporting, living largely on my own. I sought out mentors, but helpful, caring persons capable of empathizing with me on a deeply relevant level of experience were not readily available. Out of my loneliness and sense of being different, I searched out the mentor's spirit in everyone and everything. That habit served me well. It seems worth sharing. (1997, 2–3)

For a writer like Sinetar, the task of a self-help book author is to guide readers in their self-education. In this light, the practice of selecting and reading a self-help book is a procedure not so very different from that undertaken by the average undergraduate in signing up for a variety of courses in a modern university.

Until recently, with the growing reemphasis on core courses and integrated programs, most colleges and universities fell prey to what Gerald Graff calls the "course fetish." He explains, "The courses being given at any moment on a campus represent any number of rich potential conversations within and across the disciplines. But since students experience these conversations only as a series of monologues, the conversations become actual only for the minority who can reconstruct them on their own" (1992, 106). It is this "reconstructing" of the integrative conversation *on their own* that is essential for students who seek to be educated. In effect, the integration of knowledge into an education—into wisdom—is something they must do on their own, as they themselves integrate the thinking they have engaged in through each course into a cohesive whole.

How is the situation different or similar for an individual who chooses to "take a course" offered in the form of a readable self-help book? The subject matter may be quite different from that of a typical college course, but the process of solitary integration of the learning—of self-education—is surely similar. The goal in the case of the self-help book reader is to learn a more effective way of dealing with life's problems and at the same time to integrate that new knowledge into an emerging personal philosophy of life. The process is both educational and informal or folkloric. It is an often unrecognized but integral part of the process of lifelong learning.

Self-Help Books and the Construction of a Personal Philosophy

An important assumption here, then, is that self-help books are written and read for the purpose of helping individuals build a personal philosophy. There are other goals and motives as well, of course, but the objective of contributing to the construction of a personal philosophy looms somewhere behind the decision to write or read self-help books. A book such as Ronald Gross's *Peak Learning: How to Create Your Own Lifelong Education Program for Personal Enlightenment and Professional Success* (1999) offers some practical guidance to readers of self-help books, but in general, the process of building a personal philosophy itself has been neglected as an area of study.

In part, this neglect can be explained by the difficulty in studying a process, any process. People are certainly aware of the notion of "process" and often have an intuitive sense of how a given process works. But discussing process requires a movement from the concrete to the abstract and back to the concrete again. In Peter Senge's insightful study of systems theory, *The Fifth Discipline,* the author uses a series of diagrams to examine and represent a process—in this case, flow within a system. Unfortunately, even diagrams must use abstract terms and concepts, and the people asked to fill in the abstractions with concrete examples may not "see" those slots as others would. Though such visualizations are often more memorable than verbal discussion, inevitably diagrams oversimplify. But Senge's book does effectively illustrate the need to identify fundamental principles that define a process.

By convention, when any process is so defined, it is also classified by the kind of materials involved as well as the principles of selection—as in naming the flow of capital an "economic" process or the decisions on time use a "time management" process. The process involved in building a personal philosophy is a personal learning process or what I would call a folklore process. The process entails our exercising principles for combining cultural and personal belief into a coherent philosophy, and it is accomplished in large part through unofficial channels. To call something a "folklore process" is to characterize that process as central to the creation of an individual's sense of identity but also as both informal and traditional. Often things that are so characterized tend to be neglected and taken for granted. A few folklorists have examined the lives of individuals to see if a dominant worldview can be extracted from their narratives and commentary, but rarely has the process of building a personal philosophy been studied. An introductory consideration of this process is one objective I hold in writing this book.

The Skill of Asking the Right Question

A cursory glance through the titles of the books in the bibliography at the close of this study would suggest that the authors see their books as functioning in many different ways—some to help people achieve financial or career success, some to guide people toward better health, some to inform people on what God or the world is really like, some to instruct people in how to overcome certain faults or addictions, some simply to advise people on how to be happy and get along in the world. I would argue that, despite their varied titles and specific topics, the roughly three hundred books of popular nonfiction I have read for this study all share one practical objective: to teach readers to see reality and to respond to that reality rather than to the ineffective "truths" and misinformation their culture has given them. In other words, self-help writers hope to guide readers toward a reliable personal philosophy, a reasoned and wise philosophy, rather than toward the unexamined and faulty set of cultural assumptions they inherited along with all of the other folklore, useful or not, that fills their heads and hearts.

And to do this, they seem most consistently to encourage their readers to ask the very questions that advice-seekers usually ask—but with the recognition that the answers will always reflect the values of this American culture, or, as Peter Kramer said, our generalized answers will simply give us "news about norms" (1997, 36). In other words, the practical concerns of self-help books are the very issues that draw into the readers' conscious thought the values that will form the basis of their emerging personal philosophies. We will know how to behave, we will know how to respond, because we will know the fundamental principles of our own working personal philosophies. Thus would self-help writers tie together practical wisdom and shared ideas and teach their readers to discover ways to answer their own questions.

What are these questions? When we think of how personal philosophies are formed, we may envision the lone seeker climbing to the mountaintop and asking the reclusive guru, "What is the meaning of life?" Instead, self-help writers imply in their works that the more mundane questions, what Herbert Gans called "prosaic issues," are the ones that, when answered, reveal and articulate our personal philosophies. Taking a cue from Kramer, I see his question "Should I leave?" as one of these essential philosophy-invoking questions. I might reverse the question to its opposite: "Should I stay?" In either case, the answer is simple and for most writers always the same— no, you should not leave; yes, you should stay.

In effect, the advice is almost always to stay the course—at least until an important life skill is learned, one that will serve in all other such situations. The argument is that if a person learns this important life skill, he or she will no longer need to ask an expert, "Should I leave?" Ultimately, the one life skill everyone needs is confidence—the ability to trust, to love, to accept what is. Whatever it is called, it is a competence rather than a feeling, and therefore it can be taught. Advice-givers see their role as coaching others in their efforts to gain competence in love, in trusting others, in accepting the world as it is, and ultimately, as Robert Solomon says, in redefining and improving oneself (2001, 155). Self-help writers are rhetorically effective cheerleaders on one hand and probing teachers on the other. The aim is to guide individuals along a path of personal development that continues after the book is finished, or as Gregg D. Jacobs explains in his book *The Ancestral Mind,* to teach them skills that they "can use without relying on the intercession of a doctor or a medication" (2003, 82). To do that, self-help writers must ask readers to envision every action (or inaction) in their lives as part of a long chain of illustrations tied to a principle that accepts life the way it really is, without fear but instead with ample confidence.

In other words, self-help writers offer to teach their readers not simply practical competence in life activities but also the positive attitude that bolsters the likelihood of success. Self-help writers teach readers to be confident and to display an attitude of love—love of self, love of others, love of the planet, love of the universe, love of God, and, in particular, love of life as it really is (or at least as the writers endeavor to explain that "it really is"). They teach readers to substitute this capacity for love and optimism in place of the much too common response of fear, with its many ill effects on daily behavior and general attitude. Not all authors have stated this goal so bluntly— characterizing as a skill or competency something that is more often viewed as an emotion—but all seem to assume that what they have to offer must be taught, that an individual is not born knowing what they have to teach, not born knowing how to love life, other people, or even themselves.

Theirs is an educational thesis with a stable structural formula, similar to what folklorist Alan Dundes has identified as the basic structure of all narrative: lack and lack liquidated. As suggested in the introduction, when applied to popular nonfiction, this basic structure becomes a suggestion that something is wrong with us, with the culture that guides or programs us, or with our information about the world (lack), and a suggestion of what might be done to correct this problem (lack liquidated). In more conventional terms, then, all statements of the "problem" call for our seeing reality more clearly, and all "solutions" offered are some form of teaching the skill of loving life as it really is—a conscious practice of acceptance, trust, and care. And I would like to suggest as well that people who read these books in an effort to right the wrongs of their lives and learn the skill of loving life as it really is are engaging in the folklore process of building a personal philosophy.

The abundance and variety of books can be explained in part precisely because the books are used in a folklore process. One of the defining characterstics of folklore is variation: witness the many parodies of "Roses are red . . ." or the many recipes for the world's best chili or the variety of duck decoys or quilt patterns. Similarly, the authors of these many self-help books may be offering answers or solutions that can be abstracted to the single functional skill of learning to see reality more clearly and practice trust and love, but their formulation of "what is wrong" with society or individuals—their critique that needs to be addressed—takes many forms. Each author, in other words, describes in a different way the problem to which the answer is always "to learn to see reality clearly and to practice the skill of love"—even if "love" in this case simply means caring enough about one's performance in the world to be careful and competent. These discrete formulations of everyday problems, then, are responsible for the great variety of self-help books, and this variety is what makes the whole enterprise of writing such books a creative and productive one—or, as folklorists would say, a creative use of cultural resources.

Self-Help Books and the Folklore Process

Books of popular nonfiction imply a folklore process at work in two ways. One is in the writing of the books. Though some books of popular nonfiction are strikingly original in tone or voice, the process involved in their composition can be compared to the performance of highly formulaic folklore, such as the epic. Like the griot singing an epic, the writer of a self-help book makes use of certain traditional resources and combines them in ways that have come to be expected by the audience or reader. Self-help books are formulaic and didactic; that is, they all follow a basic pattern of critique and solution. Other kinds of popular literature are often compared to folklore because of their formulaic nature—romances, mysteries, adventure stories, rags-to-riches sagas. But, as we saw in chapter 2, there is no one predictable style or subtype of popular nonfiction. Self-help books take a variety of forms—some parables or framed stories, some sequential steps in a guidebook, some analytical segments built upon a well-known text, some a series of short essays expanding upon a list of insights or themes. The formulaic structure of self-help books is more abstract, tied as it is to the overarching objective of teaching the reader to replace fearful and ineffective thinking and behavior with insight and acceptance of reality along with love and confidence and its many positive effects. However, many other elements of the books are more concrete and clearly traditional, and these other traditional elements are significant in our understanding of how writers create rhetorically effective self-help books.

If I were concerned only with the process of writing such books, we could move immediately to a discussion of what these traditional elements are and how they figure in the process of composition. In fact, chapters 5, 6, and 7 do exactly that; they examine the proverbs or sayings, the stories, and the traditional beliefs used in popular nonfiction. But my focus here is not simply on the authors and their performances as reflected in the variety of self-help books—or texts—examined in this study. Rather, I have argued that an equally important question asks how these books are used by readers in their efforts to build a personal philosophy. This question highlights a second way the folklore process is implicated in the study of popular nonfiction. And, strangely, it is a question that strains our current understanding of what is meant by the "folklore process."

Normally, folklorists engage in ethnographic research in an effort to address how "artistic communication in small groups" happens. Even when we stretch the "small group" to include mass media productions or museum exhibits, we still expect to deal with "artistic communication" in some way—specifically, in what we can treat as a "text." We record a bluesman singing, a storyteller talking, children riddling; we photograph quilts and carvings, houses and barns; we videotape people dancing, teenagers playing the dozens, graffiti artists painting, healers healing, worshipers worshiping. Always we expect to provide ourselves with a text, an artifact, a performance we can then study. One of the best examples of this research practice can be seen in Richard Bauman's *Story, Performance, and Event: Contextual Studies of Oral Narrative* (1986), a book in which the author looks at a few oral stories and discusses at great length how the context affects the text—how everything in the storyteller's cultural surrounds conspire to give us those very particular texts.

I could treat each of the self-help books I have read for this study as a text ripe for the process of deconstruction. I could work back from each book and try to account for its final form and content by citing the cultural and personal elements that influenced each author's literary "performance." In doing this, I would be invoking two assumptions currently a part of most folklore research: that the artifact we study is composed *in performance* and that the performer uses the cultural frame of reference shared with his or her audience to create a performance that is meaningful. There is no reason to quibble with these assumptions; they work very well for any "artistic" text—actually any artifact at all that can be captured in some form that allows us to examine it. The problem here is that these assumptions derive from a verbal model. Performance theory grew out of studies of oral epic and the ethnography of speaking. It helps tremendously with the analysis of texts. Even the performance of a traditional ballad like "Barbara Allen," in which the singer tries to sing the song just as she learned it, benefits from attention to what happens as the performer brings to bear all of her cultural frame of reference as she sings.

An author like Wayne Dyer, writing his tenth best-selling self-help book, could fruitfully be studied using the methods associated with performance theory. Dyer even helpfully cites other writers whose self-help books he has read. Careful analysis would reveal how the cultural context and the genre of self-help books have been incorporated, consciously or not, into the writing of his latest book. But when we look at how Dyer's book is used by an individual reader, our understanding of the process is complicated by the fact that there is no performed "text" to analyze, no artifact from which to work backward toward the act of composition. A reader does not create a text but rather builds a personal but tacit belief system. And possibly, the reader uses not only Dyer's tenth best-seller but also all his other books and the books of many other writers, not to mention cultural resources quite apart from the assortment of self-help books read.

The process of creating this tacit belief system, this nonverbalized text, is a folklore process as well, but we might want to identify its basic steps in a slightly different way. There is another conceptualization of the folklore process that uses a material rather than a verbal model. I was first introduced to this way of articulating the folklore process when I sat years ago as a student in a class taught by Henry Glassie, a folklorist who often studies material culture—folk crafts, folk art, folk architecture. Glassie was attracted to Claude Lévi-Strauss's metaphor of the artisan as *bricoleur*—someone who brings together materials that happen to be at hand and uses them to carry out the task of building what needs to be built. If we think of an individual reader as a *bricoleur,* we can imagine that person gathering information and wisdom from a variety of sources and using them in the task of "building" a personal philosophy. Of course, the philosophy thus created is no more material than it is verbal, but the metaphor of the *bricoleur* allows us to envision the process, much as Peter Senge's diagrams helped in explaining that process. The question then is how the *bricoleur* selects the materials that he or she ends up using.

The process of selection is constrained by culture, as Lévi-Strauss argues, but it is also influenced by the reader's own personal history and goal in reading. These three elements each contribute in a significant way to the overall choices that are made. We could outline this alternative model of the folklore process as follows:

1. The *bricoleur* brings together the materials that are at hand for working on a project.
2. Three things affect the process of selection:
    a. The *bricoleur's* cultural frame of reference
    b. The *bricoleur's* self, personal history, or personal narrative
    c. The goal of the project
3. The *bricoleur* carries out the project, but the end product may remain unarticulated; it may instead be a tacit belief system that supports and influences behavior.

The easiest ingredients to study are those that make up the cultural frame of reference—the traditional elements. And, the goal of the project is a rough approximation of the stated assumption of this study—that the reader hopes to build a personal philosophy. The wild card is the reader's own self and life history. In every case, the reader must supply concrete examples to flesh out the principles discussed by reflecting upon his or her own life.

Some insights can be gained from looking at research in adult education, in particular the work of French scholar Pierre Dominicé. Along with American educators interested in what Jack Mezirow calls "transformative learning," Dominicé examines the role that reflection on an individual's life history plays in solidifying learning. In Dominicé's book *Learning from Our Lives: Using Educational Biographies with Adults* (2000), we can see how the practice of creating "educational biographies" encourages adult learners to examine the effects of various educational experiences on their understanding of life. In other words, there is an increasing awareness among adult educators that the process of reflection—of building a personal system of understanding, a personal philosophy—is essential to the overall process of adult education. And Dominicé's book discusses at length the advantages in requiring adult learners to tie together their own life stories and their sense of themselves as people who have learned from the lives they live.

We can see, then, that without such required and formalized reflection, the more typical folklore process at play when a reader reads a self-help book leaves us with an unarticulated "text." The object or thing that grows out of an individual's reading and thinking remains an unexpressed amalgam of inchoate ideas, a personal but tacit belief system. Nevertheless, this "product"—this unarticulated educational biography—functions well for the reader. And within it are some components that we can more easily identify and study—the traditional elements that make up the cultural frame of reference.

The Cultural Frame of Reference

The notion of a "cultural frame of reference" derives from two separate concepts in the field of folklore research. When the two concepts are brought together, we have a particularly rich analytic tool. The first concept is tied to the common phrase "frame of reference." Usually, in day-to-day speech, this phrase is used to identify a set of accepted values or a body of shared information that allows a person to interpret the meaning or relative importance of a given item. Thus, in his book *Frame Analysis,* Erving Goffman sets out "to isolate some of the basic frameworks of understanding available in our society for making sense out of events" (1974, 10). Having a frame of reference allows us to understand; without one, we have only our instincts and raw senses to guide us. The source of a frame of reference is thus either subjective experience or interaction with other people, a reference group.

The concept of a folk or culture group is the second part of the larger concept of a cultural frame of reference. Dan Ben-Amos, in offering a definition of folklore in context, wrote, "For the folkloric act to happen, two social conditions are necessary: both the performer and the audience have to be in the same situation and be part of the same reference group" (1972, 12). To be part of the same reference group may mean something so limited as to be members of the same nuclear family, or it may mean simply to be members of the same country. Ultimately, what decides whether one person is part of the same reference group as another person is whether they share the "stuff" that would be referred to—in effect, whether they share traditions. E. D. Hirsch Jr., in his book *Cultural Literacy* (1987), capitalizes on this notion of a shared cultural frame, emphasizing the advantages to students in being a part of the "educated" group whose cultural references are most highly valued and most often alluded to in our society.

Sometimes the traditions that are referred to are not easily identified; often they might more correctly be called "patterns" or "worldview" or "folk ideas," and often, especially in those instances, the "reference" is not a conscious one but rather a functional but unconscious use. Still, some specific kinds of folklore—a group's corpus of sayings, stories, practices, and beliefs—do constitute much of the cultural frame of reference. I would offer the following as a definition for the concept: A cultural frame of reference is a mental framework that holds the cumulative repertoire of traditions and cultural patterns of behavior and thought shared by members of a group. Tied to this definition are three assumptions:

1. There must be *something to refer to:* the traditions.
2. The frame of reference is group-based (cultural) rather than idiosyncratic.
3. Though the frame is culture-based, not everyone will share every element that makes up the frame with everyone else who is a part of the group; furthermore, because every person has a separate life history, each individual's constellation of groups to which he or she belongs is unique.

The cultural frame of reference is what allows a listener to make sense of communications from other people, and often it is what attracts people, by its very familiarity, to the message conveyed or convinces them of its truth.

The cultural frame of reference is used at both ends of a communication—by the encoder and the decoder. But, again, the resources used in this way are not simply verbal ones but all traditions. The field of folklore study is essentially a two-hundred-year-old effort to identify the traditions that make up the world's discrete and cumulative cultural frames of reference. It is important to view this accumulation of cultural knowledge as only one portion of the whole that contributes to the individual's construction of a personal philosophy. As suggested earlier, the individual's own life and experience (including biological, psychological, and environmental factors) and the goal of self-education itself influence the process. The cultural frame of reference is a significant portion nonetheless; it is the part that both feeds and draws upon socially constructed reality. In this study of popular nonfiction, it is the cultural frame of reference shared by the majority of Americans that is most influential. It is the cultural frame that adds a social dimension to the solitary act of reading a self-help book.

Self-Education and the Concept of a Learning Project

Self-help books are read primarily by adults but only rarely as part of the regular college and university curriculum. Such books certainly *could* be a part of the college curriculum. Edward LeRoy Long Jr., in *Higher Education as a Moral Enterprise,* suggests that there are three functions or responsibilities that must be addressed by any college or university: (1) "maturation and enrichment of selfhood"; (2) "discovery/construction, extension, and dissemination of knowledge and culture"; and (3) responsibility for "the well-being of society" (1992, 6). Most often, the second function is allowed to dominate, with the first and third seen as less significant aspects of college life. While some colleges are making efforts to balance these three functions, most have not incorporated all three into the curriculum. The enrichment of the "self" in particular is left to the individual as an extracurricular choice.

Still, the current decade promises to be a period of great change among institutions of higher learning. Curriculum is being reexamined. Perhaps more striking than curriculum revision is the growing attention to vocational training, service learning, human and organizational management, continuing education, "returning" students, distance education, and on-line courses; these and other emerging features of the contemporary expanding university are bringing a new challenge to the enterprise of higher education in America. One aspect of this challenge is a renewed and more urgent interest in practical rather than theoretical questions about how learning happens, no matter what the subject. Does learning happen best in well-organized group presentations? Can learning happen in solitary programs or one-on-one interactions via the Internet? Should learning be participatory, or are lectures effective? Are adult learners more likely to set their own goals for learning rather than depend upon the institution to tell them what is most important?

As institutions of higher education are grappling with these issues, the unofficial self-help "movement" has found ways of addressing them as well, especially as these issues affect learning about the self and the learner's own behavior. A major consideration in either case is whether the individual learner will work with others in a group or instead independently, with only authoritative resources and his or her own learning goal as a guide. Looking at my own involvement with the learning process as an example, I can say that for all but the first five years of my life, I have been a student or a teacher; my own experience with the process of learning clearly has involved the context of a group—the typical classroom setting. I appreciate and endorse the advantages of learning in a group setting; there is nothing in a solitary learning situation to match the effects of a stimulating discussion.

Nevertheless, circumstances cannot always offer that ideal. Joseph Kett's 1994 study chronicles the emergence of adult education and attests to the efforts people have made to find group contexts for learning, even in nonacademic settings. In America, from the colonial period on, there has been a strong interest in clubs, library societies, books, and institutions that support self-improvement among adults not enrolled in regular schooling—in other words, in self-education. Kett's survey takes account of the group venues historically available for intellectual, social, and spiritual improvement of the self. Today, churches, synagogues, health clubs, library discussion groups, noncredit college workshops, even bookstore coffee shops continue this tradition. In addition, there are a growing number of institutions, such as the California Institute of Integral Studies or the Whidbey Institute in Clinton, Washington, dedicated to the process of "transformative learning," as Jack Mezirow named this self-developmental adult learning practice some years ago (1978).

Kett mentions as well the positive response people in the earlier decades of the twentieth century had to the few self-help books just beginning to appear on publishing lists—books such as Dale Carnegie's *Art of Public Speaking* (1915) and *How to Win Friends and Influence People* (1936). Such books attested to an increasingly popular independent self-help reading practice that grew up alongside the group-oriented venues for self-education. By the 1960s, there began a surge in publishing such books of popular nonfiction that continues unabated into the present. Readers are now offered a wide selection of books that can be discussed in group settings or, more often, read in private and used by the individual as part of a self-directed learning program. As noted earlier, by 1994, the abundance of books had already created a need for *The Authoritative Guide to Self-Help Books,* which culled through more than one thousand self-help books available in order to help people decide which would be most worth reading.

To be worth reading, according to John W. Santrock, Ann M. Minnett, and Barbara D. Campbell, the authors of the *Authoritative Guide,* a self-help book would have to be judged beneficial for the reader by a group of professional mental health experts. In other words, their concern in rating the books was whether the authors offered sound psychological information and advice and whether the content was presented effectively. In effect, once again, Long's second function—the responsible dissemination of knowledge and culture— is the primary goal, and it is a worthy one. But the books are not assessed for their effectiveness in conveying a perspective on the self nor in instilling a desire to work for the well-being of society—the other two charges Long identifies with educational enterprises. I would argue that most readers expect self-help books to serve all three educational functions. And increasingly they seek out books that have something to say about the spiritual dimension of life, in other words, books that help them build a philosophy of life. They expect such books to serve their own unofficial and sometimes unrecognized plan for self-education.

K. Patricia Cross, in her classic study *Adults as Learners,* devoted several pages to a discussion of the incidence of "self-directed learning," reviewing in particular the work of Allen Tough, who, in the early 1970s, had introduced the concept of a "learning project." Tough's definition of a learning project brings together a series of related episodes: "In each episode more than half of a person's total motivation is to gain and retain certain fairly clear knowledge and skill, or to produce some other lasting change in himself" (qtd. in Cross, 1981, 63). Other researchers have considered more generally the way learning projects function within the sphere of adult education. Malcolm Knowles identifies the "problem-centered orientation" as most characteristic of adult learning in general. It is in the articulation of the problem itself that most adult learners seek assistance through outside sources—paid experts, friends, and books. According to research in the late 1970s, books were the third most common resource consulted in individual learning projects. I would suspect that they are an even more common resource today, along with a growing dependence on the Internet.

A typical learning project is self-initiated, self-planned, and self-directed. However, the individual learner, as Knowles suggested, often has trouble articulating the problem he or she feels compelled to address. Self-help books serve this need well. As I suggested earlier, every author states a lack that needs liquidating, a problem that needs solving, and the problem is stated in terms that are personally relevant to the individual reader. In choosing and reading a book, readers recognize the theme or problem addressed in the book as their own, or at least as one related to the question at the heart of the often unorganized but yet compelling learning project guiding the choice of reading matter. Self-help books are not bought on whim but rather on purpose. And that purpose is to serve the goal of the reader's learning project, even if that learning project has not yet been clearly outlined, even if it is implicit and emergent rather than explicit and fixed.

Philosophical Self-Help as a Learning Project

I have construed the goal of building a personal philosophy as an educational but also a philosophical or spiritual endeavor, an activity that serves the individual's need to understand reality and personal experience and learn to live a good and enjoyable life. I have included most self-help and other popular nonfiction books among the resources used in such a project. How does reading yet another book on career choices or how to break an addiction or how to manage after a divorce represent an attempt to build a personal philosophy? The *bricoleur* will seek out and use what is at hand. These are the books that are available, and their usefulness can be assumed to some degree by their popularity. The implication would be that people who are undertaking their own learning projects are buying and reading the self-help books that stay in print, and especially the books of authors who more than once make the best-seller list. Still, we must assume that something other than simply availability determines which books are found most useful. The book needs to fit into each reader's individual learning project.

A learning project that involves self-help books may take on different guises at various times. Someone working on a learning project may choose to participate in workshops or discussion groups in which a particular book is used. For example, Linda J. Vogel stresses the importance of the group in adult religious education: "Teaching and learning in communities of faith must incorporate a dialogue—where all have an opportunity both to listen and to be heard. Teaching begins with what people already know and offers tools for working toward a consensus where all can benefit. . . . [This process] compels us to listen to others, to build community, to clarify problems, and then to work toward a more just world" (1991, xii). Often such involvement in community is as important as the subject matter itself. Some people learn much more easily through dialogue and discussion and the stimulation of a workshop. But, in general, Americans seek a balance between community involvement and individualism, as Robert Bellah and his colleagues suggest in *Habits of the Heart*. Clearly, for many readers, reading a book in solitude and pondering its message in private can be equally satisfying.

A number of writers of self-help books have assumed this second alternative and have offered throughout their books opportunities for reflection, questions or assignments that readers may or may not use in their own learning projects. Sam Keen and Anne Valley-Fox's early success with the 1973 version of *Your Mythic Journey* (1989) speaks to the need many people (authors and readers) feel for having a "text" or artifact that captures the reader's learning in some fixed form. Drawing upon their work with Joseph Campbell, Keen and Valley-Fox introduced the notion of a "personal mythology" and encouraged readers to answer questions and build a story (or several stories) that would represent the reader's own expressive myth. Some books leave open spaces on the page for readers to write their own thoughts. Some encourage readers to keep a daily journal. Some suggest ways that readers might express their thoughts through various creative activities—art, dance, poetry, or music. Some direct people toward social service. In every such case, one objective is to have some "thing" to show for the learning that has taken place.

As we discussed earlier, often the *bricoleur's* task is to build a formless system of belief, a personal philosophy that cannot be (or at least is not) expressed in a concise and fixed text. In this case, the learning project has a clear goal, but that goal does not entail the creation of a text, artifact, or performance. Our query becomes that of the tree falling in the forest—is there a philosophy if it is never expressed, never written down or given voice, even in a rudimentary way? As a teacher, I will argue that better learning is achieved when learners articulate what they have learned. So I will side with those writers who offer opportunities for readers to record their own thoughts in some way. On the other hand, we must assume that reading alone also has its effect. Self-help books are useful in learning projects that seek to build for the reader a personal philosophy, even if that philosophy remains in the tacit dimension. Furthermore, the real "application" of a tacit belief system or personal philosophy occurs in the personal behavior of the individual, in real life, rather than in the creation of a written or performed text. Life lived becomes the true application, the text.

In the next chapter, we shall look at some of the nonverbalized ideas behind this tacit application—some of the often hidden themes that lurk in the background when readers take the lessons of self-help writers to heart.

5. Memes, Themes, and Worldview

At the heart of all self-help books is a professed disenchantment—profound or mild—with conventional ways of thinking, with the worldview that is a part of American culture. The authors of self-help books universally adopt the premise that what they have to offer is a new way of thinking that will—to the benefit of the reader and ultimately the world—replace the old. Their task is a rhetorical one; they must persuade their readers to adopt the new and cast off the old. As have teachers and prophets from earlier times, they claim to bring a new philosophy to the common people, and they want to present it in a way that people will find convincing. This means that some aspects of the presentation will have to be already familiar to the audience. Like Jesus in the New Testament, many writers have used the everyday genres of story and aphorism to teach and persuade. But they have also simply addressed directly the faulty "ways of thinking" they deem in need of revision. They have identified and challenged the "folk ideas" that comprise our American worldview.

Are We Talking about Myth?

In the first few paragraphs of his article "Folk Ideas as Units of Worldview," Alan Dundes explains the distinction folklorists make between the category "myth" and other larger, more amorphous and inclusive notions often called "myth" by people outside the field of folklore studies. He admits that the practice of using the term "myth" to refer only to sacred oral narratives is confined to folklorists and anthropologists, and he raises the question of what might be done about the looser view of myth that includes ideas, beliefs, faulty reasoning, themes, and other general elements of worldview. He proposes that the term "folk ideas" be used for some aspects of this loose category and offers the following definition: "By 'folk ideas,' I mean traditional notions that a group of people have about the nature of man, of the world, and of man's life in the world. Folk ideas would not constitute a genre of folklore but rather would be expressed in a great variety of genres" (1972, 95). Clearly, as his title indicates, Dundes is searching for a unit of analysis but is also implying that these "folk ideas" are recognizable, autonomous entities, each with a history of its own. They may or may not depend on narratives, on myths, for their most potent means of expression. And any given folk idea may be summarized in a single word (for example, "individualism") or a sentence ("Science can solve any problem") or phrase ("the principle of unlimited good").

Not all ideas routinely called "myth" by media writers would be "folk ideas," and not all folk ideas would find their way into the stories folklorists call myths. However, collectively, the folk ideas that are taken up and given expression through popular self-help books may well function as does myth—to allow for the expression and evolution of a significant set of beliefs. In 1926, noted anthropologist Bronislaw Malinowski wrote the following observations on myth in his *Myth in Primitive Psychology:*

> Myth fulfills in primitive culture an indispensable function: it expresses, enhances, and codifies belief; it safeguards and enforces morality; it vouches for the efficiency of ritual and contains practical rules for the guidance of man. Myth is thus a vital ingredient of human civilization; it is not an idle tale, but a hard-worked active force; it is not an intellectual explanation or an artistic imagery, but a pragmatic charter of primitive faith and moral wisdom. ([1926] 1954, 101)

The role of myth as pragmatic charter of faith and wisdom is easily seen in the penchant of self-help book writers for examining folk ideas.

Yet as Dundes warned us, folk ideas are not easily identified. They do not have a single form, style, or genre. A folk idea must be recognized purely on the basis of content. And that person doing the "recognizing" cannot simply surmise that a given notion is a folk idea; the classifier must also be able to demonstrate that the idea is traditional, that it has a "history" of transmission through time and space. The process is similar to that of identifying "cultural patterns" or, more recently, "memes" in culture and perhaps even themes in works of literature or music. In fact, the well-worn term "theme" often used in literary studies is probably most appropriate to our study of self-help books since they are a genre of literature. But the process of transmission more closely follows that of folk motifs in oral literature.

Many of the same concerns that folklorists have brought to their study of folktales have reemerged in the "new science of memes." Aaron Lynch, in his book *Thought Contagion,* offers the following observations:

> Like a software virus in a computer network or a physical virus in a city, thought contagions proliferate by effectively "programming" for their own retransmission. Beliefs affect retransmission in so many ways that they set off a colorful, unplanned growth race among diverse "epidemics" of ideas. Actively contagious ideas are now called *memes* . . . by students of the newly emerging science of *memetics.* (1996, 2)

One thing that is clear in Lynch's choice of words (and in the language of other writers on the topic as well) is the sense of human inadequacy in the face of this challenge by a hostile, invading force. Memes, according to the theory, take on a life of their own and simply "use" people as a means of transmission.

It is instructive, I think, to remember the words that Mihaly Csikszentmihalyi used in writing of the historical path of memes: "Once a meme is well-established, it tends to generate inertia in the mind, and forces us to pursue its logical consequences to the bitter end" (1993, 124). It may seem surprising that researchers would adopt so easily such a pessimistic perspective, viewing people as rather spineless creatures willing and eager to do the bidding of powerful ideas. Certainly we do have the evidence of the Holocaust in World War II and even more recent genocides to point to. Still, the fear that that is the direction all humans will go when taken on by a hostile meme is itself a belief. And interestingly, it is the rhetoric-based community of self-help book authors rather than theoretical scholars that has relentlessly challenged that belief.

Let me return briefly to the process of transmission as studied by folklorists, for it is in that early study of folk narrative that we can see the most telling parallel to how researchers understand the process of "handing on" and changing established ideas. One of the clearest discussions of the "automigration" problem in folktale study was offered by Linda Dégh and Andrew Vázsonyi in their 1975 article, "The Hypothesis of Multi-Conduit Transmission in Folklore." As Dégh and Vázsonyi point out, the question of the transmission of intangible ideas—in this case, the plots of folktales—was already an issue when the Grimm Brothers published their famous collection of *Kinder- und Hausmärchern* in 1812.

But it was not until early in the next century that significant theoretical discussion focused on the process and the "thing"—in this case, the folktale "type" or plot—that was being spread, supposedly through some superorganic mechanism that simply used humans as vehicles of transmission. Thus it was postulated that a fairy tale plot such as "Cinderella" could move about as "the wave rings on water" or as an independent and steady stream. Challenges to this theory took the form of reminders that real individuals are the tellers and real people are the audiences for stories and that proper study of the process requires observation of the natural context in which stories are told. Dégh and Vázsonyi were still cautious about the conclusions one could make, but they argued that "we can safely say that investigations neither justify the contention that oral transmission inundates like a stream covering everything, nor support the thesis that the once-established 'perfect' form of tradition is perpetuated merely by multiple and manifold reinforcement" (1975, 211).

In effect, folklorists battled the too-ready acceptance of the metaphor of the meme a long time ago. I point this out again only to emphasize how very seductive that metaphor is; it tempts us to see only that an idea marches relentlessly to "its bitter end." We lose sight of our own role as individuals who choose what we will do with an idea. Nevertheless, recognizing the meme or the theme or the folk idea as a real and powerful idea is important, is essential, if we are to choose wisely. If we see clearly what would likely happen if we continue to follow a path that leads toward a "bitter end," perhaps we can individually and collectively choose not to follow that path, even though it might offer us a personal or political advantage right now. That is the message of self-help book writers. And because awareness of the possible bitter end is so important, we must, they would argue, be very careful in identifying what the problem is before we consider how to solve it.

Cultural Ambiguity

We have seen that there is a process that allows folk ideas to emerge and evolve and become a part of the worldview of a culture. As we might guess, given his suggestion of a term for analysis of worldview, Alan Dundes has spent much of his career identifying folk ideas, establishing their longevity and pervasiveness, and assessing their effect on the rest of culture. And he has named some folk ideas as particularly characteristic of American culture: an orientation toward the future; a tendency to value and trust vision over other senses; an active bias favoring males over females; even a need to think and group things or ideas in threes (see Dundes, 1980).

Other researchers have identified various cultural patterns that fall easily into the category of folk ideas. Richard M. Dorson names four "impulses" that characterize each of four periods in American history (*America in Legend* [1973]); Edward C. Stewart and Milton J. Bennett discuss a number of behavior patterns characteristic of Americans, such as pragmatism, competition, an orientation to action, informality, materialism, and individualism (*American Cultural Patterns: A Cross-Cultural Perspective* [1991]); and Robert Bellah and his colleagues have addressed at length the conflict between individualism and commitment to community (*Habits of the Heart*). These and other works speak directly to the assumption that there are accepted beliefs or ideas that are so pervasive in American culture as to be characteristic of the culture as a whole.

Still, it is clear that while one can identify customary ways of thinking, individuals in contemporary America are bombarded with many conflicting ideas. America is not a homogeneous culture, even if there is a majority whose ideas on what is right and good seem to dominate. People are acquainted with many points of view. As Kenneth J. Gergen writes: "Beliefs in the true and the good depend on a reliable and homogeneous group of supporters, who define what is reliably 'there,' plain and simple. With social saturation, the coherent circles of accord are demolished, and all beliefs thrown into question by one's exposure to multiple points of view" (1991, xi). In contemporary American culture, there is a tendency for ideas to exist in a constant state of opposition or conflict, even when one side of the conflict seems to be stronger than the other.

This incidence of opposition between folk ideas is not unique to American culture, however, or even to the modern period. Perhaps no other writer has had a more profound impact on contemporary thinking about the construction of cultural ideas than Claude Lévi-Strauss, and he was adamant about the universality of mythological thinking. In "The Structural Study of Myth," he says, "Some claim that human societies merely express, through their mythology, fundamental feelings common to the whole of mankind, such as love, hate, revenge" (1972, 170). He contends that it is not so simple as that; he goes on to say that "the kind of logic which is used by mythical thought is as rigorous as that of modern science" (194). And that logic always involves the mediation of opposites. In other words, mythical thinking requires that folk ideas be both traditional and opposed, usually in a fairly complicated and richly creative way.

Where does this take us in our discussion of self-help books? First, we can agree to think of self-help books collectively as a cumulative expression of mythical thinking in contemporary American culture, much as Lévi-Strauss was willing to include Freud's use of the Oedipus story as part of the cumulative cultural material comprising the Oedipus myth. Though the books are written rather than passed along orally, the work of individuals rather than tribal property, and, for the most part, expository rather than narrative, we can still acknowledge their functioning as vehicles for mythical thinking. And, we can assume that there will be identifiable units—folk ideas—that we can, with effort, name and corroborate as existing in American culture and recognize when we encounter them in self-help books. Finally, we can anticipate at every turn a mediation of opposites, or, in fact, an ambiguity in the culture about which folk idea is right and good—a disagreement about how we are to feel about the ideas our culture has provided.

This cultural ambiguity is precisely what engages self-help book writers. They are eager to offer their interpretations, and those interpretations will always require a consideration of their opposites, of the "old" point of view. At a more popular level, they are doing what Alan Dundes determined to do in his book *Interpreting Folklore:* to discover patterns of culture and thus "provide the means of raising levels of consciousness" (1980, x). And, the self-help book writers usually go beyond this exercise in consciousness-raising and suggest expansions and applications that make this awareness of folk ideas more directly relevant to the lives of their readers. They offer New Age answers to the cultural ambiguity that accompanies these highlighted folk ideas.

Themes of the New Age

It should be clear that the topics of self-help literature are not necessarily the same thing as the folk ideas addressed by self-help writers. For example, in Santrock, Minnett, and Campbell's *Authoritative Guide to Self-Help Books,* only a few of the thirty-two topics listed in the table of contents represent actual belief-based practices or attitudes that the authors hope to challenge with opposing ideational rhetoric—topics such as anger, anxiety, codependency, or depression. A few topics do represent the New Age themes the self-help books are particularly noted for addressing—understanding death and dying, finding love and intimacy, raising self-esteem, and improving motivation. But in general, the folk ideas central to the didactic purpose of self-help books are to be found embedded in the texts themselves, much as Dundes proclaimed folk ideas to be scattered and often camouflaged within the various genres of folklore.

More telling are the titles of many of the self-help books themselves (*Positive Solitude* [André, 1991]; *Stop Being Mean to Yourself* [Beattie, 1997]; *Minding the Body, Mending the Mind* [Borysenko]; *Feel the Fear and Do It Anyway* [Jeffers]) or their subtitles (*How to Transform Your Life by Telling the Truth* [Blanton, 1994]; *When Being in Control Gets Out of Control* [Mallinger and DeWyze, 1992]; *Getting Out of Your Own Way* [Sills, 1993]; *Creating Trust, Luck, and Joy* [Sinetar]). Ultimately, as with the paradigmatic structures Lévi-

Strauss identified in myths, the themes developed and challenged by self-help books are in the eye of the beholder. The few writers or editors who have directly addressed the self-help book phenomenon as a topic of research have helped identify several themes.

Gary Greenberg, in *The Self on the Shelf,* for example, focuses exclusively on the theme of codependency—in this case, an "old" belief or behavior pattern that the many relevant self-help books hope to replace with a more effective philosophy. Greenberg is quick to point out the problems in the "new" ideas offered by the self-help writers; he acknowledges the continuing ambiguity of the culture. Most self-help book writers themselves are less inclined to recognize the need for mediation between the old and the new. A more recent study by Elizabeth Lesser, *The New American Spirituality: A Seeker's Guide* (1999), is clearly supportive of the folk ideas promoted by the spiritual self-help books she reviews for her readers. She incorporates the themes she identifies into her own story of spiritual renewal, much more in the way that Lévi-Strauss would envision a myth emerging in an individual's telling. The sense of mediation of opposites is left, in this case, up to the reader.

Perhaps more helpful to our purpose here—identifying some of the primary folk ideas or themes at the heart of the self-help movement—is a book produced by Ronald S. Miller and the editors of *New Age Journal.* The book, *As Above, So Below* (1992), is published by one of the noted New Age publishers, Jeremy P. Tarcher of Los Angeles, and it includes as subtitles for each of its chapters phrases that, to my mind, identify the folk ideas Miller and the editors recognize as central to the New Age movement (and thus certainly a significant part of the self-help tradition). Often immediately apparent in the combination of chapter title and subtitle is that declaration of opposites so essential in mythical thinking. For example, chapter 1 is titled "The Emerging Spirituality," and its subtitle is "Falling in Love with Our World." Implied in the word "emerging" in the title is the suggestion that previously—before the new spirituality began to emerge—people were not "in love with our world." Or again, in chapter 12, the title is "Awakening Creativity," and the subtitle is "Liberating the Inner Artist." That creativity or artistry needs to be awakened or liberated again suggests that the old folk idea restrained such expression.

In writing *50 Self-Help Classics,* Tom Butler-Bowdon groups books into six general themes: The Power of Thought (change your thoughts, change your life), Following Your Dream (achievement and goal-setting), Secrets of Happiness (doing what you love, doing what works), The Bigger Picture (keeping it in perspective), Soul and Mystery (appreciating your depth), and Making a Difference (transforming yourself, transforming the world). The sub-titles, again, reveal the points of challenge and ambiguity. If to be happy, one must start "doing what you love," then clearly an older and contrasting belief is that to be happy, one must be dutiful or moral or obedient. While the writers are not ambiguous about which beliefs are right, the culture is. The themes that are central to self-help literature reflect the ambiguity of conflicting beliefs.

My own articulation of the themes I see most clearly is influenced to some extent by my adherence to the notion of syncretism in folklore and anthropological research. "Syncretism" is a term used to identify the blending or reconciliation of differing beliefs systems. Usually the term has been used when the blend has been more obvious, as when belief in a fertility goddess is replaced with adoration of the Virgin Mary. In this instance, I view the emergence of New Age themes in self-help books as an accommodation of and response to folk ideas that have long been a part of American worldview but have been increasingly brought into question and held in a state of ambiguity. Self-help books make that ambiguity—that conflict of beliefs—apparent.

The writers of self-help books themselves are more often eager to challenge the old and promote the new. It is the reader's responsibility to reconcile the differing beliefs in his or her own evolving philosophy. Robert Wuthnow, in *After Heaven: Spirituality in America since the 1950s* (1998), suggests that in recent decades, people have adopted a "spirituality of seeking"—one that emphasizes negotiation rather than the security of a settled and shared belief system and worldview. Even with regard to more secular themes, people choose to seek out a variety of perspectives and reconcile the old and the new beliefs in their everyday behaviors. Writers of self-help books feed this practice of negotiation by presenting arguments that invoke the dominant folk ideas, only to challenge them and offer their opposites.

In keeping with their role as problem-namers and problem-solvers, self-help book writers address a number of concerns individuals are likely to themselves identify as their own problem. Readers often pick up a self-help book specifically because it is about their self-identified problem with insecurity, timidity, guilt, worry, shyness, underachievement, rigidity, lack of creativity, lack of intimacy, a sense of failure, fear of death, depression, or simple lack of faith in much of anything. Others look for even more specific problem areas: inadequacy in parenting, overeating, poor health, poor performance on the job, and especially poor performance or lack of satisfaction with regard to sexuality and personal interactions. Simply listing these concerns does not really bring these issues into the arena of mythical thought.

We can do this more effectively by returning to the framework of folk ideas presented in opposition—the framework of cultural ambiguity.

While recognizing the many specific concerns viewed as problems by both writers and readers of self-help books, I am going to suggest here that there are eight "mythic" themes, themes that are in conflict in American culture and to which self-help writers have offered and promoted the "new" perspective along with challenging the old. In effect, these are eight themes that are intended to evoke a mythical, or mediating, response from the reader, a response of informed choice, an enlightened and personally negotiated response. And I would argue that, despite the energetic efforts of self-help book writers, each of these themes will remain ambiguous in American culture— though for those of their readers who are persuaded by their rhetoric and examples, personal philosophies may well change to accept the new and challenging side of the folk idea.

The eight themes can be presented as single-word concepts: (1) fear; (2) control; (3) competition; (4) judgment; (5) dishonesty; (6) individualism; (7) violence; (8) impatience. It may seem that culture gives us a clear attitude to bring to each of these. In American culture, competition and individualism are good; dishonesty and violence are bad. Generally, we would argue, control and judgment are good; fear and impatience are bad. However, in fact, there is an ambiguity tied to each of these. Fear is bad if it produces cowardice but good if it produces obedience to God or a law of nature. Control is good if it leads to effective work but bad if it stifles innovation. Competition is essential in a capitalist system, but it just might not be so good if it leads to suicide or war. Our system of justice requires that all citizens be prepared to judge their peers; on the other hand, the Bible teaches us to "judge not, that ye be not judged." Everyone knows that dishonesty is bad—even a very young George Washington could not tell a lie—but then there are times when the truth must not be spoken (Are you hiding Jewish war-victims in your attic?). Individualism is the backbone of American culture, yet Robert Bellah and his colleagues in *Habits of the Heart* point to its many negative effects, including the loss of a sense of community. Violence is awful, of course, but we resort to it time and again, thus reinforcing its real value. And impatience is if nothing else bad practice—"All things come to those who wait"—and yet our culture is strongly geared toward action, speed, and being first in line.

Most of the concerns that self-help writers address can be grouped under one of these eight themes. In fact, a number of writers suggest that all concerns or problems are a result of the first theme—fear, that eliminating fear or at least learning to respond more appropriately to it is the one answer to all questions posed by self-help books. Ivan Hoffman writes, "Happiness, loving, caring, feeling about a situation in a positive manner, looking at the world without fear are all about the same thing" (1993, 69). Susan Jeffers, in her book *Feel the Fear and Do It Anyway,* says, "The fear will never go away as long as I continue to grow." But she adds, "Pushing through the fear is less frightening than living with the underlying fear that comes from a feeling of helplessness" (1987, 30). In other words, pushing through the fear (eliminating it) is what is needed in the end.

James Kitchens brings a number of the themes together in one summary comment on this common process of coming under the spell of a fear-inspired set of folk ideas:

> As we grow older, we lose our souls. We learn about failure and disapproval and rejection, and we begin to fear. We risk less, and our natural creativity is swallowed up in our worry about inadequacy. We become careful and controlling as we compare ourselves to others, evaluate and grade ourselves, and compete in order to avoid being perceived as a failure. Caution and suspicion replace trust and openness. We live in order to collect things and achievements, which become badges we wear. We hope to prove to ourselves and to anyone else who might be looking that we are not losers. We forfeit ourselves, and life becomes hard. (1994, 20)

This dismal litany evokes the dominant folk ideas very clearly, if completely negatively. No quarter is granted to the idea that sometimes fear is good, that sometimes competition produces desired results, that the meme of judicious control leads to progress. All that this writer sees is the "bitter end" to which such a fear-based belief system leads.

We must remember that it is the self-help writers' task to identify the problematic "old" beliefs and promote the opposite and "better" new beliefs they would hope their readers will come to espouse. Kitchens, in his review above of the fear and control, competition and judgment that make life hard, offers essentially one folk idea in contrast and as a solution. He calls his solution "joy"; he subtitles his book *Rediscovering the Joy and Meaning in Your Life.* But he goes on to say that "joy is a way of proceeding" (1994, 39), and his description of that process is in fact the "folk idea" he hopes to promote: the process of eliminating fear, refraining from judgment, and loosening control brings joy, and we realize joy only by learning to trust—trust ourselves, trust the universe, trust God—and accept life.

Most of the writers who address the problem of fear in any of its guises—timidity, insecurity, fear of death, fear of failure, a sense of inadequacy, doubt and disbelief—offer as a contrast and solution the idea of learning to trust the universe and accept life as it is. The folk idea asserts that life can be trusted—not necessarily that things will go as one might wish or that there will be no suffering, but rather that there is nothing to fear. In the larger perspective, life will provide what is needed, and what is given can be accepted as right and good.

A perhaps not-so-subtle corollary here is the idea of the soul, the idea that what is of ultimate concern is not the fate of the body but rather the fate of what we identify as a "self." Some writers do not identify this "self" as an eternal soul but rather as a kind of psychological self-referential entity; however, a large number of writers do in fact write of the soul as a preexisting, death-surviving reality. Interestingly, in either case, the assertion is made that one must learn to trust that the "self" is safe, that the self cannot be harmed by life. Like Alexander Pope in the eighteenth century, self-help book writers assure us that "whatever is, is right." On the other hand, a fairly large number of "spiritual" writers (as distinguished from popular psychology writers) do also address the question of God or life after death, or both. But, again, the folk idea involved is less one of describing or even recognizing "God" and more a matter of general faith in the proposition that the universe is not to be feared but rather accepted.

This folk idea of trust is also offered, perhaps more indirectly, by writers addressing the issue of too much control or the perceived need to evaluate and judge. For example, in their book *Too Perfect: When Being in Control Gets Out of Control*, Allan E. Mallinger and Jeannette DeWyze draw a picture of the obsessive individual as someone who maintains a "myth of control":

> They come to believe that, through control of themselves and their personal universe, they can protect themselves against the dangers in life, both real and imagined. If they could articulate the myth that motivates their behavior, they might say: "If I try hard enough, I can stay in control of *myself,* of *others,* and of all the *impersonal dangers* of life (injury, illness, death, etc.). In this way I can be certain of safe passage." (1992, 15)

And while the authors offer some very specific suggestions of how to overcome the compulsive behavior associated with this kind of thinking, in general their message is tied to the larger idea of learning that control is ultimately not in our hands, that we must trust life rather than try to control it.

Similarly, the "issues" of judgment, prejudice, even dishonesty itself are seen as responses to the problem of fear, or the lack of trust. Often, the self-help book writers remind us, we prejudge people because we fear that if we don't, they will take advantage of us in some way. We are convinced that we need to be in control; we do not trust that we are safe in situations in which we must deal with people who are different from us. We may manipulate people or even lie directly when we fear that simply trusting the universe will not work to our advantage. Americans tend to applaud "street smarts," and openness is often seen as naïveté. Even in our most intimate relationships, deception is often the choice we make. As Harriet Goldhor Lerner says, "The human capacity to hide the real and display the false is truly extraordinary, allowing us to regulate relationships through highly complex choices about how we present ourselves to others" (1993, 118).

Lerner goes on to echo the observation of many self-help writers: "Trust evolves only from a true knowledge of our partner and ourselves and a mutual commitment to increasing levels of sharing and self-disclosure" (170). In other words, what we call trust in an intimate relationship develops only when the fear of self-disclosure is abandoned, when we no longer fear being honest rather than cagey. For many of the self-help writers, the contrast between fear and trust, between dishonesty and trust, soon pulls into its domain a related worry over what happens when trust is absent—competition, self-centeredness, and isolation, and even violence. As I mentioned earlier, these ideas are often celebrated or at least consciously tolerated in American culture. "It's lonely at the top" is often seen as the price of competition and individualism, but Americans are loath to give up any hard-won victories on behalf of the rights of the individual.

The answering folk idea that many self-help writers offer in response to these very ambiguous cultural icons of competition, individualism, and violence is an assertion that *the universe and all in it are one*. In particular, many writers argue that there is a unity among all people, among all living beings, and that awareness of that unity will restrain the individual from the imbalances of aggressive competition, arrogance and self-centeredness, and violence. There are, however, surprisingly few practical suggestions offered for how to implement this folk idea in daily life. Those who seem most easily able to make such suggestions are writers who adopt from the very start an Eastern rather than Western stance. Ram Dass (previously Richard Alpert), noted counterculture figure of the 1960s, for example, took from his long immersion in teachings of India a new sense of how to respond to the "separateness" so characteristic of America. In *Compassion in Action*, reporting on his work with AIDS victims, he speaks very directly to the problem of how fear compels us to remain separate and also how we can overcome it:

> When people are dying they often feel alone in their pain and fear. Those around them are not going through what they are, so how could they understand? It takes a lover who is not afraid of the pain to be present and wipe away the loneliness.

For over twenty-five years I have been often in the company of dying people. In the course of all those moments I have come to see just how in love I can stay with other beings in the face of their suffering. If I am afraid of pain, then in a subtle and sometimes not-so-subtle way I distance my heart from the dying person with whom I am sitting. If I am afraid of dying, then the very dying process of another awakens my fear and inevitably I push that person away so I can remain safe in my own "not dying" illusion. (80–81)

He goes on to speak of the disturbing experience of recognizing that he is distancing himself from the dying patient. He speaks of coming to grips with his own failure to be open and then describes the process of moving from this distancing to a sense of compassion: "I go deeper within myself, far behind my identification and fears, back into awareness, mindful of our predicament but no longer lost in it. The humanity is there, but so, too, is the spacious awareness. I have come into love, and I feel the barriers between me and this other being dissolve" (81).

When self-help books treat the question of unity, often apparent is some confusion of individuality and separation with the notion of subjectivity. Again, the message or folk idea that New Age writers are sending is one that advocates cutting through subjectivity to see that people are all "the same" under the skin, all a precious expression of life—even, as Neale Donald Walsch tells us in *Conversations with God: Book 1*, an incarnation of the divine—and all, therefore, worthy of our love. Some of this confusion is apparent in Barbara Sher's book *It's Only Too Late If You Don't Start Now*. In discussing romantic love, she offers the following very effective "exercise" for understanding how self-centeredness clouds the ability to love people in the more general sense:

> To experience real love is to understand that a unique creature, separate and different from you, is standing in front of you. When you can see another human that way, you can't help loving him. To do that, however, you need a stable identity, a sense of knowing who you are, and no desperation in your heart. . . . You can get a very brief glimpse of what I mean if you try this experiment. Sometime when you're out in the world, take a look at an ordinary stranger: a bus driver, or someone sitting near you on a train or in a restaurant. Spend a few seconds looking at him. Then imagine you just got a message from the future and found out he was going to die the next day.
>
> Suddenly that person looks different. In an instant his value becomes clear to you and you see how unusual and unique he is. It's only a trick you've played on your senses, but it gives you an idea of how miraculous people will look to you one day, once you've learned how to see without the fog of self-interest. That's love. The real thing. To see someone else clearly, not to look into the

mirror of your own desire or to dress up the beloved with the scrim of your
favorite fantasy, or to reinvent him for your own uses. (1998, 130–31)

Here, seeing the other as a separate being seems to be a goal rather than an
obstacle, and yet despite the language used, we are still being coached to see
the unity of all persons and to not, in this case, let our subjectivity deny that
unity and instead substitute a mirror image. We need to escape our own is-
land of perception and see that we are not the only real person in the universe. Or, as Jon Kabat-Zinn says in his book *Wherever You Go, There You Are,*
"One practical way to do this is to look at other people and ask yourself if
you are really seeing them or just your thoughts about them" (1994, 26).

Ideally, one of the significant contributions that the fields of anthropology
and folklore make to the world is in their promotion of the concept of unity
in the midst of diversity. In general, self-help writers are looking not so much
at unity in the face of cultural differences as at an awareness of unity in the face
of a philosophy of separatism. Even intimate partners who share many aspects
of culture may feel a sense of alienation, competition, self-centeredness, a need
to withhold or deceive, shame or arrogance, and even violence that comes from
seeing each other as entirely separate. Self-help writers are eager to offer a philosophy that ties all human beings together, and yet they find it difficult to
suggest practical applications of that idea. Perhaps that is why James Redfield
felt it necessary to offer his insights in the form of a fictional story. In his second parable, *The Tenth Insight,* he has one of his characters, Wil, respond to
the narrator's question "Aren't some people just inherently bad?" with the
following comment:

> No, they just go crazy in the Fear and make horrible mistakes. And, ultimately,
> they must bear the full responsibility of these mistakes. But what has to be
> understood is that horrible acts are caused, in part, by our very tendency to as-
> sume that some people are naturally evil. That's the mistaken view that fuels
> the polarization. Both sides can't believe humans can act the way they do with-
> out being intrinsically no good, and so they increasingly dehumanize and alien-
> ate each other, which increases the Fear and brings out the worst in everyone.
> (1996, 134)

And later the same character adds: "We know that no matter how undesir-
able the behavior of others is, we have to grasp that they are just souls at-
tempting to wake up, like us" (149).

One surprising application of this awareness of unity is in Peter Senge's
popular business handbook, *The Fifth Discipline.* Among his many other
insights, Senge observes that "systems thinking" eliminates the need for casting others as villains.

In mastering systems thinking, we give up the assumption that there must be an individual, or individual agent, responsible. The feedback perspective suggests that *everyone shares responsibility for problems generated by a system.* That doesn't necessarily imply that everyone involved can exert equal leverage in changing the system. But it does imply that the search for scapegoats—a particularly alluring pastime in individualistic cultures such as ours in the United States—is a blind alley. (1990, 78–79, emphasis in original)

In effect, Senge's practical advice presupposes a philosophy or folk idea that views all individuals as interdependent, as equally tied to the system that sustains their interactions. From Redfield's rather mystical notion of unity to Senge's pragmatic one, there is a New Age reinforcement of the idea of unity and an awareness of its importance in overcoming self-centeredness. It represents a shift in awareness similar, Senge argues, to that "so ardently advocated by ecologists in their cries that we see ourselves as part of nature, not separate from nature" (78). It is the second major folk idea advanced by the writers of self-help books.

The third folk idea is tied to the previous two but includes the dimension of time in a new way. In his book *Soul Search,* David Darling quotes Albert Einstein to summarize the new philosophy to which Einstein was so clearly a contributor.

A human being is part of the whole, called by us "Universe"; a part limited in time and space. He experiences himself, his thoughts and feelings as some thing separated from the rest—a kind of optical delusion of his consciousness. The delusion is a prison for us, restricting us to our personal desires and to affection for a few persons nearest to us. Our task must be to free ourselves from this prison by widening our circle of compassion to embrace all living creatures and the whole of nature in its beauty. Nobody is able to achieve this completely but the striving for such achievement is, in itself, a part of the liberation and a foundation for inner security. (1995, 134–35)

Einstein saw time as part of the prison that confines people to a sense of separation and a mistrust of the universe. He does not offer suggestions one might follow to achieve release from this "prison" of time, but of course our self-help book writers do.

The most famous articulation of the contrasting folk idea to the confining awareness of time is Ram Dass's classic statement in his 1971 book *Be Here Now.* In *The New American Spirituality,* Elizabeth Lesser writes of a meeting between Ram Dass and Indian-English spiritualist Pir Vilayat Kahn:

At one of Omega's first programs Ram Dass joined Pir Vilayat and other spiritual teachers to lead a meditation retreat. I recall a conversation around the dinner table between Ram Dass and Pir Vilayat that I call the "to be here now or not to be here now" debate. In his erudite British accent, Pir Vilayat wondered aloud why anyone would want to only "be here now."

"There are so many glorious planes of existence. The angelic realms are refreshingly different from the one *here*, and they are available to us at all times," he argued. "Why not leave *here*, and go *there?* That's what meditation is for."

"That's not why I meditate," said Ram Dass.

"Well, I meditate to transcend the experiences of pain and separation of the here and now. Why remain in our stale, fossilized state of being, when we could dance in cosmic ecstasy?"

Ram Dass, always ready with an answer, said, "Pain and separation occur when we regret the past or worry about the future. Here and now *is* ecstasy. And about those 'glorious planes of existence'? Those 'angelic realms'? I'm afraid I'm not familiar with them." (1999, 95)

As Ram Dass suggests, problems such as guilt, worry, pain, alienation, and perhaps even anger and depression may reflect our inability to "be here now." I would see this third New Age folk idea as contrasting with the eighth theme above—impatience. In some ways this theme is second only to individualism as "the" mythic theme of American culture. Like individualism, impatience is viewed with great ambivalence by Americans. Certainly we do not want to be forever worrying or feeling guilty or harried by the future. We do not want to be forever hurdling, as James Kitchens says—forever jumping one hurdle after another, always focusing on the next (1994, 39). And yet even many self-help writers speak of the need to control time. Often lack of creativity or underachievement or dissatisfaction on the job is linked to the mismanagement of time.

It might seem that a writer such as Alan Lakein in his book *How to Get Control of Your Time and Your Life* is advocating, if not outright impatience, at least an overseer's manipulation of this quantity—time. But even Lakein, after speaking of ways to better use the time we have, suggests something very like the notion of "be here now":

I think you will find that if you arrange things so that you find time to relax and "do nothing," you will get more done and have more fun doing it.

One client, an aerospace engineer, didn't know how to "do nothing." Every minute of his leisure time was scheduled with intense activity. He had an outdoor-activities schedule in which he switched from skiing and ice hockey to water-skiing and tennis. His girlfriend kept up with him in these activities, although she would have preferred just to sit by the fire and relax once in a while. Like too many people, he felt the need to be doing something all the time—doing nothing seemed a waste of time. His "relaxing by the fire" consisted of playing chess, reading *Scientific American,* or playing bridge. Even his lovemaking was on a tight schedule.

For an experiment I asked him to "waste" his time for five minutes during one of our sessions together. What he ended up doing was relaxing, sitting quietly and daydreaming. When he was finally able to admit that emotional reasons caused him to reject relaxing as a waste of time, he began to look more critically at that assumption. Once he accepted the fact that relaxing was a good use of time, he became less compulsive about being busy and started enjoying each activity more. (1973, 53)

Lakein's "relaxing" may seem a far cry from the deep, meditative experience of "being" that Ram Dass and other New Age writers advocate. And yet the experience of "be here now" is pretty much whatever one makes of it. It is the one folk idea that is entirely subjective. Jon Kabat-Zinn begins one of his chapters with the following description of a *New Yorker* cartoon: "Two Zen monks in robes and shaved heads, one young, one old, sitting side by side cross-legged on the floor. The younger one is looking somewhat quizzically at the other one, who is turned toward him and saying: 'Nothing happens next. This is it'" (1994, 14). Kabat-Zinn goes on to say that meditation is not a "doing" but rather a "being." And this "being" allows us "to let go of the past and the future and wake up to what we are now, in this moment." And washed away as well in this experience of "being here now" are many of the physical ills associated with stress and anger and, of course, that hallmark of "type A" personalities, impatience.

One of the more interesting developments of the "be here now" idea is the expansion of the general principle of engagement or "mindfulness" into what Mihaly Csikszentmihalyi calls "flow." In his book *Finding Flow: The Psychology of Engagement with Everyday Life,* Csikszentmihalyi writes of the "autotelic" personality. Here are some of his observations:

> Applied to personality, autotelic denotes an individual who generally does things for their own sake, rather than in order to achieve some later external goal. . . . They are more autonomous and independent, because they cannot be easily manipulated with threats or rewards from the outside. At the same time, they are more involved with everything around them because they are fully immersed in the current of life. . . .
>
> If there is one quality that distinguishes autotelic individuals, it is that their psychic energy seems inexhaustible. Even though they have no greater attentional capacity than anyone else, they pay more attention to what happens around them, they notice more, and they are willing to invest more attention in things for their own sake without expecting an immediate return. Most of us hoard attention carefully. . . . The result is that we don't have much atten-

tion left over to participate in the world on its own terms, to be surprised, to learn new things, to grow beyond the limits set by our self-centeredness. (1997, 117–18, 123)

Flow is not so much a state achieved through meditation as it is a strong sense of engagement applied as consistently as possible throughout the day.

Studies prove that people in a "flow" state do not notice the passage of time; they are too absorbed. As Ram Dass would have it, they are "being here now." Furthermore, there is no evaluative dimension to their experiences until those experiences are over. People in a state of flow recognize their experiences as "ecstatic" or "satisfying" or "peaceful" only afterward. Like a jazz musician, they avoid self-consciousness lest they pull themselves out of the "now" experience and break the frame of engagement. Flow is the difference between the ecstasy of sex and the victory of conquest; it is the difference between the high of creative performance and the pride of accomplishment, the rapture of a religious swoon and the confession of awe and contrition. It is the difference between the excitement of thinking and the congratulations for impressive thought.

Csikszentmihalyi concludes his discussion of the process of finding flow with a reflection on how being present, being "in flow," can serve the good of humanity:

> The more psychic energy we invest in the future of life, the more we become a part of it. Those who identify with evolution blend their consciousness with it, like a tiny creek joining an immense river, whose currents become as one.
>
> Hell in this scenario is simply the separation of the individual from the flow of life. It is clinging to the past, to the self, to the safety of inertia. . . . Within an evolutionary framework, we can focus consciousness on the tasks of everyday life in the knowledge that when we act in the fullness of the flow experience, we are also building a bridge to the future of our universe. (147)

It is perhaps ironic that Csikszentmihalyi himself feels compelled to attach a future goal to the "practice" of flow experiences in the everyday context. The point, of course, is that these experiences happen for their own sake; people are engaged not for a reason but for a fact.

Still, *Finding Flow*, for all its intellectual complexity and the erudition of its author, is in effect a self-help book. The writer suggests certain practices that will, if followed faithfully, lead to a life more replete with experiences of flow and a more autotelic personality. The three "new" folk ideas of trust, unity, and "be here now" come through in Csikszentmihalyi's book as clearly as in many of the other books written in response to the "old" themes of fear, control, competition, judgment, dishonesty, individualism or separation, violence, and impatience. These are the aspects of worldview examined, challenged, and interpreted by the self-help book writers. These are the ideas that are in the culture and used by self-help authors in what seems to be an entirely acceptable "creative cultural plagiarism." No one will fault even three hundred self-help authors for all offering their readers the traditional advice to "let go" and trust the universe.

In the next chapter, we shall look at how these same authors use narrative—one of the most ancient and familiar of rhetorical devices—to persuade their readers that these "new" folk ideas are more effective guides to the good life than the old themes so pervasive in America's worldview.

6. Stories

Though self-help books are works of nonfiction and are cast, in general, into what composition teachers would call "expository prose," they very often use stories by way of illustration. In fact, so common is this use of narrative that many reviewers of popular psychology books raise the issue of stories, testimonials, or case studies as reason to mistrust the arguments presented through such books altogether. Psychologist Keith E. Stanovich offers the following observation:

> Talk shows and paperback book racks are full of psychological theories based on the clinical experience of the originator. Many of the therapies presented to the public through these outlets are backed by nothing more than the testimonials of individuals who have undergone them and considered themselves improved or cured. . . . [W]e shall develop a principle of great use to consumers of psychological information: Case studies and testimonials are virtually worthless as evidence for the evaluation of psychological theories and treatments. (1992, 55)

Not all self-help books address psychological issues, of course, but Stanovich's critique could likely apply in most cases anyway—if, as he assumed, the objective were to convince other researchers or even "consumers" of the validity of a theory or method of analysis.

To return to the didactic goal of the self-help book writer, we can see that persuasion sufficient to inspire a reader's own constructive action is the writer's objective; persuasion, rather than rigorous verification, is the writer's aim. And stories are very persuasive, despite their singularity, despite their lack of comparative or control group instances. It is almost as though people not bound by "professional standards of research" are more free to indulge their innate appreciation for the universal truth of any story—or the universal fiction of all stories, including those claiming to be scientific explanation. At issue for the scientist in any field is the level of consistency or repetition considered necessary for scientific proof. At issue for the reader of a self-help book is the level of familiar "good story" structure, drama, and appropriateness the writer brings to the application. If the writer is successful, the story included as illustration will attract and engage the reader and just perhaps lead the reader to accept a new point of view. Writers know the power of stories.

For Love of Drama

In *A Chorus Line,* the popular 1980s musical about American choreographer Bob Fosse, one of the dancers sings the song "What I Did for Love." Interestingly, the song is not about an intimate relationship but rather about the singer's love for her work, her creative expression, her profession. The song itself is a story, and like all stories, it illustrates our seemingly inescapable need for drama. In effect, what we do for love—what we do to convince ourselves that we are alive—is create drama, over and over again, story after story, every moment of our lives. When it gets out of hand, we speak of people as "overly dramatic," but when drama is absent, we think of ourselves as dead, or at least as bored, and we seek ways to put drama into our lives, sometimes by seeing or creating problems where there are none, sometimes vicariously through video games or television, or sadly, sometimes through violence or drugs.

But most often, we create for ourselves stories, narratives that help us "see" the dramatic logic of what we are doing or have done or intend to do. Stories tie pieces of information together into a meaningful sequence, explanation, or coincidence. These stories may range from a simple pattern such as "In the past when the bell rang, I got food; when it rings again, I can expect food" (even Pavlov's dogs tell stories) to complex chains of cause and effect or instances of synchronicity. At the Duke University Institute for Parapsychology, for example, staff members record accounts of seeming coincidences that their informants find significant, usually as proof of extrasensory perception or precognition. Always the storytellers decide that their experiences are so dramatic, so unusual, as to be worth telling the researchers at the institute. Richard S. Broughton, director of research at the institute, makes the following comments:

> While we all know people who seem inclined to impart mystical significance to any two events that seem remotely connected, the fact is that most adults can keep coincidence in reasonable perspective in their daily lives. The cases that were volunteered to the Duke lab were given precisely because they seemed to

exceed the threshold of chance. In general what makes the cases stand apart
from simple coincidences is the *preciseness of the fit* between the experience and
the event. (1991, 23, emphasis in original)

In other words, dramatic instances of synchronicity are worth telling, and
for the tellers at least, the stories are likely accepted as "proof" of some fact
of nature, such as the possibility of ESP, precognition, or life after death.

Again, as with Stanovich's dismissal of clinical "cases" earlier, we might
view such stories as inadequate evidence for parapsychological realities. But
for self-help book writers, it is the dramatic success of the stories themselves—the preciseness of the fit—that makes them useful to their enterprise.
The stories make a good "case" because they are so dramatic, so well-con-
structed—almost too good to be true. In *There Are No Accidents: Synchronicity and the Stories of Our Lives,* Robert H. Hopcke argues that stories that
relate meaningful coincidences are constructed from the teller's own feelings,
that "our feelings are the mainspring of our stories, and it is our feelings that
drive the plot forward" (1997, 34). For Hopcke, it is the tellers' own need to
find coherence in their lives that motivates them to understand their experiences as though they were stories—as unusual, dramatic, and meaningful
events. And, as a self-help writer, he advises them to do exactly that—to see
dramatic concurrence in the events of their lives and to allow that sense of
synchronicity to lend to each life the "quality of a single, unified story" (213).
In effect, he encourages people to expect in their own lives the kind of coincidences he presents as stories in his book. He uses stories to teach a lesson
in faith, personal vision, and self-esteem.

Besides creating our own stories, we listen to or read or watch other people's stories—anecdotes, novels, films. We learn to seek out narratives and
use them in formulating our response to life. Little wonder, then, that self-
help book writers rely so heavily on stories. Authors draw upon a great variety of sources for the stories they use in their books, and they make use of a
number of specific narrative genres that work particularly well as illustrations or what medieval priests called "exempla"—stories that underscore a
point or lesson. While some of the stories self-help writers include or refer
to are short stories or are from novels or films, many are the circulating plots
of traditional stories or are the authors' own newly created plots of personal
narratives or case studies. And self-help writers use these stories in a conventional way, in a way teachers and mentors have used them for centuries: they
use them to reinforce a point; they use them rhetorically.

One entertaining yet telling metafolkloric record of the clear tie between
stories and moral lessons to be learned is the rise of the "shaggy dog story"
as a popular joke tradition. In such stories, there is usually a long, drawn-

out narrative involving absurd characters doing absurd things. Finally, when the listener's patience with the nonsensical story is wearing thin, the story-teller offers a "moral" in the form of a punning variation on a familiar saying, such as "People who live in grass houses shouldn't stow thrones."[1] The joke patterns itself after (and parodies) the ancient fable, which also offers a "moral" in which the person recounting the fable (Aesop, or later La Fontaine) suggests a suitable interpretation or application of the narrative in the context of human affairs. The "shaggy dog story" simply keeps this didactic genre alive in contemporary society, playfully reminding us that stories and messages or "morals" have always been paired in our collective experience. The appeal of stories and the need (or at least the opportunity) to interpret them to specific moral or political ends have long been recognized by rhetoricians like Aesop who hope to sway their listeners (or readers) toward a particular opinion or understanding of advisable behavior.

In a similar vein, Christianity justly celebrates Jesus as a master storyteller and teacher. Like modern self-help writers, Jesus knew the power of stories. Even people who have never set foot in a Sunday school classroom will know the parable of the sower, the parable of the talents, or the story of the prodigal son. Jesus' effective use of parables very likely accounts for much of his popularity in his own time. He was an educator, a rabbi, who knew how well a story conveys what mere preaching cannot. And he appreciated the appeal and memorable quality of stories; he was eager to enlist everyone's love of drama, of narrative, in his own mission to teach a new philosophy.

Parables are only one kind of story, but they are especially effective when used in a teaching context, or in any context in which the storyteller hopes that a particular message comes through. In a classic folklore study, Barbara Kirshenblatt-Gimblett writes at length about the relationship between a specific parable and a specific context in which it was told. In this case, the parable was used by the storyteller (Dvora Katz) to comment indirectly on her brother's actions and to suggest how disappointing his behavior was to his children. The brother had promised several times to take the children to a show but had been too busy each time to carry through with his promise. Finally, one day when it was late in the evening and the children were already engaged in other activities, he invited them to the show. Dvora told him that it reminded her of one of their mother's stories. Here is the story she tells:

> A man once came to a rabbi to ask a *shayle* (question regarding ritual purity), forgiveness.
>   He says, "What is it? What did you do?"
>   He says, "I didn't wash . . . I didn't say the prayer before the meal."
>   He says, "How come?"

He says, "Because I didn't wash my hands."
He says, "Well, why didn't you wash your hands?"
He says, "Because I wasn't eating Jewish food."
He says, "How come you weren't eating Jewish food?"
"Because I was eating in a Gentile restaurant."
He says, "How come?"
"Because it was *Yonkiper* and the Jewish restaurants were closed." (1975, 110)

Yom Kippur is the Jewish Day of Atonement, a most solemn fast day on which every person's fate for the coming year is to be decided. It becomes apparent only at the end of the story how gravely inappropriate the man's action was. He made much of not praying or washing his hands when in truth his greatest offense was that he had gone to eat in a Gentile restaurant when he should have been observing a most holy day of fasting and repentance. The storyteller herself makes the connection between the story and the "frame" of the real situation (in which her brother protests that his children are ungrateful when he finally says he will take them to the show), and she reports both pieces as yet another story—about how she smoothed out a tense situation with a humorous yet pertinent story. She was well aware of both the power and the appeal of the story and its appropriateness to the context.

Parables are a special genre of narrative, rather like fables. They are simple yet puzzlelike tales that are intended to be applicable to a variety of situations. One unfortunate note in the history of religious studies is tied to the fact that for many years the parables of Jesus were seen as allegories with specific meanings rather than as parables. As Joachim Jeremias explains, "Even in the very earliest period, during the first decades after the death of Jesus, the parables underwent a certain amount of reinterpretation. At a very early stage the process had begun of treating them as allegories—of attributing some special significance to every detail . . . and for centuries that kind of allegorical interpretation obscured their real meaning like a thick veil (1966, 10). Jeremias goes on to lament the years of scholarly writing in which the parables were not viewed as simple didactic tales but rather as obscure texts with hidden, specific and esoteric meanings. Jesus himself understood the role such stories could play in guiding people toward the new insights he hoped to share. And he knew that equally important was the listener's connection between the story and the theme of his sermons or discourse. Among our contemporary self-help book writers a similar understanding prevails, and it includes many other stories besides the parables.

Psychologist Robert Sternberg's *Love Is a Story: A New Theory of Relationships* makes the following direct comment on the ties between story and our understanding of the kind of life problems addressed by self-help books:

A clean separation of fact from fiction simply isn't possible in the context of personal relationships, because we shape the facts of a relationship to conform to our personal fictions. As Immanuel Kant pointed out in *The Critique of Pure Reason,* if there is an objective reality, it is unknowable. All we can know is the reality we construct. That reality takes the form of a story.

Love really is a story, then—only we, rather than William Shakespeare or Gabriel Garcia Marquez or Erich Segal or Barbara Cartland, are the authors. . . . We relate better to love stories—whether in novels, plays, soap operas, or elsewhere—than we do to self-help books or magazine articles containing lists of generic steps we are supposed to take to understand and improve our relationship. (1998, 5)

Most self-help book writers have noticed, as does Sternberg, how much more effective stories are than lists, and they have used stories rhetorically to convince readers of the wisdom of their philosophy and suggested practices.

Einfache Formen

When I first studied folklore in graduate school, I was fascinated by a theory put forth in the early 1900s by German scholar André Jolles. His argument was that there exists a series of nine "simple forms" (*einfache Formen*) that serve as archetypal genres underlying all literature. Each form or genre, he explained, had a singular attitude or basic mental concern associated with it, and that concern remained at the core even as each genre developed into the more complex literary forms we see in written literature today.[2] The theory was hotly debated, of course, but my fascination was sparked by the idea that, like Jung's psychological archetypes, narrative archetypes may be inherent in the human species. It would go far in accounting for the effectiveness of stories in the process of informal education. Stories are a natural part of our learning tool kit. We are easily persuaded by stories.

Among the stories used throughout the corpus of self-help books I have examined, common are many of the "simple forms" Jolles identified: life stories, legends, myths, jokes, fairy tales, personal narratives, and anecdotes or "cases." Whether Jolles is right or not, these simple narrative forms are repeatedly employed in the context of self-help books because of that same effective core of essential meaning that seems to attach itself to each genre. In other words, self-help book writers are eager and willing to capitalize on our inherent love for drama and our human programming that favors simple stories.

What are some of these simple stories, and how have they been used in self-help books? There are at least a dozen different kinds of story that are

used successfully in the self-help books I have read: parables, fables, life stories, fairy tales, even novels and creation myths, as well as anecdotes, personal
narratives, and what we might call testimonials or case studies, along with a
few children's stories, supernatural tales, and legends. All of the stories serve
as didactic illustrations. In each case, the story has been chosen, presented,
and often interpreted by the author with the aim of supporting the point or
theme under discussion. No matter what kind of story, its form and dramatic
appeal are tools in the service of the author's educational objective. Readers
are expected to find the stories not simply entertaining or moving but also
effective, convincing, and, most important, memorable. The very process of
moving from the story's simple beginning through the dramatic plot toward
the goal or climax catches the reader's attention and makes the author's point
seem somehow exactly right and reasonable, perhaps even familiar.

Let me first discuss a few examples of the parable, since these have figured
so prominently in didactic literature all along. Parables show up in self-help
books either as short narratives embedded in a thematic discussion or as long
stories that comprise the whole of the book. One of the most memorable of
this last sort is James Redfield's *Celestine Prophecy*. The author offers us what
he calls an *adventure parable*. The story begins with the narrator (a man who
remains nameless throughout) meeting a friend at a restaurant. The friend
tells him of a recent conversation with a priest in Peru and introduces some
information about a mysterious ancient manuscript found there. The manuscript, written in Aramaic but translated quickly as each segment is found,
is considered dangerous by the Peruvian government, and the military has
joined forces with the ruling clergy in an attempt to keep knowledge of the
manuscript from spreading. The rest of the book revolves around the narrator's adventures as he tracks down the nine segments, or insights, that make
up the manuscript. Each insight, of course, is an important lesson or message the author hopes to convey to the reader, and the sequence in which they
are presented is essential for constructing the comprehensive psychological
theory and spiritual philosophy that is the author's "message."

The characters in Redfield's book are one-dimensional, rather like the
characters in a fairy tale, and yet the adventures of the main character are
compelling enough to keep the reader's interest. There is less an aim of realism than of structural support for the goal of finding each of the insights and
testing their wisdom through narrative action. Through dialogue and action,
the author's intended interpretation of the story emerges as the reader moves
through each chapter of the extended parable. The book has been immensely
successful, and Redfield produced two sequels—*The Tenth Insight* and *The
Secret of Shambhala*—as well as a coauthored guidebook to make sure that

the lessons taught by the parable are clearly spelled out and put into practice. In many ways, *The Celestine Prophecy* mimics the success of John Bunyan's seventeenth-century classic, *Pilgrim's Progress,* with its aim of demonstrating, through obvious allegory in Bunyan's case, how the average human
can live a faithful and satisfying life.

Another example of an extended (though shorter) parable is Dan Millman's *Laws of the Spirit.* In it, his also unnamed narrator goes for a hike in
the mountains near his home and encounters a mysterious "sage"—a woman who dresses in green and claims to have known Merlin. She leads the
narrator through a sequence of adventures or experiences that are, for the
most part, not fanciful but rather made significant through the sage's commentary. The larger story provides a frame for the twelve parable/adventures
that the sage and narrator reflect upon together. Each internal parable serves
to illustrate one of the twelve laws the sage hopes to pass along to the narrator (and the book's readers).

A number of other writers have tried their hand at such extended parables, some framing their narratives less as adventure stories and more as
novels—for example, Paulo Coelho's *Alchemist* (1988) or Wayne Dyer's *Gifts
from Eykis.* Another successful parable is Spencer Johnson and Kenneth Blanchard's *One Minute Manager,* a short story with a "young man" as the main
character. In this and other of Johnson's *One Minute* parables, various pieces
of management advice are presented in the context of the young man's interviews with other representational characters. Again, the narrative serves
to make the advice seem more concrete and memorable. The reader's identification with the man and his goals is important in conveying the dramatic significance of each piece of advice. As readers, we want to see the man learn
what he needs to learn through each action or piece of discourse. For example, the One-Minute Manager tells the young man a story (parable) about
training a pigeon, which he uses to teach the man about the principle of
"catching someone doing something right." By the end of the book, the reader is hooked into the young man's learning adventure, even though the characters are one-dimensional and the plot very thin.

Rather than create an extended parable and use it to present her self-help
advice, Marsha Sinetar in *Living Happily Ever After* adopts the Brothers Grimm
version of "Hansel and Gretel" as the centerpiece of her book and goes through
the tale step-by-step, interpreting the actions depicted in the tale as they teach
us to experience "trust, luck, and joy." The whole question of the relationship
between fairy tales and psychological theory is itself a separate issue, one that
has sparked such well-known studies as Bruno Bettelheim's *Uses of Enchantment: The Meaning and Importance of Fairy Tales* (1976) or Joseph Campbell's

Hero with a Thousand Faces (1949). As Ruth B. Bottigheimer points out in her own study, *Grimms' Bad Girls and Bold Boys,* most such Freudian or Jungian scholars use the Grimms' collection to "illustrate or substantiate their theories of human behavior" (1987, 16). The use of fairy tales by self-help book writers such as Sinetar is similar and yet notably different; their objective is rhetorical effectiveness rather than the validation of theory within academic discourse.

Sinetar, for example, introduces her book's second chapter with the following sentences taken loosely from Margaret Hunt's translation of "Hansel and Gretel":

> [When the children awoke in the forest it was pitch dark.] Gretel began to cry. "How are we ever to get out of the wood?" she said. Hansel comforted her. "Wait a bit," he said, "until the moon is up, and then we'll find our way sure enough."

In chapter 1, she had discussed Hansel's creative and effective response of collecting and then dropping stones that would show up as a path in the moonlight. In this chapter, she ties this "lost in the woods" segment of the story to the development of a basic attitude of confidence and self-assurance. She offers the following commentary:

> Like Hansel and Gretel we develop our threshold for happiness and even our problem-solving muscles early in life. The person who during childhood knows himself to be energetic on his own behalf will face setbacks in life in a healthier, more optimistic way. Hansel's comment, "We'll find our way sure enough," depicts how this energy transmits itself into problem-solving skill and attitudes. (1990, 36)

Thus, segment by segment, Sinetar ties ideas and pieces of advice to the story of Hansel and Gretel. Her hope, of course, is that as readers take in the well-known story, they will hear it not simply as an entertaining tale but as a familiar touchstone for the messages, the lessons, she is teaching.

Similarly, many other kinds of story are used as exempla in self-help books. Stephen Covey in his bestseller *The Seven Habits of Highly Effective People* makes excellent use of the Aesopic fable "Goose That Lays the Golden Eggs." Or, again, the popular *Chicken Soup for the Soul* (and *Chicken Soup* collections for various special groups, such as Christians or teenagers or women) by Jack Canfield and Mark Victor Hansen is an interesting case in point. The editors offer no commentary on the selections but simply expect the stories to speak for themselves. In their brief introduction, they explain: "In our seminars and workshops we take more time to set up and discuss the implications of each story. There are more explanations and explorations of how to apply the lessons and principles to your everyday life" (1993, xvi). Other writers are more concerned to make sure that the reader gets the intended message. Stories, in fact, are so very effective as rhetorical devices that this difference in how stories are used becomes an intriguing indicator of each self-help book writer's working assumption about the process of learning. This point can be seen more clearly if we look at how writers use the personal narrative.

Prime Time for Personal Narratives

The use of narrative by self-help writers is so very rich that I can only suggest as a fruitful area of further research this fascinating tie between story and lesson or message. Attention to just how writers decide which story might best illustrate a given point or reinforce a specific idea or value is an important goal for continuing nonfiction studies. For now, one kind of story cries out most forcefully for this kind of attention—the personal narrative. I must admit that I am particularly attuned to hear this cry as I have been interested in the personal narrative as a folklore genre for many years. The personal narrative offers an especially telling instance of narrative illustration in self-help books.

If scholarly reviewers are annoyed with the abandonment of scientific rigor that characterizes self-help books, if they find it inexcusable that authors offer testimonials and case studies as illustrations without first subjecting them to experimental controls that would ensure their repeatability, those reviewers are sure to be incensed at the writers' use of personal narratives—their own stories created from their own experience, included with no apologies for breaking the cherished rule of objectivity. Yet in the context of self-help books, personal narratives have proved to be very effective, given that the desired effect is rhetorical persuasion rather than scientific demonstration. And there are several reasons why personal narratives in particular have so easily found their niche in this genre of nonfiction.

In studying verbal folklore, folklorists have always been fascinated by the choices performers make—why they pick certain songs to sing or stories to tell and how they decide what contexts would be appropriate or even ideal for performing certain items from their repertoire. Even more intriguing is the case of the performer who creates a narrative seemingly out of whole cloth from his or her own experience or observation and tailors that story to a very specific context, at least the first time it is told. When I first became interested in the personal narrative as a folklore genre, I was hopeful that I would at last be able to see in such stories a kind of literary intentionality at work in its seedling stage whenever anyone first articulated an experience in the form of a story. I would be able, in a natural conversational setting, to see an ur-form created on the spot, and the relationship between the story and the context that inspired it would be single-stranded and obvious. The motivation for creating the story and the teller's process of manipulating the mix of experience and convention would be revealed as clearly as though in a controlled science lab. That hope has long since been dashed, but in its place is a perhaps less ambitious hope that such stories told in the context of didactic nonfiction might be more cooperative in telling us about the relationship between story and context and between intention and meaning.

Narrative performance in an oral context presents a wonderful challenge to the folklorist. One response to the challenge is to consider such performances in light of reception theory, a kind of modified reader-response theory—in other words, the response of the listener. The listener builds a response as the performance progresses toward its close, drawing at each moment upon a vast array of cultural and personal references that are sparked by the overall structure and by the tiny details and nuances of the performance—an amazingly complex participation by each individual hearing the story. In other words, the listener has as much work to do as the teller when a story is told.

The skillful performer will welcome and play upon those many and varied strands of reference and meaning. That is what makes the performance "artistic." When someone tells a personal narrative, that person is absolutely dependent upon this process. Listeners must fill in their own personal and cultural tags of meaning if the story is to be successful as entertainment. In effect, in most oral contexts, the storyteller gives up interpretive control of his or her story in order to create a successful performance, one in which the listener does truly participate.

Contrast with this, then, the case of the author of a self-help book. Most such writers have learned the power of personal narratives. In many cases, the writers are counselors who deal with narrative on a daily basis as clients tell their own stories and hopefully discover some new and helpful meaning in them. But the stories I am interested in here are the ones authors choose to include in their books. Very often, of course, these are reworked stories originally told by their clients. But surprisingly often, the stories are the authors' own personal narratives, ones created perhaps only for this specific context—the popular self-help book.

The authors of such books face a peculiar dilemma: if they tell their stories well—that is, if they offer memorable, artistically successful stories—then their readers will respond in the usual way, from within the richness of their own varied frames of reference. On the other hand, if the author seeks above all to control the interpretive response of the readers, to guide them directly toward a specific understanding of the "meaning" of the story, then most often the story that emerges seems to lack something in the way of memorable story content, or more simply, "artistry."

In an effort to consider why this situation develops, we might ask first why the authors choose to include stories in the first place. The authors obviously have certain expectations. They assume above all that the stories will be effective in the didactic sense: stories will teach the lesson or make the point they intend. And stories are memorable. If the reader remembers the story, then he or she may remember the author's commentary that accompanied it as well. A story provides the author with an opportunity to introduce or repeat a point that is made elsewhere more directly without seeming to be repetitive and dull. Furthermore, authors know that people are more likely to believe in or trust information conveyed through the familiar format of a story. And, perhaps most telling of all, they know that stories help sell their books. People enjoy reading stories more than dry homilies with little entertainment value.

But why do authors choose their own stories? Why not simply use those of their clients? Many do, of course, but there are advantages in using their own stories. Personal narratives are, after all, more personal, and the author achieves a degree of intimacy with the readers by relating personal narratives. Furthermore, as with oral personal narratives, listeners tend to believe that someone speaking from personal experience is telling the truth. But, more important to the author is the fact that personal narratives seem to offer the writer greater control over the interpretation and application of the story.

I say "seem to offer" because, despite what writers may believe about the control they gain from choosing to include personal narratives, they in fact do not always succeed in controlling the interpretive context to the extent that they expect. After surveying the many books included in this project, I have found that there are varying degrees of effectiveness in establishing a correspondence between stories and their intended object lessons. The advantage to me as a researcher is that authors do make each object lesson perfectly clear. Somewhere in the vicinity of the story they state clearly the point they are trying to make. Nevertheless, their assumption that the story itself somehow makes that same point is not always justified. And it is interesting to see why.

There are a number of structural types or subgenres of personal narrative that are used in the books. Most common are the following five: the didactic exemplum, the insight tale, the personal parable, the memorate, and the entertaining or striking anecdote or joke. By far the most common is what I am calling the didactic exemplum. The didactic exemplum exhibits the earmarks of a story created to suit the requirements of the commentary that follows or precedes it, a "commentary-requires-story" form. It makes sense that this would be the most common form. We can easily imagine the author sitting at his or her computer with the intended point clearly visible, trying to remember some bit of personal experience that would serve as an appropriate illustration. And generally authors do come up with something—though usually the story itself is not particularly impressive, often related with little dramatic flair and reflecting heavy-handed manipulation of slim content.

One writer who uses many such stories is Wayne Dyer, author of *Your Erroneous Zones, Pulling Your Own Strings* (1978), *The Sky's the Limit, What Do You Really Want for Your Children?* (1985), *You'll See It When You Believe It, Real Magic, Your Sacred Self* (1995), *Manifest Your Destiny, The Power of Intention* (2004), and many other books. Dyer actually uses numerous stories of various kinds, and obviously to good effect. He has made the national best-seller list many times, and most of his books are still in print. The high number of personal didactic exempla in his works is, it seems, simply a result of his tendency to use stories whenever possible. For example, in one passage in *You'll See It When You Believe It,* Dyer is discussing the concept of giving rather than taking. To illustrate, he tells the reader that recently he backed off on a financial misunderstanding that cost him nearly two hundred dollars. But he relates the information as a story; he creates a narrative by casting the information into a sequential plot that can be manipulated to serve his point of illustration. Here is his story:

> I recently purchased an automobile and found after the closing that the dealer had added a charge of almost two hundred dollars into the contract, over and above the price that we had agreed upon. I did not discover this until I had returned home and looked over the final papers more carefully. For me, this was a perfect opportunity to practice all that I have been writing about in this book. Years ago, I probably would have been angry, felt cheated, and had an unpleasant exchange with the car dealer. Not this time. I simply called, and expressed my opinion to the salesman about what had happened, and explained that I did not feel that he had acted from integrity in the closing. I also talked to the owner, and I again expressed how I felt about it, without any anger or bitterness. We had a pleasant exchange, and the dealer apologized, but felt that he could not refund the money since we had signed the papers and after all a "deal is a deal." I told him that I did not respect this particular business practice, and I then let it go. I did not need to forgive him, since I was not owning any anger about the situation. I vowed I would look more carefully at contracts before closing in the future. That was the end of it. Until the following letter arrived some ten days later.

Dear Wayne:

After giving our conversation on the phone further thought, I have decided to refund the $188.50 that is in question. I feel that it was a misunderstanding and not an attempt to mislead. However, our customers' positive feeling toward us is very important and I hope that this refund will be evidence of that.

If I can be of any other assistance, please let me know. (1989, 252–53)

In the paragraphs before relating this story, Dyer presents the theme he hopes the story will illustrate:

What you think about expands. Thus, if your thoughts are on getting all that you can and beating the other guy who you believe is trying to do you in, then you are constantly thinking about, worrying about, and planning on the notion of deception. Your thoughts are focused on the dishonesty of the other guy and the callousness of the world. That is what will expand in your life, because that is what you are thinking about. Consequently, you will find yourself getting more and more fearful about being cheated, insuring yourself against the possibility, hiring attorneys to protect you, and loading yourself up with adversaries. You literally put yourself in an adversarial relationship with almost everyone that you meet. And sure enough, you find this sort of thing continuing to expand. (250)

The story, then, is a concrete example of someone (himself) resisting this mistrustful, adversarial kind of thinking. He is less concerned with the dramatic appeal of the story itself (which is fairly low) than with the appropriateness of the story to his theme. This theme is central to his book—in fact, to a number of his books. He tries to find many ways to express the idea that "what you think about expands," and this personal exemplum is one that allows him to express the idea in a concrete rather than abstract way.

However, such personal exempla are not very memorable, even if they do make the point effectively. Somewhat more memorable is the personal insight tale. Such stories are not necessarily more impressive as narratives, but because the author ties the experience at the base of the story to a telling personal insight, the story stays with the reader. In this case, often the story is "memorable" simply because the reader is impressed with how significant the experience or revelation was for the author. This is one instance in which the intimacy of the personal narrative works to the author's advantage. Early in the twentieth century, Irish novelist James Joyce borrowed the term "epiphany" to identify such personally revelatory experiences. In self-help books, the author who chooses to use such personal insight tales is often obligated to weave into the story (or at least conclude with) some commentary on the significance of the event relative to the "insight" gained. Otherwise, the plot may seem thin since the "action" is actually a sequence of thought rather than the more usual dramatic event.

For example, in his book *Talking to Ducks,* James Kitchens relates a long story recounting mostly his feelings on a specific Saturday night two years after his divorce from his wife and subsequent separation from his children. He writes in minute detail of his thoughts about his efficiency apartment where he was living, his observations of people walking below as he stood on his balcony, his sense that maybe he wasn't even there. He tells how, after crying uncontrollably for some time, he went to a nearby convenience store and bought some gum, just to see if the clerk would acknowledge that he existed. The clerk's "Thank you" as she took his change was, he said, "among the sweetest words I ever heard." Kitchens summarized the insight he drew from the experience as follows: "My life had been a morass of attempts to be someone else, someone whom other people wanted me to be. That night of pain and fear unmistakably dramatized that I did not know me, that I was not being me. And I knew that I had better do something about it" (1994, 26). His epiphany, his insight, would likely not have been apparent to his readers without his commentary, and, indeed, the bare content of the story would likely not have made any impression without the author's guidance on why the rather simple actions—crying, standing on the balcony, and purchasing gum at the convenience store—were important.

Another example of the personal insight tale is the following story from the classic self-help book *The Road Less Traveled* by Scott Peck.

> Almost all of us from time to time seek to avoid—in ways that can be quite subtle—the pain of assuming responsibility for our problems. For the cure of my own subtle character disorder at the age of thirty I am indebted to Mac Badgely. At the time Mac was the director of the outpatient psychiatric clinic where I was completing my psychiatry residency training. In this clinic my fellow residents and I were assigned new patients on rotation. Perhaps because I was more dedicated to my patients and my own education than most of my fellow residents, I found myself working much longer hours than they. They ordinarily saw patients only once a week. I often saw my patients two or three times a week. As a result I would watch my fellow residents leaving the clinic at four-thirty each afternoon for their homes, while I was scheduled with appointments up to eight or nine o'clock at night, and my heart was filled with resentment. As I became more and more resentful and more and more exhausted I realized that something had to be done. So I went to Dr. Badgely and explained the situation to him. I wondered whether I might be exempted from the rotation of accepting new patients for a few weeks so that I might have time to catch up. Did he think that was feasible? Or could he think of some other solution to the problem? Mac listened to me very intently and receptively, not interrupting once. When I was finished, after a moment's silence, he said to me very sympathetically, "Well, I can see that you do have a problem."

I beamed, feeling understood. "Thank you," I said. "What do you think should be done about it?"

To this Mac replied, "I told you, Scott, you do have a problem."

This was hardly the response I expected. "Yes," I said, slightly annoyed, "I know I have a problem. That's why I came to see you. What do you think I ought to do about it?"

Mac responded: "Scott, apparently you haven't listened to what I said. I have heard you, and I am agreeing with you. You do have a problem."

"Goddammitt," I said, "I know I have a problem. I knew that when I came in here. The question is, what am I going to do about it?"

"Scott," Mac replied, "I want you to listen. Listen closely and I will say it again. I agree with you. You do have a problem. Specifically, you have a problem with time. *Your* time. Not my time. It's not my problem. It's *your* problem with *your* time. You, Scott Peck, have a problem with your time. That's all I'm going to say about it."

I turned and strode out of Mac's office, furious. And I stayed furious. I hated Mac Badgely. For three months I hated him. I felt that he had a severe character disorder. How else could he be so callous? Here I had gone to him humbly asking for just a little bit of help, a little bit of advice, and the bastard wasn't even willing to assume enough responsibility even to try to help me, even to do his job as director of the clinic. If he wasn't supposed to help manage such problems as director of the clinic, what the hell was he supposed to do?

But after three months I somehow came to see that Mac was right, that it was I, not he, who had the character disorder. My time *was* my responsibility. It was up to me and me alone to decide how I wanted to use and order my time. If I wanted to invest my time more heavily than my fellow residents in my work, then that was my choice, and the consequences of that choice were my responsibility. It might be painful for me to watch my fellow residents leave their offices two or three hours before me, and it might be painful to listen to my wife's complaints that I was not devoting myself sufficiently to the family, but these pains were the consequences of a choice that I had made. If I did not want to suffer them, then I was free to choose not to work so hard and to structure my time differently. My working hard was not a burden cast upon me by hardhearted fate or a hardhearted clinic director; it was the way I had chosen to live my life and order my priorities. As it happened, I chose not to change my life style. But with my change in attitude, my resentment of my fellow residents vanished. (1978, 39–41)

In didactic exempla, such as Wayne Dyer's story of the extra $188.50 charge above, the plot, such as it is, is responsive to the author's need for an illustration. The reader's participation in the creation of meaning of the story is limited by the author's fairly heavy-handed manipulation of the plot and the author's commentary. The reader is never allowed to forget that the reason for the story is to illustrate some specific object lesson. In contrast, Scott Peck's insight tale is closer in a number of ways to the traditional, transmission-polished story. In this case we have a "story-yields-commentary" form, similar to the tradition associated with the fable. And in Peck's case, he tells the tale very much as though he were telling an oral story. The personal insight tale is different from the didactic exemplum simply in its invitation to the reader to respond to the story as an account of the process of revelation. The author takes some risk in telling of a very personally significant event that may or may not seem significant to others. The author gives some interpretive control to the reader. Granted, Peck jumps right in with his own commentary, but only after the reader has already taken in a complete and well-told story, which, by the way, includes the requisite structural features of the seeming villain and the reversal or twist at the end that makes the story artistically effective.

The third kind of personal narrative often found in self-help books is similar to the personal insight tale. I am calling it the personal parable, though we might simply view it as what is commonly identified as the single-episodic personal experience story. It functions to characterize the storyteller, often somewhat ironically, and, like the traditional parable, it is much more widely applicable to various situations than is the insight tale. The example I would like to share here is much too long to include in this chapter, so I will offer an abridged version and encourage readers to find the original and enjoy the full version at leisure. The story is one that is included in David Whyte's 1994 book *The Heart Aroused: Poetry and the Preservation of the Soul in Corporate America*.

> During a long month of bird-watching in the Nepalese Himalayas, I had been moving slowly up the Marsyandi river valley on the eastern side of the Annapurna range. I had parted from my two companions, a Belgian ornithologist and a Sherpa guide, telling them I needed a little time to myself, and then taking a parallel trail, I had promised to meet them farther up the valley in a few days.
>
> On the afternoon of the second day, exhilarated by the clear, thin air and the ever-nearing white peaks rising around me, I turned sharply from an eroded cliff path high above an immense black gorge and found myself on a grassy shelf where the path turned from the rock wall and attempted to cross the drop. I say attempted, because to my utter dismay, the bridge itself was broken. The taut metal cables on one side of the narrow footbridge had snapped and the old rotted planks that made up its floor had concertined into a crazy jumble in the middle. Looking down through the gaps, I could see the dizzying three- or four-hundred-foot drop into the dark lichened gorge below.

Whyte then relates at length how stymied and humiliated he felt by this "intractable problem," given his many other adventures in which he had overcome what seemed to be insurmountable obstacles. He even explains that he has been a rock climber since his early teens. He concludes as follows.

> After an hour had passed, I had finally faced up to defeat, made an attempt to swallow my pride, and determined that there was nothing for it but to shoulder my pack and start back down the path. As I reached for my pack, I noticed the silhouette of a small but strangely shaped figure shuffling into view along the same cliff path that had brought me to the bridge. I saw her but she did not see me. An old bent woman, carrying an enormously wide-mouthed dung basket on her back, she saw nothing but the ground she was so intent on searching. In these bare high places, denuded of trees and fuel, yak dung dries quickly in the parched air and is harvested as a valuable fuel.
>
> She shuffled, head bent, toward me, and seeing at last the two immense booted feet of a westerner, looked up in surprise. Her face wrinkled with humor as she registered her surprise, and in the greeting customary throughout Nepal, she bowed her head toward me with raised hands, saying, "Namaste." The last syllable held like a song. "I greet the God in you."
>
> I inclined my head and clasped my hands to reply, but before I could look up, she went straight across that shivering chaos of wood and broken steel in one movement. I saw her turn for a moment, smile almost mischievously, and then to my astonishment, she disappeared from the sunlight into the dripping darkness of the opposing cliff. Incredulous, but without for one moment letting myself stop and think, I picked up my pack and went straight after her, crossing the broken bridge in seven or eight quick but frightening strides. (47–51)

Because the story includes the almost symbolic image or motif of the broken bridge as well as the contrast between an old but wise woman and a young but frightened man, we can imagine any number of applications for the implied lesson. Whyte himself expands on the idea of seeming impasses in the workplace and how courage and confidence (and perhaps a good example) are needed if individuals are to work through problems. The story itself is well told and memorable. The reader's invitation to identify with the storyteller and the storyteller's thoughts and actions is clear, and the author is free to make fun of his own fearful feelings while at the same time celebrating the dramatic and inspiring end to the story.

The personal insight tale and the personal parable are similar in function; their differences lie primarily in what we might call the quality of dramatic narrative and the sense of traditional motif. Again, since the stories are personal narratives rather than traditional tales, their content in both cases is based on actual experience of the narrator and should not, therefore, exhibit the hallmarks of traditional narrative—specifically, a recognizable, traditional plot and culturally stereotyped characters. However, in the case of the

personal parable, the close approximation to the content or motifs of traditional tales and to the archetypical behavior or actions of traditional dramatis
personae make the story seem more traditional and in fact more satisfying,
"better," or worthy of repetition. The personal parable can stand on its own
simply as a good story, even though it has that quality of instruction that
makes it particularly effective in a didactic context.

Another kind of personal experience story that has that quality of traditionality is the memorate. The term "memorate" was suggested in the 1930s
by Swedish folklorist Carl Wilhelm von Sydow to identify stories based on
personal experience, usually involving the supernatural. Embedded within a
memorate is a belief that is demonstrated through the events recounted in
the story. In the past, folklorists and anthropologists often collected such stories purely for the sake of abstracting and recording the beliefs involved. But
as stories, such narratives have the advantage of being regarded as highly dramatic and significant, and thus they can be useful to self-help book writers
not so much as evidence for a belief as a memorable rhetorical device for
underscoring a piece of advice or a more general attitude or perspective.

Many personal experience stories that recount coincidences would be of
this sort. Often the stories are themselves so striking that the point the author is trying to make gets lost, even though the story has great impact. The
underlying belief, in other words, stands out as the primary message, whether
the author particularly intends to promote that belief or not. For example,
consider the following story related by Wayne Dyer. He offers the story for
the first time in his book *You'll See It When You Believe It,* but he refers to it
again in later books (*Real Magic, Your Sacred Self,* and *Manifest Your Destiny*), always with the clear intention that the reader associate the story with,
in this case, the theme of forgiveness. It is Dyer's own story—in fact, his own
special kind of insight tale—and there is little reason to doubt that in his mind
the story and the theme of forgiveness are inextricably linked. However, I
would argue that without his commentary, his readers would not necessarily connect the two. Instead, they would very likely simply take away from
the story some reinforcement of a belief in the mystical workings of synchronicity, or perhaps even in messages or actions from beyond the grave. I mentioned Wayne Dyer's story in chapter 2, but let me offer a few excerpts that
tell the rest of the story.

> I was born in 1940, the youngest of three boys, all under the age of four. My
> father, whom I have never seen, abandoned this family when I was two. From
> all accounts, he was a troubled man who avoided honest work, drank exces-
> sively, physically abused my mother, and had run-ins with the law and spent
> some time in prison.

Dyer explains how resentful he became about this abandonment and how he hoped to some day find and confront this man, his father.

> In 1970 I received a call from a cousin I had never met, who had heard a rumor that my father had died in New Orleans. But I was in no position to investigate it. . . . Then came the turning point in my life. In 1974 a colleague of mine at the university invited me to take an assignment in the South. . . . When I decided to go I telephoned the infirmary in New Orleans where my cousin had reported my father to have been, and I learned that Melvin Lyle Dyer had died there ten years earlier of cirrhosis of the liver and other complications, and that his body had been shipped to Biloxi, Mississippi.

He then resolves to seek out his father's burial place, and he reflects upon whether or not his father had even given any thought to him and his brothers.

> I rented a brand-new car in Columbus to make the drive to Biloxi. I mean *brand*-new! The odometer read 00000.8 miles. As I settled in behind the wheel I reached for the lap belt and discovered that the right-hand belt was missing. I got out of the car, took out the entire bench seat, and there was the belt, attached to the floorboard of the car with masking tape, the buckle encased in plastic wrapping, and a rubber band around the plastic wrapping. When I ripped off the tape and the plastic, I found a business card tucked inside the buckle. It read: "Candlelight Inn . . . Biloxi, Mississippi," and had a series of arrows leading to the inn. I thought it was odd, since the car had not been used before I rented it, but I stuck the card in my shirt pocket.
>
> I arrived at the outskirts of Biloxi at 4:50 P.M. on Friday and pulled into the first gas station I saw to call the cemeteries in Biloxi. There were three listed, and after a busy signal at the first and no answer at the second, I dialed the third and least impressive listing. In response to my inquiry, an elderly-sounding male voice said he would check to see if my father was buried there. He was gone for a full ten minutes, and just as I was about to give up and wait for Monday morning to do more research, he came back with the words to end a lifetime journey. "Yes," he said, "your father is buried here," and he gave me the date of his interment.
>
> My heart pounded with the emotion of this powerful moment. I asked him if it would be all right if I visited the grave right away.
>
> "Certainly, if you will just put the chain up across the driveway when you leave, you are welcome to come now," he said. Before I could ask for directions, he continued, "Your father is buried adjacent to the grounds of the Candlelight Inn. Just ask someone at the station how to get there."
>
> Shivering, I reached into my shirt pocket and looked at the business card and the arrows on it. I was three blocks from the cemetery.
>
> When I finally stood looking at the marker on the grass, MELVIN LYLE DYER, I was transfixed. During the next two and a half hours I conversed with my father for the very first time. I cried out loud, oblivious to my surroundings.

And I talked out loud, demanding answers from a grave. As the hours passed, I began to feel a deep sense of relief, and I became very quiet. The calmness was overwhelming. I was almost certain that my father was right there with me. I was no longer talking to a gravestone, but was somehow in the presence of something which I could not, and still cannot, explain. (1989, 3–6)

The story is well told, and as with Whyte's story, I can only recommend reading the original story in full. Nevertheless, I think even from this short-ened version, it is apparent that the story itself is memorable, that the cen-tral theme of coincidence is both elegant and chilling. I do believe that Dyer succeeds in tying the theme of forgiveness to the story, but that connection is likely not so permanent as is the memorable quality of the story itself. People will remember the story far longer than they will the reason it was told (or in this case, written). Like Whyte's personal parable, the story itself seems to have the strength of narrative drama inherent in its structure. The author's commentary is icing on a very solid and delicious cake.

Finally, as we might expect, some authors more or less give in to the pow-er of certain stories and include them with little real hope that the theme or lesson to which they are tied will be remembered much beyond the page. Rather, they seem simply to delight in the opportunity to tell a good story. Such stories clearly could stand on their own as an entertaining anecdote or joke. Though an anecdote is technically about someone else and a joke is fictional, I refer to this last kind of personal narrative as a humorous personal anecdote. Typically, the story has that quality of counterpoint between two worlds of discourse and expectation that characterizes the joke. And, because it is a personal narrative, some of the humor comes as well from the reader's knowing that the author is making fun of himself or herself and actually offering some of that friendly psychological exposure that creates intimacy.

One very short example comes from the book *What Love Asks of Us* by husband and wife Nathaniel and Devers Branden. The authors introduce the notion of avoiding too much seriousness and its inhibiting effects, especial-ly in sexual relations. Devers Branden then relates the following story:

> By way of illustrating what we mean by lightness of spirit, I will just men-tion an occasion when Nathaniel believed we had finished making love while I entertained the notion that perhaps we hadn't. Borrowing one of the tools I sometimes use in therapy, a Snoopy hand-puppet (I will not attempt to explain), I improvised a new use for it in bed that neither of us had contemplated be-fore. (1987, 138)

With this story, the folklorist can almost imagine adding a few new motifs to the shunned X700–X749 section of the *Motif-Index of Folk Literature*, the section that Stith Thompson, in publishing his six-volume work from 1955 to 1958, left vacant for humorous but obscene motifs future scholars might want to include. For example, we might suggest such motifs as X705.12, Snoopy puppet as sex toy, or X715, Wife uses unusual object to trick husband into longer sex play. That fanciful expansion of the index aside, we can easily identify the story as a personal anecdote, more memorable for its humorous content than its didactic application.

Let me close this long chapter on stories in self-help books with one final example of a personal experience narrative, one that arguably could be placed among the personal anecdotes simply because it can stand alone as a well-told story. However, in this specific context it serves as a personal parable. Clearly the author has related it with that intention. The story is actually taken from a collection of sermons, and as implied earlier, exempla in sermons are probably the prototype for the use of narratives in self-help books. Rev. David Owen's 1995 book *Getting There from Here: Meditations for the Journey* includes one meditation called "Elephants in Our Living Room." In the course of that meditation, he relates the following personal narrative:

> When I lived in Indianapolis before moving to Bloomington—we lived in the Broad Ripple area—I enjoyed biking early in the morning several days a week and my route usually carried me straight north out College Avenue. Within two miles of home however there was a big, unchained dog that often lurked at the top of a steep hill. Just as I came to the top of this big hill, nearly exhausted, the large and vicious dog would come charging out of its front yard intending to attack me and I had to peddle as fast as I could to escape him. The hill was so steep and the dog was so big that biking was becoming less and less fun. Indeed I began biking less because of the beast.
>
> One day as my wife and I were driving north on that same street, I said, "Now here's that big hill where the dog often waits for me at the top." "What hill?," she asked. "This hill!," I answered. "This great big hill!" But now that my wife was along observing and rolling her eyes, it didn't look like much of a hill, but more like God's attempt at an incline. When we crested the incline I said, "Now there's where the dog often waits" and I pointed toward the white house with the red shutters. And there the beast was, out in the driveway, except that he wasn't huge any more but had somehow become a miniature schnauzer that looked as though he had been purchased because he was especially good with children. My wife said, "That's the beast?" I tried to recover by saying, "Well, when you're on a bike and are exhausted from this incline, he looks pretty big and vicious." (56–57)

The author ties the story to the theme of his essay: "My point is this: if we dare to speak aloud about what is bothering us, everyone may not agree as to the size and shape of the beast. When we keep our grievances to ourselves, they tend to become inflated. Sometimes what we think is an elephant in our living room is a miniature schnauzer blown up."

Stories such as these are essential for helping writers persuade readers to accept a new perspective or alter an old one. Personal narratives have, as I suggested, found a particularly hospitable niche in the pages of self-help books, but all of the various kinds of stories used in these works of popular nonfiction are there because of their effectiveness. In the next chapter, we shall examine how a closely related genre of folklore—the proverb or traditional saying—is also used to good effect in many books of popular nonfiction.

7. Proverbs, Quotes, and Insights

In creating self-help books, writers are eager to tap the great store of cultural resources that makes their works more effective. Some of these resources are more easily identified than others. As we have seen, traditional ideas are often hard to spot because such memes or themes are amorphous and ambiguous; the culture holds them uneasily in an invisible ether of worldview. Stories are concrete and dramatic; they are effective though at times unwieldy since they typically must be recounted in full. Another indispensable tool self-help writers have among their many cultural resources is the memorizable saying. Again, because the purpose of self-help books is always didactic, the sayings must be not simply memorable but, if possible, memorizable. That is, the sayings must be easily memorized so they can be brought to mind and perhaps even stated aloud whenever applicable. Like schoolchildren who learn mnemonic devices to help them spell properly or remember the colors of the spectrum, so too are self-help book readers encouraged to memorize phrases or sayings that incorporate various helpful pieces of advice that can be easily retrieved. Writers often put advice into language that most easily serves that purpose—into "poetic" language.

More precisely, the sayings that most successfully serve to recall and encapsulate useful self-help advice usually exhibit such features as metaphor, pithiness or conciseness, parallelism, alliteration, rhyme or assonance, and often traditional referentiality. This is not to say that all self-help book writers are necessarily aware of the added value of such poetic language. One successful writer, Ken Keyes Jr., states clearly his advice that readers memorize the "twelve pathways to the higher consciousness planes of unconditional love and oneness," which he presents in a number of his books as the cornerstone of his Living Love System. In introducing the twelve pathways in his *Handbook to Higher Consciousness*, he states:

> The Twelve Pathways are presented on the previous two pages. Memorize these Twelve Pathways in order to implant them deeply into your consciousness. Memorizing helps you use them as programming in shaping your perceptions below conscious levels. Just reading them for intellectual understanding will not permit you to use them as dynamic tools that can make your life work. Use the Pathways in interpreting your moment-to-moment stream of consciousness. They can lead you straight into higher consciousness and enable you to find the love, happiness, wisdom, and fulfillment that is your birthright in life. (1975, 17–18)

Unfortunately, at least to my mind, the actual language of each of those "twelve pathways" is thick and abstract; there is little that is striking or poetic, little that is easily memorizable about the twelve statements.

His first pathway, for example, is: "I am freeing myself from security, sensation, and power addictions that make me try to forcefully control situations in my life, and thus destroy my serenity and keep me from loving myself and others." I actually tried memorizing this statement and found it a substantial challenge. I was much too easily discouraged by the cumbersome language from trying to memorize the other eleven. To some extent, Keyes intends for his "pathways" to require "work" of his readers, much as one might have to work to attain the tools that would help with any other sort of addiction. Still, the hard work of self-education is challenging enough without this kind of learning obstacle. Other counselors working with people we might regard as "addicted" to a poor worldview are much more cooperative in offering easily memorized, easily recalled sayings that accomplish the goal Keyes has set for his readers.

Tim B. Rogers, a member of the psychology department at the University of Calgary in Canada, offers in an article in the yearbook *Proverbium* the following comments on the role that memorizable sayings can have in "therapeutic communities" (TCs) convened to treat drug abuse:

> TCs have amassed an impressive collection of techniques oriented toward maintaining the group. Charismatic leadership, ordered discipline, emphasis upon personal responsibility, shared labour, public confession, [and] creating an air of elitism are just some of the procedures employed—each oriented toward strengthening the group and the members' commitment to it. One particularly interesting technique is the use of slogans, colloquialisms and proverbs.
>
> Alexander Bassin documented the use of these devices in a number of TCs.

Describing his introduction to a TC he noted the slogan "Hang Tough" prominently displayed upon the entry to the facility. Discussions of the meaning of such sayings were an important part of the Alcoholics Anonymous (AA) programme. In some TCs the therapeutic principles take the form of cryptic comments such as "No cop outs," "Act as if," "Turn around," and "No free lunch." A book entitled *The Tip of the Iceberg: Slogans and Sayings About Alcoholism, Drug Abuse, and Recovery,* includes a large number of sayings and proverbs that can be applied to TCs. Examples of slogans popular in these ends of support communities are:

> It's better to give than to receive.
> Water seeks its own level.
> We mock the things we are to be.
> What goes around, comes around.

These types of sayings, which include proverbs and proverb-like expressions, have emerged as a significant aspect of the TC. (1989, 104)

The poetic devices that make such expressions memorizable surely must account for some of their effectiveness in therapeutic situations. Such poetic language would be helpful in self-help books as well. The "twelve pathways" Keyes asks his readers to memorize would have benefited from the poetry of proverbial language. It would have made the task of remembering and using the advice much easier.

I was recently visiting a United Methodist nursing home where the social director was entertaining some of the residents while they waited for their meals to be served. She was reading from a book of Bible quizzes, and one quiz asked the listeners to finish the sentences of the Beatitudes Jesus offered in the Sermon on the Mount (Matthew 5:3–11 KJV). I was impressed to hear a number of the residents successfully finish all of the verses, as in "Blessed are they that mourn: *for they shall be comforted*" or "Blessed are the meek: *for they shall inherit the earth*" or "Blessed are the merciful: *for they shall obtain mercy.*" Granted, most of those who knew the verses grew up in an era when many people were routinely encouraged, even required, to memorize poems as well as Bible verses. Still, it struck me that Jesus had made it easier for people to do just that by putting the Beatitudes into poetic language that included (even in translation) active agency, striking images, and parallelism. It still takes some effort to memorize, but poetic language makes the task easier and perhaps even an end in itself.

Proverbs and their various linguistic kin are, of course, the quintessential memorizable and memorable sayings. We might expect to see self-help book writers using proverbs and slogans throughout their works because of their proven effectiveness. And yet, proverbs themselves—in their pure traditional state—are not featured in popular nonfiction so often as are their modern adapted parodies, literary equivalents, and personalized imitations.

Proverbs

Proverb scholar Wolfgang Mieder offers the following definition for proverbs:

> Proverbs are concise traditional statements of apparent truths with currency among the folk. More broadly stated, they are short, generally known sentences of the folk that contain wisdom, truths, morals, and traditional views in metaphorical, fixed, and memorizable form and which are handed down orally from generation to generation. Although proverbs are recognizable through such "markers" as structure, shortness, metaphor, and style (i.e., alliteration, rhyme, parallelism, ellipsis, etc.), their actual traditionality and currency will always have to be established before they can in fact be called "proverbs." This requirement differentiates proverbs from such literary genres as aphorisms, epigrams, maxims, quotations, and slogans. (1998, 525)

Paremiologists (those who study proverbs) and folklorists are reluctant to identify as proverbs those sayings that have not been a part of oral tradition or even those traditional sayings that are not metaphorical and expressed in a full sentence. As Mieder suggests, terms such as "maxim" or "slogan" or "aphorism" might better be reserved for these related categories. And the reason is not merely academic nit-picking. True proverbs are clearly derived from and honed by the culture; other kinds of popular sayings may or may not be.

The reason this matters at all in our consideration of self-help books is that one would expect proverbs to be central to the conception and construction of such books since their function and aims are so very similar—to convey wisdom in an accessible, even appealing manner. But true proverbs— "A new broom sweeps clean," "Don't count your chickens before they hatch," "Don't throw the baby out with the bathwater," "Birds of a feather flock together," "Look before you leap," or "It's always darkest before the dawn"— are rarely found in self-help books. And the reason they are largely absent is interesting. True proverbs are stubbornly embedded in discourse; they lose their full meaning when elicited or proclaimed without a surrounding context. The meaning of a proverb emerges only in the context of discourse, and the individual who uses a proverb has learned how to use it only from other contexts of discourse. Thus, proverbs—for both readers and writers of self-help books—are part of the frame of reference of the culture they share, but proverbs are rarely set out by themselves; rather, they are used only in response to a specific situation. Like Dvora Katz's parable recorded by Barbara Kirshenblatt-Gimblett, the context must tell us the reason why the proverb is recalled and used; the situation must give us the "performance meaning," which may be much more specific than the "base meaning" (see Kirshenblatt-Gimblett, 1981). Ghanan folklore scholar Kwesi Yankah offers the following folk explanation:

> A newly installed Akan chief once invited to his palace a well known orator to tell proverbs to the chief. The orator asked the chief to close his eyes for a few seconds and open them; whereupon he asked the chief, "what did you dream on closing your eyes?" The chief replied that since he did not sleep, he could not possibly have dreamed. The orator replied, "Without sleep there is no dream; without discourse there is no proverb." (1989, 167)

Yet clearly the Akan chief had a reason to want the orator to "tell" him proverbs. Proverbs by definition bear the weight of cultural endorsement. By their very traditionality they can claim an important "proven" status; they are collective wisdom, even if their application may remain ambiguous. Self-help writers are understandably in a quandary when faced with the possibility of using proverbs in their books. As mentioned earlier, they typically claim to be challenging rather than promoting the status quo, the current worldview, and proverbs are unquestionably part of the "old" worldview. An interesting consideration of the role of proverbs emerges in self-help writer Scott Peck's book *Further Along the Road Less Traveled*. In reflecting on the way Alcoholics Anonymous teaches people to move forward with their lives, he points out that one way they teach is

> through the use of aphorisms and proverbs. I have mentioned a few of them, "Act as if," and "I'm not okay and you're not okay, but that's okay." But there are many others—all marvelous gems: "The only person you can change is yourself." Or "One day at a time."
> I will tell you a personal story of why I am so convinced that proverbs are important. I had the kind of grandfather every boy should have. He was not a particularly smart man, and his speech was seldom more than a series of clichés. He would say to me, "Don't cross your bridges until you've come to them," or, "Don't put all your eggs in one basket." Not all were admonishments; some were consoling, like, "It's often better to be a big fish in a little pond than a little fish in a big pond," or, "All work and no play makes Jack a dull boy."
> He was not above repeating himself, however. If I heard "All that glitters is not gold" once, I have heard it a thousand times. . . . It was on walks with my grandfather, back and forth to the double features, that I was able not only to hear but to digest and absorb his proverbs, and their wisdom has stood me in

very good stead over the years. As he himself might have put it, "A spoonful of sugar helps the medicine go down." (1993a, 141–42)

Peck's grandfather did at least have the option of interpreting the proverbs to his grandson, or of using them in specific situations. In his books, Peck does occasionally include proverbs, but he always amplifies them with a story or explanation. He says, for example, "Unfortunately, when you react against something that is sinful, you will often go to the other extreme, and you can get into as much trouble as you were in before. You can jump from the frying pan into the fire, or, as I often put it, throw out the baby with the bathwater" (197). Here he is purposefully using proverbs to underscore his general comment on "reaction formation." But far more often, self-help writers use not straight traditional proverbs but rather parodies or "perverted proverbs," and then only sparingly, often in the title of a book or a subheading.

When Wayne Dyer titles one of his books *You'll See It When You Believe It,* he is clearly assuming that his readers "get" the allusion to the traditional proverb "I'll believe it when I see it." But the point of the parody or reversed proverb is tied to our understanding that the idea of believing first and letting that belief determine what we see is quite different from the traditional notion that we will only believe what we can see. Dyer is using the weight of culture inherent in the traditional proverb to add a kind of rhetorical surprise and freshness to the "new" idea he is introducing through the reversed or "perverted" proverb. He is, in fact, drawing attention to the proverb and its traditionality and then spinning it around in an effort to jolt his readers into a new point a view.

People as diverse as Ralph Waldo Emerson and cult leaders in the 1960s have used altered or perverted proverbs to express new perspectives.[1] Like "shaggy dog stories" with their reversals and spoonerisms based on proverbs, perverted proverbs depend on the readers' previous knowledge of the proverb being parodied. But in the more didactic context of self-help literature, as in Emerson's speeches or the litany of the LSD cult, the reversal is supposed to be taken seriously; it represents a purposeful change in the message being conveyed. The process is reminiscent of a rhetorical device Jesus used repeatedly, as, for example in Matthew 5:38–39 (KJV) when he says: "Ye have heard that it hath been said, An eye for an eye, and a tooth for a tooth: But I say unto you, That ye resist not evil: but whosoever shall smite thee on thy right cheek, turn to him the other also." The parallelism and metaphorical nature of the traditional statement are retained, but the message is altered, in this case, to its direct opposite.

It might be instructive to consider in this context the writing of one of America's earliest self-help writers, Henry David Thoreau. Joseph J. Moldenhauer, in a 1967 article for the *Journal of American Folklore,* examined Thoreau's use of proverbs in his classic work *Walden.* Like Jesus, Thoreau was eager to challenge the old order or at least wake people up to the deeper meaning of phrases and ideas that had become commonplace. In his very thorough study, Moldenhauer notes the following kinds of proverblike material:

> The approximately one hundred proverbial and aphoristic items in *Walden* can be divided, for the purpose of rhetorical analysis, into three groups. The first consists of explicit, recognizable, familiar proverbs, whether or not they are subjected to distortion in their context. Expressions which are analogous in some respect to particular standard proverbs comprise the second group. The third contains Thoreau's original aphorisms, his "new proverbs." (1967, 155)

As in the writings of contemporary self-help authors, Thoreau's *Walden* rarely leaves the intended interpretation of the proverblike material up to the reader. Thoreau's use of the proverb form is sufficient to recall cultural associations for the reader, but it is the new message or the new interpretation of an old saying that Thoreau wants his reader to take away from the work. As a didactic writer, Thoreau is committed to the same goal as his modern counterparts. He recalls the culture's store of wisdom only to challenge it or modify it or take it in a new direction.

Some modern self-help writers do offer, like Thoreau, proverblike expressions that are intended to serve the reader as maxims directing their behavior. Peter Senge, in *The Fifth Discipline,* for example, includes a chapter in which he discusses the "Laws of the Fifth Discipline," which include: (1) Today's problems come from yesterday's "solutions." (2) The harder you push, the harder the system pushes back. (3) Behavior grows better before it grows worse. (4) The easy way out usually leads back in. (5) The cure can be worse than the disease. (6) Faster is slower. (7) Cause and effect are not closely related in time and space. (8) Small changes can produce big results—but the areas of highest leverage are often the least obvious. (9) You can have your cake and eat it too—but not at once. (10) Dividing an elephant in half does not produce two small elephants. (11) There is no blame (1990, see chap. 4). Number 5 is a traditional proverb; number 6 is an updated version of "haste makes waste"; number 9 is a traditional proverb with a modification. All of the "laws" are intended to function as proverbs, and only number 8 edges away from the language and style of the proverb. A few self-help writers, such as Senge, have found a way to make proverbs central to their cause.

Quotations, Aphorisms, and Bons Mots

Though they may not use traditional proverbs in their books, many self-help writers do recognize the role that proverbs can play in articulating and maintaining a personal philosophy of life. There are a few "New Age" proverbs or sayings that are included in a variety of self-help books with no alterations and no apologies for their familiarity, such as the Zen proverbs "When the student is ready, the teacher will appear" or "Before enlightenment, chop wood, carry water; after enlightenment, chop wood, carry water" or the more recent "Be careful what you pray for; you just might get it" or even the Nike slogan "Just do it." And some modern writers, following the model of Thoreau or Jesus, use the traditional proverb with clear transformations or obvious irony to challenge accepted ideas.

More often, however, self-help writers offer their readers literal maxims or aphorisms that dispense advice directly, without the ambiguity we associate with traditional, metaphorical proverbs. Dennis Prager, for example, in his book *Happiness Is a Serious Problem: A Human Nature Repair Manual*, includes in his discussion of helpful attitudes the adage "This too shall pass." In that same section he includes two other quotes, one from German philosopher Friedrich Nietzsche, "That which doesn't kill me makes me stronger," and one from Russian novelist Fyodor Dostoyevsky, "To live is to suffer" (1998, 118–19). Prager is careful to expand on the quotes, to offer his own interpretation. In a similar pattern, Marianne Parady, in her book *Seven Secrets for Successful Living*, selects quotations from Ralph Waldo Emerson's many works and offers commentary on their applicability to modern problems and situations.

Strange to say, however, in many self-help books, literary quotes of the sort Prager or Parady include are offered with little or no explanation, often as epigrams at the head of chapters or as independent sidebars or pages. The thick volume *You Can't Afford the Luxury of a Negative Thought* by John-Roger and Peter McWilliams (1990) is a running series of such quotes with unrelated discussions of a variety of topics on opposite pages. Almost always when writers include such sayings, the quotes are simply ascribed to an author with no documentation identifying the specific source. Often these quotes are ones that show up in other self-help books. Just a few of the most common are:

> The unexamined life is not worth living.—Plato
> Habit is habit, and not to be flung out of the window, but coaxed downstairs a
>   step at a time.—Mark Twain

I will act as if what I do makes a difference.—William James

Whatever you can do or dream you can, begin it. Boldness has genius, power,
and magic in it.—Goethe

If one advances confidently in the direction of his dreams . . . he will meet with
a success unexpected in common hours.—Henry David Thoreau

This practice of leading off with uncontextualized but vaguely relevant quotes
is a staple of the literary essay tradition. What is interesting to note in the
corpus of self-help books is just how often the quotes chosen as epigraphs
are borrowed not from venerable authors and poets of the past but rather
from other contemporary self-help writers.

Since self-help writers are often addressing the same issues, it makes sense
that specific ways of articulating an idea or piece of advice might be useful
over and over again. In his 1711 didactic poem "An Essay on Criticism," Alexander Pope gives us the handy couplet that recognizes this process:

> True wit is nature to advantage dress'd,
> What oft was thought, but ne'er so well express'd.

Some three hundred years later, writers are still eager to borrow pieces of
wisdom that have already been encapsulated in a quotable form. And, because most self-help writers are a part of the New Age "Aquarian Conspiracy," they share many of the philosophical perspectives expressed through
these increasingly familiar quotes.

In chapter 2, I mentioned the practice of metacommentary so common
throughout self-help literature, and this tendency for self-help authors to
quote each other is a part of it. Jon Kabat-Zinn, for example, is often cited
simply for the title of his book *Wherever You Go, There You Are*, as is Marsha
Sinetar for the title of her book *Do What You Love, the Money Will Follow*.
Steven Covey's "seven habits" are often cited, either singly or as a group: Be
proactive; begin with the end in mind; put first things first; think win/win;
seek first to understand, then to be understood; synergize; and sharpen the
saw. Wayne Dyer is often quoted for his observation that "what we think
about expands." It is clear that some writers do in fact hope to create quotable quotes or bons mots with some of their formulations of "what oft was
thought, but ne'er so well express'd." Some writers even quote themselves
right along with other sources ranging from the Bible to Plato to Shakespeare
as well as more recent literary figures and other self-help writers.

I was somewhat taken aback the first time I saw that such writers as Anthony Robbins (for example, in *Awaken the Giant Within*) or Susan Jeffers
(in *End the Struggle and Dance with Life*) had selected a piece of his or her

own writing as a self-attributed quote to be set apart as an insert or epigraph or that writers such as John Gray (in *How to Get What You Want and Want What You Have* [1999]) or Nathaniel Branden (in *The Six Pillars of Self-Esteem* [1999]) routinely lifted telling sentences—ones that were indeed in a more heightened language and carried the weight of a major theme—and put them into boxes or lined inserts, inviting the readers to view them as special, repeatable sayings. Of course academic writers do often cite their own previous works, but somehow in the context of a self-help book, the self-citation seemed perhaps a little too smug and self-satisfied.

And yet, there is in fact a long-standing tradition of promoting and publishing one's own aphorisms. In a recently translated volume of the aphorisms of Phia Rilke (mother of poet Rainer Maria Rilke), translators Wolfgang Mieder and David Scrase comment on the aphoristic tradition represented by such figures as Georg Christoph Lichtenberg, Goethe, Novalis, Nietzsche, Franz Kafka, Karl Kraus, or Theodor Adorno (1998, 13–14). Phia Rilke's volume of 219 aphorisms reflects both her own philosophy and many aspects of late-nineteenth-century European worldview. Aphorisms selected and published in such a volume function as very short poems. The tradition of publishing such collections of aphorisms was well established and carried no hints of hubris on the part of the authors. Instead, such books seemed to be in some ways forerunners of our modern self-help books.

Indeed, several self-help writers have produced such collections of their own aphorisms. Wayne Dyer's *Staying on the Path* (1995a) offers more than four hundred sayings. A few of them are quotes from other sources, such as "Buddha said, 'You will not be punished *for* your anger. You will be punished *by* your anger'" or "As Carl Jung reminded us, at the same moment that you are a protagonist in your own life, you are a spear carrier or an extra in a much larger drama." Most, however, are his own short, aphoristic sayings, many of which have appeared in similar form in some of his other books: "You can never get enough of what you don't want"; "It's never too late to have a happy childhood"; "Being *against* anything weakens you, while being *for* something empowers you"; "We become what we think about all day long"; "Everything that is happening is supposed to be happening"; "These are the good old days"; "When you have the choice between being right and being kind, just choose kind"; or "Circumstances do not make a man, they reveal him." There is a fine line between such aphorisms and what I am calling below "insights" or personal principles. This difference lies primarily in whether the author offers the saying as a way of stating "what oft was thought" or instead as a new insight, a personal revelation so profound that it has moved him or her to put the idea into language that readers will find memorable.

Insights

Very likely, most self-help writers would claim that the entirety of what they are offering their readers are "insights" gained from their own research, experience, and thought. These insights are shared in general through ordinary prose in a popular nonfiction format that is both understandable and persuasive. Ken Keyes's twelve pathways, for example, despite the rather abstract and dense language, do represent his primary contribution to the ideas circulating among readers of self-help literature. Not all writers have found a way to cast their ideas into memorizable sayings, but some have. The hope of each writer is, of course, that readers will remember the insights they have passed along to them. James Redfield in his *Celestine Prophecy* and *The Tenth Insight* obviously intended to have his insights pondered and used; he even offered readers a workbook and an additional commentary (*The Celestine Vision: Living in the New Spiritual Awareness* [1997]) that would allow these insights to be more easily absorbed and applied.

One very successful writer who has capitalized on the power of succinctly stated insights is Richard Carlson. In *Don't Sweat the Small Stuff . . . and It's All Small Stuff,* Carlson titles each of his short meditations with a repeatable, memorizable "insight" that he examines in a few paragraphs. The book title is the first one. Others are straight "advice" insights such as "Develop Your Compassion"; "Don't Interrupt Others or Finish Their Sentences"; "Let Others Have the Glory"; or the well-known "Seek First to Understand." Others take the form of observations, the kind of insights that clearly reflect Carlson's own philosophy: "Life Is a Test. It Is Only a Test"; "Praise and Blame Are All the Same"; or "If Someone Throws You the Ball, You Don't Have to Catch It."

Carlson's chapter titles are very much along the lines of what Mark Goulston and Philip Goldberg in their book *Get Out of Your Own Way* call "usable insights." Mark Goulston offers a distinction:

> Ordinary insights provide relief and better understanding, but they don't necessarily spark action. *Usable* insights have a more practical and lasting impact. My patients find that the insights in this book inspire constructive change and remain in their minds long after they first hear them. One patient called them "the gift that keeps on guiding." (1995, xxii)

Most of the "usable insights" have that epigrammatic quality that makes them universally applicable: sometimes the easy way out is the right way in; you can't live for others without losing yourself; sometimes the grass *is* greener on the other side; if you want what you never got from your parent, become your own grandparent; we always learn from our mistakes, but we don't always learn the right lessons; don't look where you're going, go where you're looking; there are always strings attached.

Such usable insights give the reader a sense of the condensed wisdom of the writer, the essence of personal belief based on experience and study. They are both an expression of a personal philosophy and guiding principles offered in a form that can be easily recalled and used whenever an appropriate situation presents itself. The proverblike wisdom and wide applicability of such sayings are what make them so effective in self-help books. They are a significant part of the traditional pool of resources that come together in modern self-help books and grant them an air of both ancient wisdom and modern creativity. And, as we shall see in the last chapter of this book, all such resources are potential ingredients in self-help book readers' programs of applied self-education.

8. Finding a Use for Self-Help Testimonies

One of the most astonishing books I read for this study is *The New Psycho-Cybernetics: The Original Science of Self-Improvement and Success That Has Changed the Lives of 30 Million People,* published by Prentice-Hall in 2002. The author, Maxwell Maltz, died in 1975. The 2002 publication is not simply a reprint of his 1960 classic *Psycho-Cybernetics;* instead, it is an updated revision produced by Dan S. Kennedy, CEO of the Psycho-Cybernetics Foundation and successful motivational speaker. Having read Maltz's 1960 work, I found the continuation of his "voice" in the new book somewhat ghostly, but the editors—Kennedy and the Psycho-Cybernetics Foundation—offered the following explanation:

> In addition to writing the original *Psycho-Cybernetics,* on which the new edition is based, Dr. Maltz was a remarkably prolific researcher and writer. By the time of his death, he had written over a dozen books and three complete courses of study on different aspects of Psycho-Cybernetics, thousands of pages of unpublished counseling session notes, interviews, speeches, and radio broadcasts, and more. All of this material was put into a computer, carefully sorted and organized, so that Dr. Maltz could continue contributing to new works even today. Although Mr. Kennedy has also contributed to this book, to prevent confusion and clutter, you are hearing everything spoken by one voice, Dr. Maltz's. It reads as if Dr. Maltz wrote it today, in its entirety. We are certain he would be proud of this work and that you will benefit from it enormously. (iii)

Clearly the editors are more concerned with the effectiveness of the work as a self-help therapy than with questions of authorial authenticity. The publishers chose to use this new creatively remastered voice to make the reading

seem much more a book by a single living writer than a work of collaborative scholarship. But to my mind, it raises again the issue of scholarly respect—
not so much for the author as for the genre itself. If the work Dan Kennedy
produced were to be considered a work of scholarship, convention would have
required that he cite the earlier work throughout but demonstrate at each
point where he had built upon and moved beyond his mentor. Instead, in the
new version, the writer Maxwell Maltz and the contents of his book are both
mined as resources available for reinterpretation and expansion without the
careful referencing required by scholarly publishing. Certainly there are le-
gal restrictions that were involved, but in many ways *The New Psycho-Cybernetics* demonstrates once again that self-help authors are writing in a genre
that draws upon a collectively held body of American values and worldview
for its primary content. The usual intellectual property rules seem not to apply
to the fundamental ideas treated in self-help books, writers feel free to engage in "creative cultural plagiarism," and few authors feel secure in arguing
that they were first to say "what oft was thought."

The *New Psycho-Cybernetics* is astonishing, then, both for its clever way of
combining a current and a former author into one and for its ability to highlight the reported testimonies of the "30 million people" whose lives were
changed by reading the 1960 edition. In the new version, such testimonies are
included at rhetorically effective spots throughout the book and comprise the
entire content of the last chapter, "True Stories of Lives Changed Using Psycho-Cybernetics." The testimonials included in the new edition are telling for
our study of self-help books, for unlike other stories about the effectiveness
of various therapies, these testimonies speak to the effectiveness of the book
itself. In chapter 6, I cited psychologist Keith Stanovich's complaint about
paperback book racks full of therapies "backed by nothing more than the
testimonials of individuals who have undergone them and considered themselves improved or cured" (1992, 55). Scholars clearly are wary of such anecdotal evidence. Such stories, if collected and published, might be persuasive
for lay readers, but scholars in the social sciences will demand more rigor, some
system for employing such stories not rhetorically but rather systematically
as proof or documentation in a reasoned explanation. The new version of
Maltz's book may benefit from the testimonials of the earlier book's readers,
but in the arena of academic research, such responses seem too subjective and
untested to be of much use.

Here, I would like to offer a rationale for using some of the kind of testimony readers are often eager to share after reading some of their favorite
authors, just as readers of the 1960 version of *Psycho-Cybernetics* did. I have
two concerns, however, that must be addressed before we consider how we

might use such material. First, my objective is that such testimonies be recognized not as "evidence" of the effectiveness of the practices celebrated in the testimonies but rather as valuable components of the personal philosophies of the individuals offering those testimonies. In other words, I agree with Keith Stanovich when he argues that testimonials cannot be considered as evidence for proving the effectiveness or validity of various therapies, practices, or beliefs. I do, however, believe that such testimonies can be useful in documenting what people believe to be true, what practices they have faith in. Testimonials in support of certain books individuals have found helpful are little different, for example, from testimonials in support of recognized religious practices they have also found helpful. One could collect testimonials (as well as denunciations) from readers, much as the on-line bookstores do, and use these testimonials as raw data in studies of worldview.

But I do have a second concern. I believe this use of self-help reflexivity is potentially problematic for the individuals concerned. As with other kinds of belief, when individuals testify in support of practices they have tried and found effective, they want those testimonials to be taken at face value; they want to be perceived as conveying a truth. When scholars put a different spin on the stories, even a relatively minor change from acceptance of "truth" to demonstration of "your truth," those scholars must take responsibility for altering the material, subtle though that change may be. For this reason, I am reluctant simply to use testimonies offered in support of self-help books as documentation of worldview unless the people involved are aware of the larger question being addressed. In other words, I am increasingly finding myself uncomfortable with the time-honored practice of collecting ethnographic data without first making those who would share their knowledge aware of the assumptions and interpretations that may influence its eventual presentation. I am reluctant to take what an individual regards as a unique truth and demonstrate that it is at some level universal and comparable to truths that that individual regards as quite different from his or her own. As an educator, I am happy to guide my students through this process of enlightenment, but I feel less justified in bringing research subjects into the process unawares.

In the field of folklore studies, there are two ethnographic caveats that have emerged especially with regard to the use of "personal" interview material. Elaine Lawless, in collecting life story material, has suggested that researchers employ some kind of "reciprocal ethnography" that allows research subjects to comment on and effect changes to the ethnographic texts that result from interviews with them (see Lawless 1993). And earlier than that, David Hufford (1982) had cautioned against a too-ready acceptance of the "cultural source hypothesis." His concern in his study *The Terror That Comes in the Night* was that researchers often interpret personal testimonies of "experiences" as not accurate reports of personal experience but rather tradition-based stories built upon beliefs already a part of the culture. With either of these two ethnographic cautions, there is a worry that individual commentary, whether narrative or interpretive, will be subsumed within a "tradition" whenever it is shown to correlate with patterns or themes already a part of the culture. For readers of self-help books, then, much of their individual response might be seen as simply a predictable conduit for a traditional "meme" already a part of the culture and now being passed along through the books they read.

Some readers are aware, of course, of how "traditional" much of what they have read really is. For example, in an on-line review for Spencer Johnson's best-seller *Who Moved My Cheese?* (1998), the reviewer offers the following comment: "The success of the book lies in a message that everyone agrees with anyway. We all nod our heads in agreement as we read it, and smile when we finish, knowing that from now on, we'll look at change with a whole new perspective. It might be an oversimplification, but it works. I therefore recommend it. But just remember, it says nothing new" (Linda Linguvic, July 22, 2001, amazon.com). The reviewer is well aware that Johnson's advice is traditional advice, but she does at least expect her own readers to accept her evaluation that "it works." Her motive is the same as that behind most testimonials: she hopes to persuade others to read the book because it solved her problem, answered her question, or cured her ailment.

How can we more effectively make such testimonials part of the study of American worldview? One way is simply in recognizing that the values expressed through self-help books are accepted readily because they are already shared and validated by most members of the culture. This acceptance has nothing to do with the validity of therapy or suggestions offered by the books' authors. In other words, as Lawless and Hufford warn us, we must take individuals' testimonies as genuine expressions of personal philosophy and belief even if the beliefs involved are not newly learned through the books they credit with having conveyed them. In the case of self-help books, the "borrowing" from tradition is more pronounced than it would be in works of scholarship or literary fiction, more along the lines of the kind of borrowing seen in the creation of other popular-culture artifacts, such as horror movies, hero comic books, or paperback romances. The ideational content of self-help books nearly always emerges as a kind of "creative cultural plagiarism." The originality comes in *how* the content is presented, for the content itself—the traditional American values—comes from the authors' surrounding culture. In contemporary America, self-help authors are instrumental in transmitting to a new generation the values that are central to what we think of as "American character."

Daily Life and American Character

In a recent collection of readings and commentary tying the discipline of folklore study to the larger concerns of American studies, Simon J. Bronner probes many of the issues linked to both the idea of the transmission of values and the notion of "American character" (see Bronner, 2002, 3–70). He voices, first, the continuing conflict between micro and macro that haunts the relationship between folklore and American studies. Reviewing the important earlier attempts of historian and folklorist Richard Dorson to bridge the gap between the microcosm of folklore or "folk groups" and the macrocosm of American history, Bronner writes, "Dorson worried that these minute accounts of unique performances would be difficult to compare and relate to themes or events of national historical significance" (32).

And Bronner goes on to comment on a later popularizer of traditional materials, William Bennett, whose 1993 publication *Book of Virtues* was intended to bolster the teaching of American values, American character. Recognizing that Bennett's political leanings entered into the reception of this book (and its later television series, *Adventures from the Book of Virtues*), Bronner writes, "One need go no further than look at the furor over popular uses of folktales to find political divisions over the character of American tradition. Sides in the culture wars found it essential to locate a folklore that would legitimize a claim to an authentic tradition at the heart of an American culture" (56). In short, when folklorists claim that the materials they study are not simply reflective of the values and character of some small, obscure, homogeneous "folk group" but rather reflective of the values and character of "America," then suddenly there is much more at stake.

At stake is not only the idealized self-image of the nation but also the methodological assumption that no one individual (unless he is a "great man") nor one group of people can "represent" America. Typically folklorists doing fieldwork in America do not themselves claim that their studies represent anything beyond the worldview of the individuals they study, and yet they are aware that once the folklore is out there in the public eye, it may well be seen as reflecting an American worldview, an American character. This worry over representation is a concern of public folklorists, museum curators, and others who seek ways to present folklore in public contexts (see, for example, Norkunas, 1993).

One folklorist/American studies scholar who has addressed this concern is Jay Mechling (2000). He has posited the idea of viewing various institutions as "mediating structures" and argues that there is a need to see *how* our understanding moves from individuals or folk cultures to the larger entity identified as the "civil sphere" and, by implication, American culture in general. He writes of the debate between what he calls "traditional liberals" and "communitarians" and says of their conversation:

> Most liberals and communitarians seem to agree that the debate cannot continue only in the abstract realm of philosophical and political ideas but must become ethnographic in its methods and sensibilities. That is to say, many of these authors see the close study of how Americans lead their everyday lives and of how these Americans "talk" about their lives as providing crucial evidence for understanding how Americans actually practice living in a liberal democratic state, how (for example) Americans construct an everyday morality or how they balance everyday decisions. (114)

In keeping with Mechling's assertion that the close study of concrete materials is needed, we might envision the tradition of self-help books as an "institution" and thus, potentially, a mediating structure that bridges the span between individual readers and their personal life decisions and the body of American values the writers convey through their books.

More to our purpose here, we might return to Peter Kramer's comment in his book *Should You Leave?* Prefacing his series of hypothetical interviews, he states: "One way or another, I must come to know you. Otherwise I will be limited to something that is not quite advice—perhaps the transmission of values; because what passes for advice outside the individual encounter is often just the transmission of values" (1997, 34). Here, I think, is the crux of the matter with regard to what self-help writers are actually doing when they offer to help their readers. They are participating in a literary tradition whose primary purpose is the transmission of values—in this case, American values. And, taking a cue from Mechling, we can view the voluminous body of self-help books as a shared and "mediating" structure—as a common text or secular bible—in response to which individual ideas or interpretations can be articulated.

Mechling asserts that the debate over ties between the individual and the values of the larger culture "must become ethnographic in its methods and sensibilities." This study of self-help books is only a step in that direction. My hope is that, with a clearer understanding of the texts that many Americans find so useful in their efforts to act wisely, the important work of documenting the elusive personal philosophies of typical Americans can proceed more effectively. Unlike Wendy Kaminer and Tom Tiede, who see self-help books as misleading quackery cast upon an unwary reading public, I view such texts as individually significant parts of the rich cultural frame of reference each reader draws upon as he or she absorbs, uses, and passes along the shared values that define America. Kaminer and Tiede may be right in lamenting what they perceive as poor literary discrimination on the part of contemporary Americans who eagerly devour self-help books; nevertheless, such books are the "mediating structures" that allow individuals to take in abstract values, digest and understand them, and then apply them in their daily lives. Self-help book writers are selling accessible wisdom in the best sense of the word.

The Personal Philosophies of Typical Americans

The logical next step after examining the self-help book as a cultural artifact would be to determine how individuals use examples of the genre as they construct their personal philosophies, how they incorporate their reading of self-help books into their ongoing learning projects. As I suggested earlier, the most effective kind of data would be the result of ethnographic interviews with people who read self-help books and refer to them within the context of their actual life decisions and their emerging personal philosophies. In many ways, the self-help book phenomenon itself is the mediating structure that will elicit individual responses. It is not essential that an interviewer, talking with an individual, know and have read every book the individual cites as significant in his or her thinking about what is wise and effective behavior and belief. Rather, it is important that the interviewer recognize that each self-help book the individual cites is simply a stimulant, a catalyst, for creating an individual response that combines tradition within a personal philosophy.

And my own caveat for researchers undertaking such study would be that they each, before interviewing others on such personal material, individually review and reflect upon the process through which their own personal philosophies have developed. As I wrote this study of self-help books, I continually dipped into my own thoughts on what I believe, what I hold as values, what ideas on effective behavior I encountered in self-help books vibrated with my own convictions, and I often felt tempted to illustrate the process involved through these examples from my own life. But I suspect that each of my readers will in fact create such an ongoing personal response for himself or herself; at least that would be my hope. And these internal texts will be much more effective than would be my personal illustrations. It is a lesson I learned from the self-help writers—books are most useful when they spark personal reflection.

However, let me close with a quick look at someone who has already addressed this issue of the interviewer's responsibility, especially when undertaking the study of personal philosophy and American worldview. What researchers do when they interview individuals about their personal responses to self-help books will have many parallels with the process of spiritual instruction, no matter what religious or spiritual tradition is involved. Interviewers, like religious leaders, have a responsibility to be as transparent as possible, to in effect treat the interviewee as an equal rather than as a subject. I was made aware of this responsibility through the "metacommentary" of one writer who is also a United Methodist minister, David Owen. In 1995, David Owen brought together twenty-four of the many sermons he had given over a five-year period and published them as a book, *Getting There from Here,* and more recently he offered in book form another set of twenty-seven sermons titled *Wending Our Way* (2002). In addition to these books, Reverend Owen makes his sermons available via e-mail to those who ask. Just before he moved away from the church at which he had given the sermons in his earlier book, he offered his congregation a sermon in which he outlined his beliefs about life, making the following comment:

> I have forgotten the name of the book and the author now, but I remember reading a book about Christian missions almost forty years ago. The author was responding to the question "What right do we have to impose our beliefs about life on others?" We don't have any right to impose them, he said, but we have a right to share them. Moreover, we have a *responsibility* to share them, whatever our point of view. . . . That is an important way to help one another—to share as honestly and straightforwardly as we can what we have found to be true. (1996)

He then offered ten sentences, ten themes that represent his "personal creed":

> Life is good.
> God is generous, merciful and trustworthy.
> I believe that I am accepted, valued and loved by God.
> I also believe that you and all others are accepted, valued, and loved by God.
> I believe that suffering, tragedy, and injustice are real.
> And I believe that trying to alleviate them is faithful work.
> No love is ever wasted.
> I am convinced that death is not the last word—that life often comes from
>   dying—that there is always more to life than we are able to see.
> And I believe that we are never totally hemmed in or stuck, but that a doorway

always exists—that no matter when or where we are, a path to the future is open.

And I believe that while much is occurring in this world that is not in harmony with God, nevertheless God's will shall triumph ultimately.

Interspersed throughout this bare-bones list are brief discussions of some of the points. But even with this added commentary, the starkness of the list impressed me with the great effort that must have gone into paring down the accumulated wisdom of one's whole life into a series of ten sentences. He offered them in an effort to help his congregation; he felt a responsibility to do so. But it is interesting and telling, I think, that he admits to his congregation that the list was not created originally *for them*. He says:

> It may even help us to sit down and do our best to sort out our life experiences—to sift through our lives for the kernels of truth that are our own. I have not done that formally and comprehensively for some time. I have the feeling that I will soon need to do that again. But several years ago I did sit down and tried to crystallize what I have found and believe to be true.

He then offered the list of ten beliefs outlined above. His list, at least originally, was created for himself, as part of his own learning project.

The list of themes or beliefs is sparse; we can assume that much of what is offered in David Owen's sermons is an expansion of one or more of these themes. We can assume that he has drawn upon an abundance of cultural resources in creating each sermon, including current books of popular nonfiction. In his books, he refers to some of the very authors that might be found in a list of popular nonfiction writers: Reynolds Price, Lawrence LeShan, Paul Erlich, Jacob Needleman, James W. Jones, May Sarton, Julia Cameron, Thomas More. His primary sources are, as we might expect, the Hebrew and Christian Scriptures, but clearly he has made use of a great variety of cultural resources in undertaking his own learning project. Unlike most individuals, he has been required by his profession to articulate his emerging philosophy in a growing series of sermons or essays. His congregation and we who read his books are the fortunate bystanders, the recipients of this atypically written and shared learning project.

What might we discover if we had more such "texts," more information on the personal philosophies of individuals? Would we have at least some sense of how useful self-help books have been (or have not been) in the construction of an American worldview? My hope is that this study might serve as background for collecting that kind of ethnographic material and for eventually interpreting it within a respectful, collaborative analytical framework.

Epilogue

What can we conclude, then, about why Americans continue to read self-help books? We might take the somewhat cynical stance that self-help literature is addictive and that unsuspecting readers get hooked on their fix of self-help advice as surely as smokers get hooked on purposefully interlarded nicotine. We might view readers and writers alike as participants in the revered American "pursuit of happiness." We might recognize the whole enterprise as simply a continuation of the popular expression of a shared American worldview and regard self-help books as individual performances within that collective popular culture tradition. As a researcher, I admit that I have failed to "prove" any one of these explanations—or any other, for that matter. As Thomas Kuhn warned us four decades ago, "why" questions are answered with explanations that reflect much more about the researcher's working paradigm and personal perspective than we usually acknowledge. I started with a folklorist's paradigm and a personal affinity for introspective reflection and personal narrative, and I have not abandoned either of these in writing this book. However, I have been challenged by the materials I have examined to look to the larger context—the macrocosm of American social history and the role of popular culture—and I have tried to incorporate this more inclusive dimension into my own understanding of the phenomenon of the self-help book in America.

Viewing self-help books within this larger context has convinced me that readers gain something valuable from their reading; it serves an important need. And that need is not to have an authority tell them what to do. Instead, it is to have a source of stimulation for thinking about what they believe, and, perhaps most important, it is a source of inspiration to act, to engage, to face life courageously and confidently. Americans keep reading self-help books because they benefit from the variety of ways these many texts call up their natural desire to enjoy life and become who they are meant to be, solving problems along the way and learning the wisdom of the ages in an accessible form. Self-help writers are the engaging teachers most Americans wish they had in an ongoing leisure-time Chautauqua. Though self-help readers may pick up a given book with the aim of solving a particular problem, they keep reading the latest products of their favorite authors because those authors reinforce their optimism, their typically American "can-do" spirit and hope for the future.

But, to recall someone who actually attended some of those early Chautauqua teach-ins and to indulge my own penchant for the personal (and to close this book), I will return again to the vignette in the preface in which my grandmother sat reading her Bible, thinking her thoughts, and writing in her daybook. My grandmother found inspiration, guidance, and comfort in the Bible. Unlike me, she did not feel the need to seek out other kinds of resources—what Paul Tillich calls "contemporary, secular manifestations of the sacred" (see Coles, 1999, 7). She was content to ponder the wisdom that her culture's primary sacred text had to offer, both for her spiritual enlightenment and for her psychological well-being. But it is possible she would have gladly welcomed these "contemporary, secular manifestations of the sacred" that I and many others have found useful—the self-help texts we now take so for granted.

The field of folklore has always had to contend with bridging the chasm between the "public" and the "private." In considering the role of self-help books in the process of self-education and especially in the process of building a personal philosophy, we must move constantly between these two arenas. The larger cultural frame of reference is the source of many ideas and materials that writers and readers use in creating or reading a self-help book, and yet it is the individual reader who uses such books in the private task of building a personal philosophy. As mentioned earlier, Jay Mechling has suggested we borrow the concept of "mediating structures" in our efforts to understand how concrete artifacts and specific experiences relate to and interact with abstract American culture. He reminds us, in fact, that "Americans never experience abstract 'American culture'" (1989, 347). Instead, we might view self-help books as "mediating artifacts" that allow us to see how abstract, impersonal ideas in the culture become a part of an individual's private philosophy. In their desire for self-education, people engage personally with each self-help book they read, and they allow these books to mediate between the values of the culture (both those values about which we cringe and those the writers would have us choose) and their personal values. Through the process of reading self-help books, readers "experience" abstract American culture concretely, personally. Each writer serves as a private mentor even as he or she writes in a public domain.

For me, my grandmother was one of the first of my many mentors. Among the others are people like David Owen—and the many authors of self-help books I have read for this project. The role of such mentors in the tradition of self-education is a complex one, combining as it does many aspects of the folkloric process, the more formal educational process of schools and colleges, and the many often overlooked items from our rich cultural frame of reference. I hope that this study brings greater awareness of and appreciation for the contribution such popular nonfiction makes to American culture and, of course, our individual philosophies and practical engagement in daily life.

I think the self-help writers all convey, in one way or another, the conviction that life—even life in our often violent and problematic contemporary culture—can be trusted. And, believing that, they try, as Gregg Jacobs says in *The Ancestral Mind,* to "reframe the negative monologue" that is the common theme of our cultural conditioning and instead offer hope to their readers. Though I have written here as a scholar and critic, I share the optimism of the self-help writers and their readers. These accessible and engaging books of popular advice are a good thing. People read self-help books because they feel better for having read them. Accessible wisdom is essential in America's traditional ideal of an educated citizenry, and the self-help books that just keep filling the marketplace are evidence that most Americans are not dour and down in the mouth but instead hopeful and determined to improve themselves and meet life head on. We should all have such eager students!

Notes

Chapter 1: American Popular Self-Education

1. Bercovitch, 1981, 9; see also Bercovitch's fuller discussion of the concept within the framework of the Puritan "errand into the wilderness" in his book *The American Jeremiad* (Madison: University of Wisconsin Press, 1978).

2. Senge, 1990, 5; see also the discussion of the relationship of the individual to the community as represented in adaptations of Arthur Lovejoy's "great chain of being" in Greven, 1977, 194–98.

3. Charles Taylor in *Sources of the Self: The Making of the Modern Identity* (1989) offers a full discussion of a history of "understanding of what it is to be a human agent." Though Taylor does look to some popular books, such as the influential *Passages* by Gail Sheehy, his focus is upon the development of notions of "inwardness" and subjectivism in modern philosophical thought. Contrast to this Philip Cushman's discussion of "the empty self" of the modern era in *Constructing the Self, Constructing America: A Cultural History of Psychotherapy* (1995).

4. Cross, 1981, 63–66 and 186–99; Knowles, 1978; Tough, 1971. Cross's book is the clearest survey of the consideration of self-directed adult education represented by researchers Knowles and Tough. Her bibliography includes additional references by these and other scholars.

5. Nel Noddings discusses the role of constructivism—which assumes that all knowledge is constructed and never the result of passive reception—in the overall philosophy of education in her book *Philosophy of Education*, 1995, 114–19.

6. Bruce, 1974, 63–70, discusses the "morphology" of the conversion experience as it was intuitively recognized among the people who attended church camp-meetings during the Great Revival period; essential to the experience was the phenomenon of "conviction" or an acknowledgment of the unsatisfactory life the sinner had led before and the need for divine help before a conversion could take place. By analogy, the reader "needs" the help of the writer to move from an unenlightened state to an enlightened one.

7. In his introduction to *The Art of the Personal Essay: An Anthology from the Classical Era to the Present* (1994), editor Phillip Lopate offers a distinction between the formal and informal essay and further specifies the conversational style of what he calls the "personal essay."

8. Best known is Paulo Freire, *Pedagogy of the Oppressed* (1970). Important references can be found in Berryman, 1987. An interesting interpretation of the role of "personalism" in other "radical" religious movements arising at the same time as liberation theology can be found in McCarraher, 1997.

Chapter 2: The Books, the Writers, and Metacommentary

1. For a discussion of etic and emic categories, see chapter 4, "Units of Observation," in Pelto and Pelto, 1978.

2. George L. Dillon develops this point very effectively in his book *Contending Rhetorics: Writing in the Academic Disciplines* (1991). In reviewing one English teacher's proposal to teach the "genres" and conventions of writing in other disciplines, Dillon laments that the teacher "conceives of disciplinary discourse principally in terms of forms (which pose 'constraints') along with some differences of evidence and types of argument" (3).

Chapter 3: The Critics, the Simple Self, and America's Cultural Cringe

1. Philosopher Norman Melchert wrote a clear and provocative book on relativism titled *Who's to Say?* (1994); the various views of the issue are presented in the form of a play with six different characters for the six general philosophical perspectives he presents.

2. See the discussion in a short article by Jennifer K. Ruark titled "Redefining the Good Life: A New Focus in the Social Sciences," in which she outlines an emerging shift "from a disease model to a health model" (1999).

3. See Tennant and Pogson, 1995, 131–35, for a discussion of skills a competent adult learner must have.

Chapter 6: Stories

1. See Brunvand, 1963, for a classification of shaggy dog stories.

2. See Ben-Amos's introduction to *Folklore Genres* for a concise discussion of the theory (1976, xxvii–xxx).

Chapter 7: Proverbs, Quotes, and Insights

1. See LaRosa (1972) on Emerson and Bauman and McCabe (1970) on LSD cults.

Bibliography

Aarne, Antti, and Stith Thompson. 1981. *The Types of the Folktale.* FFCommunications, no. 184. Helsinki: Academia Scientiarum Fennica.

Abrahams, Roger. 1968. Introductory Remarks to a Rhetorical Theory of Folklore. *Journal of American Folklore* 81:143–58.

Adrienne, Carol. 1998. *The Purpose of Your Life.* New York: William Morrow.

Alberti, Robert E., and Michael L. Emmons. 1986. *Your Perfect Right.* 5th ed. San Luis Obispo, Calif.: Impact Publishers.

Albrecht, Mark C. 1987. *Reincarnation: A Christian Critique of a New Age Doctrine.* New ed. Downers Grove, Ill.: InterVarsity Press.

Anderson, Clifford. 1995. *The Stages of Life: A Groundbreaking Discovery—The Steps to Psychological Maturity.* New York: Atlantic Monthly Press.

Anderson, E. N. 1996. *Ecologies of the Heart: Emotion, Belief, and the Environment.* New York: Oxford University Press.

Anderson, Walter. 1997. *The Confidence Course: Seven Steps to Self-Fulfillment.* New York: HarperCollins.

André, Rae. 1991. *Positive Solitude.* New York: HarperCollins.

Atkinson, Robert. 1995. *The Gift of Stories.* Westport, Conn.: Bergin and Garvey.

Baida, Peter. 1990. *Poor Richard's Legacy: American Business Values from Benjamin Franklin to Michael Milken.* New York: William Morrow.

Baldwin, Christina. 2002. *The Seven Whispers: Listening to the Voice of Spirit.* Novato, Calif.: New World Library.

Barbach, Lonnie. 1983. *For Each Other: Sharing Sexual Intimacy.* New York: Anchor Books.

Barrow, John D. 1992. *Pi in the Sky: Counting, Thinking, and Being.* Oxford: Clarendon Press.

Barzun, Jacques, and Henry F. Graff. 1985. *The Modern Researcher.* 4th ed. New York: Harcourt Brace Jovanovich.

Bascom, William. 1965. Four Functions of Folklore. In *The Study of Folklore,* edited by Alan

Dundes, 279–98. Englewood Cliffs, N.J.: Prentice-Hall. First published in *Journal of American Folklore* 67 (1954): 333–49.

Bateson, Mary Catherine. 1989. *Composing a Life.* New York: Penguin Books.

Bauman, Richard. 1986. *Story, Performance, and Event: Contextual Studies of Oral Narrative.* Cambridge: Cambridge University Press.

———. 1992. Performance. In *Folklore, Cultural Performances, and Popular Entertainments,* edited by Richard Bauman, 41–49. New York: Oxford University Press.

Bauman, Richard, and Neil McCabe. 1970. Proverbs in an LSD Cult. *Journal of American Folklore* 83:318–24.

Beattie, Melody. 1997. *Stop Being Mean to Yourself.* New York: HarperCollins.

Bednarowski, Mary Farrell. 1989. *New Religions: The Theological Imagination in America.* Bloomington: Indiana University Press.

Bellah, Robert N., Richard Madsen, William M. Sullivan, Ann Swidler, and Steven M. Tipton. 1985. *Habits of the Heart: Individualism and Commitment in American Life.* New York: Harper and Row.

Ben-Amos, Dan. 1972. Toward a Definition of Folklore in Context. In *Towards New Perspectives in Folklore,* edited by Américo Paredes and Richard Bauman, 3–15. Austin: University of Texas Press.

———, ed. 1976. *Folklore Genres.* Austin: University of Texas Press.

Bender, David L. 1993. *Constructing a Life Philosophy: Opposing Viewpoints.* 6th ed., rev. San Diego: Greenhaven Press.

Bennis, Warren. 1989. *On Becoming a Leader.* Reading, Mass.: Addison-Wesley.

Bennis, Warren, and Patricia Ward Biederman. 1997. *Organizing Genius: The Secrets of Creative Collaboration.* Reading, Mass.: Addison-Wesley.

Benson, Herbert, with Marg Stark. 1996. *Timeless Healing: The Power and Biology of Belief.* New York: Scribner.

Benton, Debra A. 1992. *Lions Don't Need to Roar.* New York: Warner Books.

Benyus, Janine M. 1997. *Biomimicry.* New York: William Morrow.

Bepko, Claudia, and Jo-Ann Krestan. 1990. *Too Good for Her Own Good.* New York: HarperCollins.

Bercovitch, Sacvan. 1981. The Rites of Assent: Rhetoric, Ritual, and the Ideology of American Consensus. In *The American Self: Myth, Ideology, and Popular Culture,* edited by Sam B. Girgus, 5–42. Albuquerque: University of New Mexico Press.

Berger, Peter L. 1992. *A Far Glory: The Quest for Faith in an Age of Credulity.* New York: Doubleday Anchor.

Berger, Peter L., and Thomas Luckmann. 1966. *The Social Construction of Reality.* New York: Doubleday Anchor.

Bergquist, William H. 1995. *Quality through Access, Access with Quality: The New Imperative for Higher Education.* San Francisco: Jossey-Bass.

Bernstein, Paula. 1985. *Family Ties, Corporate Bonds.* New York: Henry Holt.

Berry, Thomas. 1988. *The Dream of Earth.* San Francisco: Sierra Club Books.

Berryman, Phillip. 1987. *Liberation Theology: The Essential Facts about the Revolutionary Movement in Latin America and Beyond.* New York: Pantheon Books.

Bettelheim, Bruno. 1976. *The Uses of Enchantment: The Meaning and Importance of Fairy Tales.* New York: Alfred A. Knopf.

Blackmore, Susan. 1999. *The Meme Machine.* New York: Oxford.

Blanton, Brad. 1994. *Radical Honesty: How to Transform Your Life by Telling the Truth.* Stanley, Va.: Sparrowhawk Publications.

Bloch, Jon P. 1996. "A Realer Reality": Alternative Spiritual Ideology, Narrative, and Self-Identity. Ph.D. diss., Indiana University.

Block, Joel D. 1980. *Friendship.* New York: Collier Books.

Bly, Robert. 1990. *Iron John.* New York: Vintage Books.

Bohm, David. 1994. *Thought as a System.* New York: Routledge.

Bond, D. Stephenson. 1993. *Living Myth.* Boston: Shambhala.

Borysenko, Joan. 1987. *Minding the Body, Mending the Mind.* Reading, Mass.: Addison-Wesley.

Bottigheimer, Ruth B. 1987. *Grimms' Bad Girls and Bold Boys: The Moral and Social Vision of the Tales.* New Haven: Yale University Press.

Boyd, Stephen B. 1995. *The Men We Long to Be.* New York: HarperCollins.

Bradshaw, John. 1990. *Homecoming: Reclaiming and Championing Your Inner Child.* New York: Bantam Books.

Branden, Nathaniel. 1994. *The Six Pillars of Self-Esteem.* New York: Bantam Books.

Branden, Nathaniel, and Devers Branden. 1987. *What Love Asks of Us.* Rev. ed. New York: Bantam Books.

Brandes, Stanley. 1980. *Metaphors of Masculinity: Sex and Status in Andalusian Folklore.* Philadelphia: University of Pennsylvania Press.

Breathnach, Sarah Ban. 1998. *Something More: Excavating Your Authentic Self.* New York: Warner Books.

Brinkman, Rick, and Rick Kirschner. 1994. *Dealing with People You Can't Stand.* New York: McGraw-Hill.

Brockelman, Paul. 1999. *Cosmology and Creation: The Spiritual Significance of Contemporary Cosmology.* New York: Oxford University Press.

Bronner, Simon J. 2002. *Folk Nation: Folklore in the Creation of American Tradition.* Wilmington, Del.: Scholarly Resources.

Brothers, Leslie. 1997. *Friday's Footprint: How Society Shapes the Human Mind.* New York: Oxford.

Broughton, Richard S. 1991. *Parapsychology: The Controversial Science.* New York: Ballantine Books.

Bruce, Dickson D., Jr. 1974. *And They All Sang Hallelujah: Plain-Folk Camp-Meeting Religion, 1800–1845.* Knoxville: University of Tennessee Press.

Bruner, Jerome. 1990. *Acts of Meaning.* Cambridge: Harvard University Press.

———. 1996. *The Culture of Education.* Cambridge: Harvard University Press.

———. 2002. *Making Stories: Law, Literature, Life.* Cambridge: Harvard University Press.

Brunvand, Jan Harold. 1963. Classification for Shaggy Dog Stories. *Journal of American Folklore* 76:42–68.

———. 1981. *The Vanishing Hitchhiker: American Urban Legends and Their Meanings.* New York: W. W. Norton.

———. 2000. *The Truth Never Stands in the Way of a Good Story.* Urbana: University of Illinois Press.

Buscaglia, Leo. 1986. *Bus Nine to Paradise.* New York: William Morrow.

Butler, Gillian, and Tony Hope. 1995. *Managing Your Mind.* New York: Oxford University Press.

Butler-Bowdon, Tom. 2003. *50 Self-Help Classics: 50 Inspirational Books to Transform Your Life.* London: Nicholas Brealey.

Byham, William C., with Jeff Cox. 1988. *Zapp! The Lightning of Empowerment.* New York: Fawcett.

Cameron, Julia. 1992. *The Artist's Way: A Spiritual Path to Higher Creativity.* New York: Tarcher/Putnam.

Campbell, Joseph. 1949. *The Hero with a Thousand Faces.* New York: Pantheon Books.

Canfield, Jack, and Mark Victor Hansen. 1993. *Chicken Soup for the Soul.* Deerfield, Fla.: Health Communications.

———. 1995. *The Aladdin Factor.* New York: Berkley Books.

Capra, Fritjof. 1996. *The Web of Life.* New York: Anchor Books.

Carlson, Richard. 1997. *Don't Sweat the Small Stuff . . . and It's All Small Stuff.* New York: Hyperion.

———. 1997. *Don't Worry, Make Money.* New York: Hyperion.

Carlson, Richard, and Kristine Carlson. 1999. *Don't Sweat the Small Stuff in Love.* New York: Hyperion.

Carlson, Richard, and Benjamin Shield. 1995. *Handbook for the Soul.* Boston: Little, Brown.

Carnegie, Dale. 1936. *How to Win Friends and Influence People.* New York: Simon and Schuster.

———. 1944. *How to Stop Worrying and Start Living.* New York: Simon and Schuster.

Carter, Steven, and Julia Sokol. 1993. *He's Scared, She's Scared.* New York: MJF Books.

Castaneda, Carlos. 1968. *The Teachings of Don Juan: A Yaqui Way of Knowledge.* New York: Ballantine Books.

Catford, Lorna, and Michael Ray. 1991. *The Path of the Everyday Hero.* Los Angeles: Jeremy Tarcher.

Cawelti, John G. 1976. *Adventure, Mystery, and Romance: Formula Stories as Art and Popular Culture.* Chicago: University of Chicago Press.

Certeau, Michel de. 1984. *The Practice of Everyday Life.* Translated by Steven Rendall. Berkeley: University of California Press.

Cerullo, John J. 1982. *The Secularization of the Soul.* Philadelphia: Institute for the Study of Human Issues.

Chaffee, John. 1998. *The Thinker's Way: Eight Steps to a Richer Life.* Boston: Little, Brown.

Chalmers, David J. 1996. *The Conscious Mind: In Search of a Fundamental Theory.* New York: Oxford University Press.

Chinen, Allan B. 1992. *Once Upon a Midlife.* New York: Tarcher/Putnam.

Chopra, Deepak. 1991a. *Perfect Health.* New York: Harmony Books.

———. 1991b. *Unconditional Life.* New York: Bantam Books.

———. 1993. *Ageless Body, Timeless Mind.* New York: Harmony Books.

———. 1994. *The Seven Spiritual Laws of Success.* San Rafael, Calif.: Amber-Allen and New World Library.

———. 1995. *The Way of the Wizard: Twenty Spiritual Lessons for Creating the Life You Want.* New York: Harmony Books.

———. 1997. *The Path to Love.* New York: Three Rivers Press.

Chu, Chin-Ning. 1998. *Do Less, Achieve More.* New York: HarperCollins.

Coelho, Paulo. 1988. *The Alchemist.* Translated by Alan R. Clarke. London: HarperCollins.
———. 2000. *The Devil and Miss Prym.* Translated by Amanda Hopkinson and Nick Caistor. London: HarperCollins.
Coles, Robert. 1989. *The Call of Stories: Teaching and the Moral Imagination.* Boston: Houghton Mifflin.
———. 1993. *The Call of Service.* Boston: Houghton Mifflin.
———. 1999. *The Secular Mind.* Princeton, N.J.: Princeton University Press.
Cole-Whittaker, Terry. 1989. *Love and Power in a World without Limits.* New York: Harper.
Comte-Sponville, André. 2001. *A Short Treatise on the Great Virtues.* Translated by Catherine Temerson. London: William Heinemann. Original edition, 1996.
Cooper, David A. 1992. *The Heart of Stillness.* New York: Bell Tower.
Cousins, Norman. 1979. *Anatomy of an Illness.* New York: Bantam Books.
———. 1989. *Head First: The Biology of Hope and the Healing Power of the Human Spirit.* New York: Penguin Books.
Covey, Stephen R. 1989. *The Seven Habits of Highly Effective People.* New York: Simon and Schuster.
———. 1990. *Principle-Centered Leadership.* New York: Simon and Schuster.
Covey, Stephen R., A. Roger Merrill, and Rebecca R. Merrill. 1994. *First Things First.* New York: Simon and Schuster.
Cramer, Kathryn D. 1995. *Roads Home: Seven Pathways to Midlife Wisdom.* New York: William Morrow.
Crick, Francis. 1994. *The Astonishing Hypothesis: The Scientific Search for the Soul.* New York: Charles Scribner's Sons.
Cross, K. Patricia. 1981. *Adults as Learners: Increasing Participation and Facilitating Learning.* San Francisco: Jossey-Bass.
Csikszentmihalyi, Mihaly. 1990. *Flow: The Psychology of Optimal Experience.* New York: Harper and Row.
———. 1993. *The Evolving Self: A Psychology for the Third Millennium.* New York: HarperCollins.
———. 1995. *Creativity.* New York: HarperCollins.
———. 1997. *Finding Flow: The Psychology of Engagement with Everyday Life.* New York: Basic Books.
Cushman, Philip. 1995. *Constructing the Self, Constructing America: A Cultural History of Psychotherapy.* Reading, Mass.: Addison-Wesley.
Dahl, Lynda Madden. 1993. *Beyond the Winning Streak.* Eugene, Oreg.: Windsong Publishing.
Damasio, Antonio. 1999. *The Feeling of What Happens.* New York: Harcourt.
Damrosch, David. 1995. *We Scholars: Changing the Culture of the University.* Cambridge: Harvard University Press.
Darling, David. 1989. *Deep Time.* New York: Delacorte Press.
———. 1995. *Soul Search: A Scientist Explores the Afterlife.* New York: Villard Books.
Dass, Ram, and Mirabai Bush. 1992. *Compassion in Action: Setting Out on the Path of Service.* New York: Bell Tower.
Davidson, Cathy N., ed. 1989. *Reading in America: Literature and Social History.* Baltimore: Johns Hopkins University Press.
Davies, Paul. 1983. *God and the New Physics.* New York: Simon and Schuster.

———. 1992. *The Mind of God.* New York: Simon and Schuster.

———. 1995. *About Time: Einstein's Unfinished Revolution.* New York: Simon and Schuster.

Dawkins, Richard. 1976. *The Selfish Gene.* Oxford: Oxford University Press.

DeAngelis, Barbara. 1990. *Secrets about Men Every Woman Should Know.* New York: Dell Publishing.

Dégh, Linda. 1994. *American Folklore and the Mass Media.* Bloomington: Indiana University Press.

———. 2001. *Legend and Belief: Dialectics of a Folklore Genre.* Bloomington: Indiana University Press.

Dégh, Linda, and Andrew Vázsonyi. 1975. The Hypothesis of Multi-Conduit Transmission in Folklore. In *Folklore: Performance and Communication,* edited by Dan Ben-Amos and Kenneth S. Goldstein, 207–52. The Hague: Mouton.

Delis, Dean C., with Cassandra Phillips. 1990. *The Passion Paradox.* New York: Bantam Books.

de Mello, Anthony. 1990. *Awareness.* New York: Doubleday.

———. 1991. *The Way to Love: The Last Meditations of Anthony de Mello.* New York: Doubleday.

Dennett, Daniel C. 2003. *Freedom Evolves.* New York: Viking.

Dienstfrey, Harris. 1991. *Where the Mind Meets the Body.* New York: HarperCollins.

Dillon, George L. 1991. *Contending Rhetorics: Writing in the Academic Disciplines.* Bloomington: Indiana University Press.

Dolby, Sandra K. 1998. Activist Pedagogy: Its Role in the Academy. *Folklore and Education* (Winter): 1, 9, 12.

Dolby(-Stahl), Sandra K. 1989. *Literary Folkloristics and the Personal Narrative.* Bloomington: Indiana University Press.

Dominicé, Pierre. 2000. *Learning from Our Lives: Using Educational Biographies with Adults.* San Francisco: Jossey-Bass.

Dorson, Richard M. 1973. *America in Legend.* New York: Pantheon Books.

Dossey, Larry. 1989. *Recovering the Soul: A Scientific and Spiritual Search.* New York: Bantam Books.

———. 1993. *Healing Words.* San Francisco: HarperCollins.

———. 1997. *Be Careful What You Pray for . . . You Just Might Get It.* San Francisco: HarperCollins.

Dowrick, Stephanie. 1991. *Intimacy and Solitude.* New York: W. W. Norton.

Dundes, Alan. 1962. From Etic to Emic Units in the Structural Study of Folktales. *Journal of American Folklore* 75:95–105.

———. [1963] 1965. Structural Typology in North American Indian Folktales. In *The Study of Folklore,* edited by Alan Dundes, 206–15. Englewood Cliffs, N.J.: Prentice-Hall.

———. 1966. Metafolklore and Oral Literary Criticism. *Monist* 50:505–16.

———. 1972. Folk Ideas as Units of Worldview. In *Towards New Perspectives in Folklore,* edited by Américo Paredes and Richard Bauman, 93–103. Austin: University of Texas Press.

———. 1980. *Interpreting Folklore.* Bloomington: Indiana University Press.

Dyer, Wayne W. 1976. *Your Erroneous Zones.* New York: Avon Books.

———. 1978. *Pulling Your Own Strings.* New York: Avon Books.

———. 1980. *The Sky's the Limit.* New York: Simon and Schuster.

———. 1983. *Gifts from Eykis.* New York: Pocket Books.

———. 1985. *What Do You Really Want for Your Children?* New York: Avon Books.

———. 1989. *You'll See It When You Believe It.* New York: Avon Books.

———. 1992. *Real Magic.* New York: HarperCollins.

———. 1995a. *Staying on the Path.* Carson, Calif.: Hay House.

———. 1995b. *Your Sacred Self.* New York: HarperCollins.

———. 1997. *Manifest Your Destiny.* New York: HarperCollins.

———. 2001. *There's a Spiritual Solution to Every Problem.* New York: HarperCollins.

———. 2004. *The Power of Intention.* Carlsbad, Calif.: Hay House.

Eadie, Betty J. 1992. *Embraced by the Light.* Placerville, Calif.: Gold Leaf Press.

Easwaran, Eknath. 1992. *Your Life Is Your Message.* New York: Hyperion.

Elliott, William. 1995. *Tying Rocks to Clouds: Meetings and Conversations with Wise and Spiritual People.* Wheaton, Ill.: Quest Books.

Ellis, Albert, and William J. Knaus. 1977. *Overcoming Procrastination.* New York: New American Library.

El-Shamy, Hasan M. 1995. *Folk Traditions of the Arab World: A Guide to Motif Classification, Vols. I and II.* Bloomington: Indiana University Press.

Emerson, Ralph Waldo. [1841] 1993. *Self-Reliance and Other Essays.* New York: Dover.

Emery, Gary. 1982. *Own Your Own Life.* New York: New American Library.

Epstein, Mark. 1998. *Going to Pieces without Falling Apart.* New York: Broadway Books.

Estés, Clarissa Pinkola. 1992. *Women Who Run with the Wolves.* New York: Ballantine Books.

Farley, Margaret A. 1986. *Personal Commitments.* San Francisco: HarperCollins.

Fasteau, Marc Feigen. 1975. *The Male Machine.* New York: Delta Publishing.

Ferguson, Marilyn. 1980. *The Aquarian Conspiracy: Personal and Social Transformation in the 1980s.* Los Angeles: J. P. Tarcher.

Fiore, Neil. 1989. *The Now Habit.* Los Angeles: Jeremy Tarcher.

Fox, Matthew. 1994. *The Reinvention of Work.* San Francisco: HarperCollins.

Fox, Matthew, and Rupert Sheldrake. 1996. *Natural Grace.* New York: Doubleday.

Frankl, Viktor E. 1969. *The Will to Meaning.* New York: New American Library.

Frazier, Shervert H. 1994. *Psychotrends.* New York: Simon and Schuster.

Freire, Paulo. 1970. *Pedagogy of the Oppressed.* New York: Herder and Herder.

Fried, Stephen B. 1994. *American Popular Psychology: An Interdisciplinary Research Guide.* New York: Garland.

Friedan, Betty. 1993. *The Fountain of Age.* New York: Simon and Schuster.

Fritz, Robert. 1989. *The Path of Least Resistance.* New York: Fawcett Columbine.

Fulghum, Robert. 1986. *All I Really Need to Know I Learned in Kindergarten.* New York: Ballantine Books.

Gallagher, Winifred. 1993. *The Power of Place.* New York: HarperCollins.

Gans, Herbert J. 1974. *Popular Culture and High Culture: An Analysis and Evaluation of Taste.* New York: Basic Books.

Gardner, Martin, ed. 1994. *Great Essays in Science.* New York: Prometheus Books.

Garfield, Charles. 1986. *Peak Performers.* New York: Avon Books.

Gawain, Shakti. 1993. *The Path of Transformation.* Mill Valley, Calif.: Nataraj Publishing.

Gegax, Tom. 1999. *Winning in the Game of Life.* New York: Harmony Books.

Gelb, Michael J. 1998. *How to Think Like Leonardo da Vinci.* New York: Delacorte Press.

Georges, Robert A. 1972. Process and Structure in Traditional Storytelling in the Balkans: Some Preliminary Remarks. In *Aspects of the Balkans: Continuity and Change,* edited by Henrik Birnbaum and Spiros Vryonis Jr., 319–37. The Hague: Mouton.

Gergen, Kenneth J. 1991. *The Saturated Self: Dilemmas of Identity in Contemporary Life.* New York: Basic Books.

Goffman, Erving. 1959. *The Presentation of Self in Everyday Life.* Garden City, N.Y.: Doubleday.

———. 1974. *Frame Analysis.* New York: Harper and Row.

Goldberg, Herb. 1976. *The Hazards of Being Male.* New York: Signet Books.

———. 1983. *The New Male-Female Relationship.* New York: New American Library.

Goleman, Daniel. 1995. *Emotional Intelligence.* New York: Bantam Books.

———. 1998. *Working with Emotional Intelligence.* New York: Bantam Books.

Goswami, Amit. 1993. *The Self-Aware Universe.* New York: Tarcher/Putnam.

Goulston, Mark, and Philip Goldberg. 1995. *Get Out of Your Own Way.* New York: Perigee Books.

Grabhorn, Lynn. 2000. *Excuse Me, Your Life Is Waiting.* Charlottesville, Va.: Hampton Roads Publishing.

Graff, Gerald. 1992. *Beyond the Culture Wars: How Teaching the Conflicts Can Revitalize American Education.* New York: W. W. Norton.

Gray, John. 1990. *Men, Women, and Relationships: Making Peace with the Opposite Sex.* Hillsboro, Oreg.: Beyond Words Publishing.

———. 1992. *Men Are from Mars, Women Are from Venus.* New York: HarperCollins.

———. 1997. *Mars and Venus on a Date.* New York: HarperCollins.

———. 1999. *How to Get What You Want and Want What You Have.* New York: HarperCollins.

———. 2001. *Mars and Venus in the Workplace.* New York: HarperCollins.

Greenberg, Gary. 1994. *The Self on the Shelf: Recovery Books and the Good Life.* Albany: State University of New York Press.

Greven, Philip. 1977. *The Protestant Temperament: Patterns of Child-Rearing, Religious Experience, and the Self in Early America.* Chicago: University of Chicago Press.

Gross, John, ed. 1991. *The Oxford Book of Essays.* New York: Oxford University Press.

Gross, Ronald. 1999. *Peak Learning: How to Create Your Own Lifelong Education Program for Personal Enlightenment and Professional Success.* Rev. ed. New York: Tarcher/Putnam.

Guroian, Vigen. 1998. *Tending the Heart of Virtue: How Classic Stories Awaken a Child's Moral Imagination.* New York: Oxford.

Halberstam, Joshua. 1993. *Everyday Ethics: Inspired Solutions to Real-Life Dilemmas.* New York: Viking/Penguin Books.

Hardin, Paula Payne. 1992. *What Are You Doing with the Rest of Your Life? Choices in Midlife.* San Rafael, Calif.: New World Library.

Harman, Willis. 1988. *Global Mind Change.* New York: Warner Books.

Harris, Maria. 1989. *Dance of the Spirit: The Seven Steps of Women's Spirituality.* New York: Bantam Books.

Harvey, John. 1995. *Odyssey of the Heart: The Search for Closeness, Intimacy, and Love.* New York: W. H. Freeman.

Helmstetter, Shad. 1987. *The Self-Talk Solution.* New York: Simon and Schuster.

———. 1989. *Choices.* New York: Simon and Schuster.

Herman, Stanley M. 1994. *The Tao at Work: On Leading and Following.* San Francisco: Jossey-Bass.

Hillman, James. 1996. *The Soul's Code.* New York: Random House.

Hirsch, E. D., Jr. 1987. *Cultural Literacy: What Every American Needs to Know.* Boston: Houghton Mifflin.

Hoff, Benjamin. 1983. *The Tao of Pooh.* New York: Penguin Books.

Hoffman, Ivan. 1993. *The Tao of Love.* Rocklin, Calif.: Prima Publishing.

Hopcke, Robert H. 1997. *There Are No Accidents: Synchronicity and the Stories of Our Lives.* New York: Penguin/Putnam.

Hsu, Francis L. K. 1983. *Rugged Individualism Reconsidered.* Knoxville: University of Tennessee Press.

Hubbard, Barbara Marx. 1998. *Conscious Evolution: Awakening the Power of Our Social Potential.* Novato, Calif.: New World Library.

Hufford, David J. 1982. *The Terror That Comes in the Night.* Philadelphia: University of Pennsylvania Press.

Jacobs, Gregg D. 2003. *The Ancestral Mind.* New York: Viking.

James, Jennifer. 1991. *Visions from the Heart.* New York: Newmarket Press.

James, William. [1907] 1995. *Pragmatism.* New York: Dover.

Jampolsky, Gerald G. 2000. *Shortcuts to God: Finding Peace Quickly through Practical Spirituality.* Berkeley: Celestial Arts.

Janda, Louis. 1996. *The Psychologist's Book of Self-Tests.* New York: Berkley Books.

Janeway, Elizabeth. 1971. *Man's World, Woman's Place.* New York: Dell Publishing.

Jeffers, Susan. 1987. *Feel the Fear and Do It Anyway.* New York: Ballantine Books.

———. 1989. *Opening Our Hearts to Men.* New York: Fawcett Columbine.

———. 1996. *End the Struggle and Dance with Life.* New York: St. Martin's Press.

Jeremias, Joachim. 1966. *Rediscovering the Parables.* New York: Charles Scribner's Sons.

John-Roger and Peter McWilliams. 1990. *You Can't Afford the Luxury of a Negative Thought.* Los Angeles: Prelude Press.

Johnson, Spencer. 1985. *One Minute for Myself.* New York: Avon Books.

———. 1992. *"Yes" or "No": The Guide to Better Decisions.* New York: HarperCollins.

———. 1998. *Who Moved My Cheese?* New York: G. P. Putnam's Sons.

Johnson, Spencer, and Kenneth Blanchard. 1981. *The One Minute Manager.* New York: Berkley Books.

Kabat-Zinn, Jon. 1994. *Wherever You Go, There You Are.* New York: Hyperion.

Kafatos, Manos, and Robert Nadeau. 1990. *The Conscious Universe.* New York: Springer-Verlag.

Kaku, Michio. 1994. *Hyperspace.* New York: Oxford University Press.

Kaminer, Wendy. 1992. *I'm Dysfunctional, You're Dysfunctional.* New York: Vintage Books.

Kauffman, Stuart. 1995. *At Home in the Universe: The Search for the Laws of Self-Organization and Complexity.* New York: Oxford.

Kaza, Stephanie. 1993. *The Attentive Heart: Conversations with Trees*. New York: Fawcett Columbine.

Keen, Sam. 1991. *Fire in the Belly: On Being a Man*. New York: Bantam Books.

———. 1992. *Inward Bound*. New York: Bantam Books.

Keen, Sam, and Anne Valley-Fox. 1989. *Your Mythic Journey*. New York: Tarcher/Putnam.

Kegan, Robert, and Lisa Laskow Lahey. 2001. *How the Way We Talk Can Change the Way We Work*. San Francisco: Jossey-Bass.

Kett, Joseph F. 1994. *The Pursuit of Knowledge under Difficulties: From Self-Improvement to Adult Education in America, 1750–1990*. Stanford, Calif.: Stanford University Press.

Keyes, Ken, Jr. 1975. *Handbook to Higher Consciousness*. Coos Bay, Oreg.: Love Line Books.

———. 1980. *How to Enjoy Your Life in Spite of It All*. Coos Bay, Oreg.: Love Line Books.

Kinder, Melvyn, and Connell Cowan. 1989. *Husbands and Wives*. New York: Penguin Books.

Kirshenbaum, Mira. 1997. *Too Good to Leave, Too Bad to Stay*. New York: Penguin Books.

Kirshenblatt-Gimblett, Barbara. 1975. A Parable in Context: A Social Interactional Analysis of Storytelling Performance. In *Folklore: Performance and Communication*, edited by Dan Ben-Amos and Kenneth S. Goldstein, 105–30. The Hague: Mouton.

———. 1981. Toward a Theory of Proverb Meaning. In *The Wisdom of Many: Essays on the Proverb*, edited by Wolfgang Mieder and Alan Dundes, 111–21. New York: Garland.

Kitchens, James A. 1994. *Talking to Ducks: Rediscovering the Joy and Meaning in Your Life*. New York: Fireside.

Klagsbrun, Francine. 1985. *Married People: Staying Together in the Age of Divorce*. New York: Bantam Books.

Knowles, Malcolm S. 1978. *The Adult Learner: A Neglected Species*. 2d ed. Houston: Gulf.

Koestler, Arthur. 1972. *The Roots of Coincidence*. New York: Random House.

Koller, Alice. 1990. *The Stations of Solitude*. New York: Bantam Books.

Kopp, Sheldon B. 1972. *If You Meet the Buddha on the Road, Kill Him!* New York: Bantam Books.

Kornfield, Jack. 1993. *A Path with Heart: A Guide through the Perils and Promises of Spiritual Life*. New York: Bantam Books.

Kragen, Ken. 1994. *Life Is a Contact Sport: Ten Great Career Strategies That Work*. New York: William Morrow.

Kramer, Joel, and Diana Alstad. 1993. *The Guru Papers: Masks of Authoritarian Power*. Berkeley, Calif.: Frog.

Kramer, Peter D. 1993. *Listening to Prozac*. New York: Penguin Books.

———. 1997. *Should You Leave? A Psychiatrist Explores Intimacy and Autonomy—and the Nature of Advice*. New York: Scribner.

Kraybill, Donald B. 1989. *The Riddle of Amish Culture*. Baltimore: Johns Hopkins University Press.

Kuhn, Thomas S. 1962. *The Structure of Scientific Revolutions*. Chicago: University of Chicago Press.

Kushner, Harold. 1983. *When Bad Things Happen to Good People*. New York: Avon Books.

———. 1986. *When All You've Ever Wanted Isn't Enough*. New York: Simon and Schuster.

Lakein, Alan. 1973. *How to Get Control of Your Time and Your Life*. New York: New American Library.

Langer, Ellen J. 1989. *Mindfulness*. Reading, Mass.: Addison-Wesley.

LaRosa, Ralph C. 1972. Invention and Imitation in Emerson's Early Lectures. *American Literature* 44:13–30.

Lasch, Christopher. 1991. *The True and Only Heaven: Progress and Its Critics.* New York: W. W. Norton.

Laskow, Leonard. 1992. *Healing with Love: The Art of Holoenergetic Healing.* San Francisco: HarperCollins.

Lawless, Elaine. 1993. *Holy Women, Wholly Women: Sharing Ministries of Wholeness through Life Stories and Reciprocal Ethnography.* Philadelphia: University of Pennsylvania Press.

Lazarus, Richard S., and Bernice N. Lazarus. 1994. *Passion and Reason: Making Sense of Our Emotions.* New York: Oxford.

Lazere, Donald. 1986. Literacy and Mass Media: The Political Implications. In *Reading in America: Literature and Social History,* edited by Cathy N. Davidson, 285–303. Baltimore: Johns Hopkins University Press.

Lear, Jonathan. 1990. *Love and Its Place in Nature.* New York: Farrar, Straus and Giroux.

Lebow, Rob. 1990. *A Journey into the Heroic Environment.* Rocklin, Calif.: Prima Publishing.

Leeming, David, and Jake Page. 1999. *Myths, Legends, and Folktales of America: An Anthology.* New York: Oxford.

Lempert, David H. 1996. *Escape from the Ivory Tower: Student Adventures in Democratic Experiential Education.* San Francisco: Jossey-Bass.

Lerner, Harriet Goldhor. 1985. *The Dance of Anger.* New York: Harper and Row.

———. 1993. *The Dance of Deception.* New York: HarperCollins.

Lesser, Elizabeth. 1999. *The New American Spirituality: A Seeker's Guide.* New York: Random House.

Levine, Stephen, and Ondrea Levine. 1995. *Embracing the Beloved: Relationship as a Path to Awakening.* New York: Anchor Books.

Lévi-Strauss, Claude. 1972. The Structural Study of Myth. In *The Structuralists from Marx to Levi-Strauss,* edited by Richard and Fernande DeGeorge, 169–94. New York: Anchor Books. First published in *Journal of American Folklore* 78 (1955): 428–44.

Lieberman, David J. 1998. *Never Be Lied to Again.* New York: St. Martin's Press.

Lockhart, Alexander. 1997. *The Portable Pep Talk: Motivational Morsels for Inspiring You to Succeed.* Richmond, Va.: Zander Press.

Long, Edward LeRoy, Jr. 1992. *Higher Education as a Moral Enterprise.* Washington: Georgetown University Press.

Lopate, Phillip, ed. 1994. *The Art of the Personal Essay: An Anthology from the Classical Era to the Present.* New York: Anchor Books.

Lüthi, Max. 1976. Aspects of the *Märchen* and the Legend. In *Folklore Genres,* edited by Dan Ben-Amos, 17–33. Austin: University of Texas Press. First published in *Genre* 2 (1969): 162–78.

Lynch, Aaron. 1996. *Thought Contagion: How Belief Spreads through Society, The New Science of Memes.* New York: Basic Books.

MacLaine, Shirley. 1983. *Out on a Limb.* New York: Bantam Books.

———. 1989. *Going Within.* New York: Bantam Books.

———. 2000. *The Camino: A Journey of the Spirit.* New York: Pocket Books.

Malinowski, Bronislaw. 1954. Reprint. Myth in Primitive Psychology. *Magic, Science and*

Religion and Other Essays, 96–148. Garden City, N.Y.: Anchor Books. Original edition, 1926.

Mallinger, Allan E., and Jeannette DeWyze. 1992. *Too Perfect: When Being in Control Gets Out of Control.* New York: Clarkson Potter.

Maltz, Maxwell. 1960. *Psycho-Cybernetics.* New York: Simon and Schuster.

———. 2002. *The New Psycho-Cybernetics: The Original Science of Self-Improvement and Success That Has Changed the Lives of 30 Million People.* Edited and updated by Dan S. Kennedy and the Psycho-Cybernetics Foundation, Inc. Paramus, N.J.: Prentice-Hall.

Marcus, George E., and Michael J. Fischer. 1986. *Anthropology as Cultural Critique.* Chicago: University of Chicago Press.

Maslow, Abraham. 1964. *Religion, Values, and Peak-Experiences.* New York: Penguin Books.

Masters, William H., and Virginia Johnson. 1974. *The Pleasure Bond.* New York: Bantam Books.

May, Rollo. 1991. *The Cry for Myth.* New York: W. W. Norton.

McAdams, Dan P. 1993. *The Stories We Live By: Personal Myths and the Making of the Self.* New York: William Morrow.

McCarraher, Eugene B. 1997. The Church Irrelevant: Paul Hanly Furfey and the Fortunes of American Catholic Radicalism. *Religion and American Culture* 7:163–94.

McGraw, Phillip. 2001. *Self Matters: Creating Your Life from the Inside Out.* New York: Free Press.

McKeachie, Wilbert J. 1999. *Teaching Tips.* 10th ed. Boston: Houghton Mifflin.

McKenna, Elizabeth Perle. 1997. *When Work Doesn't Work Anymore: Women, Work, and Identity.* New York: Delacorte Press.

McMahon, James M. 1999. *Letting Go of Mother.* New York: Paulist Press.

Mechling, Jay. 1989. Mediating Structures and the Significance of University Folk. In *Folk Groups and Folklore Genres,* edited by Elliott Oring, 339–49. Logan: Utah State University Press.

———. 2000. Folklore and the Civil Sphere. *Western Folklore* 56:113–37.

Melchert, Norman. 1994. *Who's to Say?* Cambridge: Hackett Publishing.

Mezirow, Jack. 1978. *Education for Perspective Transformation: Women's Re-entry Programs in Community Colleges.* New York: Columbia University, Center for Adult Education.

Mezirow, Jack, and Associates. 2000. *Learning as Transformation.* San Francisco: Jossey-Bass.

Mieder, Wolfgang. 1998. Proverbs. In *Encyclopedia of Folklore and Literature,* edited by Mary Ellen Brown and Bruce A. Rosenberg, 525–27. Santa Barbara: ABC-CLIO.

Mieder, Wolfgang, Stewart A. Kingsbury, and Kelsie B. Harder, eds. 1992. *A Dictionary of American Proverbs.* New York: Oxford University Press.

Miller, Adrienne, and Andrew Goldblatt. 1989. *The Hamlet Syndrome: Overthinkers Who Underachieve.* New York: William Morrow.

Miller, Ronald S., and the Editors of *New Age Journal.* 1992. *As Above, So Below: Paths to Spiritual Renewal in Daily Life.* Los Angeles: Jeremy Tarcher.

Millman, Dan. 1995. *The Laws of Spirit.* Tiburon, Calif.: H. J. Kramer.

———. 2000. *Way of the Peaceful Warrior.* Rev. ed. Tiburon, Calif.: H. J. Kramer.

Minor, Herman, IV [Franklin M. Mount]. 1994. *The Seven Habits of Highly Ineffective People.* New York: Citadel Press.

Moldenhauer, Joseph J. 1967. The Rhetorical Function of Proverbs in *Walden. Journal of American Folklore* 80:151–59.

Moore, Robert, and Douglas Gillette. 1990. *King, Warrior, Magician, Lover: Rediscovering the Archetypes of the Mature Masculine.* San Francisco: HarperCollins.

Moore, Thomas. 1992. *Care of the Soul.* New York: HarperCollins.

———. 1994. *Soul Mates.* New York: HarperCollins.

———. 2000. *Original Self.* New York: HarperCollins.

Morris, Richard. 1993. *Cosmic Questions: Galactic Halos, Cold Dark Matter, and the End of Time.* New York: John Wiley and Sons.

Moyers, Bill. 1993. *Healing and the Mind.* New York: Doubleday.

Muller, Wayne. 1992. *Legacy of the Heart.* New York: Simon and Schuster.

Murphy, Michael. 1992. *The Future of the Body: Explorations into the Further Evolution of Human Nature.* New York: Tarcher/Putnam.

Myss, Caroline. 1997. *Why People Don't Heal and How They Can.* New York: Three Rivers Press.

Naifeh, Steven, and Gregory White Smith. 1984. *Why Can't Men Open Up?* New York: Warner Books.

Needleman, Jacob. 1996. *A Little Book on Love.* New York: Doubleday.

Newman, Mildred, and Bernard Berkowitz. 1977. *How to Take Charge of Your Life.* New York: Bantam Books.

Newman, Mildred, and Bernard Berkowitz, with Jean Owen. 1971. *How to Be Your Own Best Friend.* New York: Ballantine Books.

Noddings, Nel. 1984. *Caring: A Feminine Approach to Ethics and Moral Education.* Berkeley: University of California Press.

———. 1995. *Philosophy of Education.* Boulder, Colo.: Westview Press.

Noer, David M. 1997. *Breaking Free: A Prescription for Personal and Organizational Change.* San Francisco: Jossey-Bass.

Norkunas, Martha K. 1993. *The Politics of Public Memory.* Albany: State University of New York Press.

Norris, Kathleen. 1996. *The Cloister Walk.* New York: Riverhead.

Nouwen, Henri. 1996. *The Inner Voice of Love.* New York: Doubleday.

Ogilvy, James. 1995. *Living without a Goal.* New York: Doubleday.

Oring, Elliott. 1976. Three Functions of Folklore: Traditional Functionalism as Explanation in Folkloristics. *Journal of American Folklore* 89:67–80.

———. 1987. Generating Lives: The Construction of an Autobiography. *Journal of Folklore Research* 23:241–62.

Orloff, Judith. 1995. *Second Sight.* New York: Warner Books.

Ornish, Dean. 1998. *Love and Survival: The Scientific Basis for the Healing Power of Intimacy.* New York: HarperCollins.

Orsborn, Carol. 1995. *Solved by Sunset.* New York: Harmony Books.

Owen, David. 1988. *Transparent Worship.* Indianapolis: United Methodist Church, The Women's Division.

————. 1995. *Getting There from Here: Meditations for the Journey.* Bloomington, Ind.: St. Mark's United Methodist Church.

————. 1996. Sermon of May 19. Bloomington, Ind.: St. Mark's United Methodist Church. Printed for local distribution. Personal copy.

————. 2002. *Wending Our Way.* Indianapolis: North United Methodist Church.

Parady, Marianne. 1995. *Seven Secrets for Successful Living: Tapping the Wisdom of Ralph Waldo Emerson to Achieve Love, Happiness, and Self-Reliance.* New York: Kensington Books.

Pearce, Joseph. 1971. *The Crack in the Cosmic Egg.* New York: Julian Press.

Pearsall, Paul. 1996. *The Pleasure Prescription.* Alameda, Calif.: Hunter House.

Peck, M. Scott. 1978. *The Road Less Traveled.* New York: Simon and Schuster.

————. 1993a. *Further Along the Road Less Traveled.* New York: Simon and Schuster.

————. 1993b. *A World Waiting to Be Born: Civility Rediscovered.* New York: Bantam Books.

————. 1996. *In Search of Stones: A Pilgrimage of Faith, Reason, and Discovery.* New York: Hyperion.

————. 1997a. *Denial of the Soul.* New York: Harmony Books.

————. 1997b. *The Road Less Traveled and Beyond.* New York: Simon and Schuster.

Pelto, Pertti J., and Gretel H. Pelto. 1978. *Anthropological Research: The Structure of Inquiry.* 2d ed. Cambridge: Cambridge University Press.

Pennington, M. Basil. 1987. *Thomas Merton, Brother Monk: The Quest for True Freedom.* San Francisco: Harper and Row.

Penrose, Roger. 1989. *The Emperor's New Mind.* New York: Oxford University Press.

Perry, Lewis. 1984. *Intellectual Life in America: A History.* New York: Franklin Watts.

Peters, Thomas J., and Robert H. Waterman Jr. 1982. *In Search of Excellence.* New York: Harper and Row.

Peters, Tom. 1987. *Thriving on Chaos.* New York: Harper and Row.

————. 1994. *The Tom Peters Seminar: Crazy Times Call for Crazy Organizations.* New York: Random House.

————. 1997. *The Circle of Innovation.* New York: Alfred A. Knopf.

Pieczenik, Steve. 1990. *My Life Is Great. Why Do I Feel So Awful?* New York: Warner Books.

Pirsig, Robert M. 1974. *Zen and the Art of Motorcycle Maintenance.* New York: Bantam Books.

Porpora, Douglas V. 2001. *Landscapes of the Soul: The Loss of Moral Meaning in American Life.* Oxford: Oxford University Press.

Prager, Dennis. 1998. *Happiness Is a Serious Problem: A Human Nature Repair Manual.* New York: HarperCollins.

Propp, Vladimir. 1968. *Morphology of the Folktale.* Translated by Laurence Scott. 2d ed. Austin: University of Texas Press.

Rachels, James. 1993. *The Elements of Moral Philosophy.* 2d ed. New York: McGraw-Hill.

Radway, Janice A. 1984. *Reading the Romance: Woman, Patriarchy, and Popular Literature.* Chapel Hill: University of North Carolina Press.

Randall, William Lowell. 1994. *The Stories We Are: An Essay on Self-Creation.* Toronto: University of Toronto Press.

Rapping, Elayne. 1996. *The Culture of Recovery: Making Sense of the Self-Help Movement in Women's Lives.* Boston: Beacon Press.

Redfield, James. 1993. *The Celestine Prophecy: An Adventure*. New York: Warner Books.

————. 1996. *The Tenth Insight: Holding the Vision*. New York: Warner Books.

————. 1997. *The Celestine Vision: Living the New Spiritual Awareness*. New York: Warner Books.

————. 1999. *The Secret of Shambhala: In Search of the Eleventh Insight*. New York: Warner Books.

Redfield, James, and Carol Adrienne. 1995. *The Celestine Prophecy: An Experiential Guide*. New York: Warner Books.

Reuben, David. 1969. *Everything You Always Wanted to Know about Sex*. New York: Bantam Books.

Reynolds, David K. 1995. *A Handbook for Constructive Living*. New York: William Morrow.

Rhine, Louisa E. 1961. *Hidden Channels of the Mind*. New York: William Sloane.

Riessman, Frank, and David Carroll. 1995. *Redefining Self-Help: Policy and Practice*. San Francisco: Jossey-Bass.

Rilke, Phia. [1900] 1998. *Ephemeral Aphorisms*. Translated by Wolfgang Mieder and David Scrase. Riverside, Calif.: Ariadne Press.

Ringer, Robert J. 1977. *Looking Out for #1*. New York: Fawcett Crest.

Robbins, Anthony. 1991. *Awaken the Giant Within*. New York: Fireside.

Roberts, Jane. 1974. *The Nature of Personal Reality: A Seth Book*. New York: Bantam Books.

Roberts, Wess, and Bill Ross. 1995. *Make It So: Leadership Lessons from Star Trek, The Next Generation*. New York: Simon and Schuster.

Rogers, Tim B. 1989. The Use of Slogans, Colloquialisms, and Proverbs in the Treatment of Substance Addiction: A Psychological Application of Proverbs. *Proverbium* 6:103–12.

Root, Michael. 1993. *Philosophy of Social Science*. Cambridge, Mass.: Blackwell.

Royce, Joseph R. 1964. *The Encapsulated Man*. Princeton, N.J.: D. Van Nostrand.

Ruark, Jennifer K. 1999. Redefining the Good Life: A New Focus in the Social Sciences. *Chronicle of Higher Education* 45, no. 23 (February 12, 1999): A13–A15.

Rubin, Lillian B. 1983. *Intimate Strangers*. New York: Harper and Row.

Rubin, Theodore Isaac. 1975. *Compassion and Self-Hate*. New York: Collier Books.

————. 1985. *Overcoming Indecisiveness*. New York: Avon Books.

Russell, Bertrand. [1930] 1958. *The Conquest of Happiness*. New York: Bantam Books.

Sagan, Carl. 1997. *Billions and Billions: Thoughts on Life and Death at the Brink of the Millennium*. New York: Random House.

Sanders, Scott Russell. 1993. *Staying Put*. Boston: Beacon Press.

Santrock, John W., Ann M. Minnett, and Barbara D. Campbell. 1994. *The Authoritative Guide to Self-Help Books*. New York: Guilford Press.

Sartre, Jean Paul. 1937. *The Transcendence of the Ego*. Translated by Forrest Williams and Robert Kirkpatrick. New York: Farrar, Straus and Giroux.

Schaef, Anne Wilson. 1981. *Women's Reality*. Minneapolis: Winston Press.

————. 1987. *When Society Becomes an Addict*. San Francisco: Harper and Row.

————. 1992. *Beyond Therapy, Beyond Science: A New Model for Healing the Whole Person*. San Francisco: Harper.

Scheler, Max. 1992. *On Feeling, Knowing, and Valuing: Selected Writings*. Edited by Harold J. Bershady. Chicago: University of Chicago Press.

Schlessinger, Laura. 1996. *How Could You Do That?! The Abdication of Character, Courage, and Conscience.* New York: HarperCollins.

Schrempp, Gregory. 1996. Folklore and Science: Inflections of "Folk" in Cognitive Research. *Journal of Folklore Research* 33:191–206.

Schwartz, Theodore, Geoffrey M. White, and Catherine A. Lutz, eds. 1992. *New Directions in Psychological Anthropology.* New York: University of Cambridge Press.

Schwartz, Tony. 1995. *What Really Matters: Searching for Wisdom in America.* New York: Bantam Books.

Scott, Dru. 1980. *How to Put More Time in Your Life.* New York: New American Library.

Scruton, Roger. 1996. *An Intelligent Person's Guide to Philosophy.* New York: Penguin/Putnam.

Seligman, Martin E. P. 1991. *Learned Optimism.* New York: Alfred A. Knopf.

———. 1994. *What You Can Change and What You Can't.* New York: Alfred A. Knopf.

Senge, Peter M. 1990. *The Fifth Discipline: The Art and Practice of the Learning Organization.* New York: Currency/Doubleday.

Senge, Peter M., and Art Kleiner, Charlotte Roberts, Richard Ross, George Roth, and Bryan Smith. 1999. *The Dance of Change: The Challenges to Sustaining Momentum in Learning Organizations.* New York: Doubleday.

Senge, Peter M., with Nelda Cambron-McCabe, Timothy Lucas, Bryan Smith, Janis Dutton, and Art Kleiner. 2000. *Schools That Learn.* New York: Doubleday.

Shain, Merle. 1989. *Courage My Love.* New York: Bantam Books.

Sheehy, Gail. 1974. *Passages: Predictable Crises of Adult Life.* New York: Bantam Books.

———. 1981. *Pathfinders.* New York: Bantam Books.

———. 1991. *The Silent Passage.* New York: Simon and Schuster.

———. 1995. *New Passages.* New York: Random House.

Sher, Barbara. 1998. *It's Only Too Late If You Don't Start Now.* New York: Delacorte Press.

Sher, Barbara, with Barbara Smith. 1994. *I Could Do Anything If I Only Knew What It Was.* New York: Delacorte Press.

Shostrom, Everett L. 1983. *From Manipulator to Master.* New York: Bantam Books.

Sills, Judith. 1993. *Excess Baggage: Getting Out of Your Own Way.* New York: Penguin Books.

Simon, Sidney B. 1988. *Getting Unstuck.* New York: Warner Books.

———. 1995. *In Search of Values.* New York: Warner Books.

Simon, Sidney B., Leland Howe, and Howard Kirschenbaum. 1972. *Values Clarification: A Handbook of Practical Strategies for Teachers and Students.* New York: Dodd Mead.

Simonds, Wendy. 1992. *Women and Self-Help Culture: Reading between the Lines.* New Brunswick, N.J.: Rutgers University Press.

Sinetar, Marsha. 1986. *Ordinary People as Monks and Mystics.* New York: Paulist Press.

———. 1987. *Do What You Love, the Money Will Follow.* New York: Dell Publishing.

———. 1990. *Living Happily Ever After: Creating Trust, Luck, and Joy.* New York: Villard Books.

———. 1991. *Developing a 21st-Century Mind.* New York: Ballantine Books.

———. 1995. *To Build the Life You Want, Create the Work You Love.* New York: St. Martin's Press.

———. 1997. *The Mentor's Spirit: Life Lessons on Leadership and the Art of Encouragement.* New York: St. Martin's Press.

Smedes, Lewis B. 1990. *A Pretty Good Person.* San Francisco: HarperCollins.

Smith, Perry M. 1998. *Rules and Tools for Leaders.* Garden City Park, N.Y.: Avery Publishing.

Solomon, Robert C. 2001. Reprint. *About Love.* Lanham, Md.: Madison Books. Original edition, 1994.

Sparrow, G. Scott. 1995. *I Am with You Always: True Stories of Encounters with Jesus.* New York: Bantam Books.

Spence, Gerry. 1995. *How to Argue and Win Every Time.* New York: St. Martin's Press.

Spock, Benjamin. 1946. *Baby and Child Care.* New York: Simon and Schuster.

Staguhn, Gerhard. 1992. *God's Laughter: Man and His Cosmos.* New York: HarperCollins.

Stanovich, Keith E. 1992. *How to Think Straight about Psychology.* 3rd ed. New York: HarperCollins.

Starker, Steven. 1989. *Oracle at the Supermarket: The American Preoccupation with Self-Help Books.* New Brunswick: Transaction Publishers.

Sternberg, Robert J. 1998. *Love Is a Story: A New Theory of Relationships.* New York: Oxford University Press.

Stewart, Edward C., and Milton J. Bennett. 1991. *American Cultural Patterns: A Cross-Cultural Perspective.* Yarmouth, Maine: Intercultural Press.

Stiller, Ben, and Janeane Garofalo. 1999. *Feel This Book: An Essential Guide to Self-Empowerment, Spiritual Supremacy, and Sexual Satisfaction.* New York: Ballantine Books.

Stoddard, Alexandra. 1995. *The Art of the Possible.* New York: William Morrow.

Swimme, Brian, and Thomas Berry. 1992. *The Universe Story.* San Francisco: HarperCollins.

Talbot, Michael. 1991. *The Holographic Universe.* New York: HarperCollins.

Tannen, Deborah. 1990. *You Just Don't Understand: Women and Men in Conversation.* New York: William Morrow.

———. 1994. *Talking from 9 to 5: How Women's and Men's Conversational Styles Affect Who Gets Heard, Who Gets Credit, and What Gets Done at Work.* New York: William Morrow.

Taylor, Charles. 1989. *Sources of the Self: The Making of the Modern Identity.* Cambridge: Harvard University Press.

Tennant, Mark, and Philip Pogson. 1995. *Learning and Change in the Adult Years.* San Francisco: Jossey-Bass.

Thompson, Stith. 1955–58. *Motif-Index of Folk Literature.* 6 vols. Bloomington: Indiana University Press.

Thrall, William Flint, Addison Hibbard, and C. Hugh Holman. 1960. *A Handbook to Literature.* Rev. ed. New York: Odyssey Press.

Tiede, Tom. 2001. *Self-Help Nation: The Long Overdue, Entirely Justified, Delightfully Hostile Guide to the Snake-Oil Peddlers Who Are Sapping Our Nation's Soul.* New York: Atlantic Monthly Press.

Tipler, Frank J. 1996. *The Physics of Immortality.* New York: Doubleday.

Toelken, Barre. 1996. *The Dynamics of Folklore.* Rev. ed. Logan: Utah State University Press.

Tolson, Andrew. 1977. *The Limits of Masculinity.* New York: Harper and Row.

Tompkins, Jane P., ed. 1980. *Reader-Response Criticism: From Formalism to Post-Structuralism.* Baltimore: Johns Hopkins University Press.

Tough, Allen. 1971. *The Adult's Learning Projects: A Fresh Approach to Theory and Practice in Adult Learning.* Research in Education Series, no. 1. Toronto: Ontario Institute for Studies in Education.

Tussman, Joseph. 1969. *Experiment at Berkeley.* New York: Oxford University Press.

Tylor, Edward Burnett. [1880] 1924. *Primitive Culture.* New York: Brentanos Publishers.

Urban, Hal. 2002. *Life's Greatest Lessons.* New York: Simon and Schuster.

Van de Castle, Robert L. 1994. *Our Dreaming Mind.* New York: Ballantine Books.

Vaughan, Diane. 1986. *Uncoupling: Turning Points in Intimate Relationships.* New York: Oxford University Press.

Viscott, David. 1971. *Feel Free.* New York: Simon and Schuster.

Vogel, Linda J. 1991. *Teaching and Learning in Communities of Faith.* San Francisco: Jossey-Bass.

von Sydow, Carl Wilhelm. 1965. Folktale Studies and Philology: Some Points of View. In *The Study of Folklore,* ed. Alan Dundes, 219–42. Englewood Cliffs, N.J.: Prentice-Hall.

Vyse, Stuart A. 1997. *Believing in Magic: The Psychology of Superstition.* New York: Oxford University Press.

Waitley, Denis. 1979. *The Psychology of Winning.* New York: Berkley Books.

———. 1992. *Timing Is Everything.* Nashville: Thomas Nelson Publishers.

Wallace, Doris B., and Howard E. Gruber, eds. 1989. *Creative People at Work.* New York: Oxford University Press.

Walsch, Neale Donald. 1995. *Conversations with God: An Uncommon Dialogue, Book 1.* Charlottesville, Va.: Hampton Roads Publishing.

———. 1998a. *Conversations with God: An Uncommon Dialogue, Book 2.* Charlottesville, Va.: Hampton Roads Publishing.

———. 1998b. *Conversations with God: An Uncommon Dialogue, Book 3.* Charlottesville, Va.: Hampton Roads Publishing.

———. 1999. *Friendship with God: An Uncommon Dialogue.* New York: Putnam.

———. 2000. *Communion with God: An Uncommon Dialogue.* London: Hodder and Stoughton.

Wegela, Karen Kissel. 1996. *How to Be a Help Instead of a Nuisance: Practical Approaches to Giving Support, Service, and Encouragement to Others.* Boston: Shambhala.

Weil, Andrew. 1995. *Spontaneous Healing.* New York: Alfred A. Knopf.

Weiner-Davis, Michelle. 1995. *Fire Your Shrink!* New York: Simon and Schuster.

Wetzler, Scott. 1992. *Living with the Passive-Aggressive Man.* New York: Simon and Schuster.

Wheatley, Margaret J. 1992. *Leadership and the New Science: Learning about Organization from an Orderly Universe.* San Francisco: Berrett-Koehler Publishers.

Whiteley, Richard C. 2002. *The Corporate Shaman: A Business Fable for the Modern Age.* New York: HarperCollins.

Whyte, David. 1994. *The Heart Aroused: Poetry and the Preservation of the Soul in Corporate America.* New York: Doubleday.

Wicks, Robert J. 2000. *Sharing Wisdom: The Practical Art of Giving and Receiving Mentoring.* New York: Crossroad Publishing.

Wiggins, Grant, and Jay McTighe. 1998. *Understanding by Design.* Alexandria, Va.: Association for Supervision and Curriculum Development.

Williams, Arthur L., Jr. 1988. *All You Can Do Is All You Can Do but All You Can Do Is Enough!* New York: Ballantine Books.

Williamson, Marianne. 1992. *A Return to Love.* New York: HarperCollins.

Wolf, Sharyn. 1997. *How to Stay Lovers for Life.* New York: Dutton.

Wordsworth, William. 1992. *Favorite Poems.* New York: Dover.

Wuthnow, Robert. 1998. *After Heaven: Spirituality in America since the 1950s.* Berkeley: University of California Press.

Yankah, Kwesi. 1989. Proverbs: Problems and Strategies in Field Research. *Proverbium* 6:165–76.

Yankelovich, Daniel. 1981. *New Rules: Searching for Fulfillment in a World Turned Upside Down.* New York: Bantam Books.

Young, Jeffrey E., and Janet S. Klosko. 1993. *Reinventing Your Life.* New York: Dutton/Penguin Books.

Zohar, Danah. 1990. *The Quantum Self: Human Nature and Consciousness Defined by the New Physics.* New York: William Morrow.

Zukav, Gary. 1979. *The Dancing Wu Li Masters: An Overview of the New Physics.* New York: Bantam Books.

———. 1999. *The Seat of the Soul.* New York: Simon and Schuster.

Index

SANDRA K. DOLBY is a professor of folklore and American studies at Indiana University, Bloomington. She recently spent a year in Norway as a Roving American Studies Scholar for the Fulbright Program and earlier spent six months in Australia as a fellow at the National Library in Canberra. She is the author of *Literary Folkloristics and the Personal Narrative* and previously taught in the English department at the University of Houston.

The University of Illinois Press
is a founding member of the
Association of American University Presses.

Composed in 10.5/13 Minion
by Celia Shapland
for the University of Illinois Press
Manufactured by Thomson-Shore, Inc.

University of Illinois Press
1325 South Oak Street
Champaign, IL 61820-6903
www.press.uillinois.edu